Our first visit
Wofford together

Made a great   May 13-14
choice for   Mother's Day 2007
her future.   Weekend

Virtus, repulsae nescia sordidae,
intaminatis fulget honoribus

True worth, that never knows ignoble defeat,
shines with untarnished honor

Though existing records do not indicate precisely when it was adopted, the Wofford College motto already was in use as part of the seal of the college on a diploma dating from 1857. The motto is a quotation from Horace's Odes (III.2.18), published around 23 BCE. The poem is a famous one, the source of the phrase *dulce et decorum est, pro patria mori* ("it is sweet and befitting to die for one's country"). It would have been familiar to faculty and students at any college of that era. In fact, based on early course catalogs in the archives, sophomores would have read the complete poem in the original as part of the normal course of study.

"Untarnished, she shines with honor," Wofford's traditional translation of the motto, captures the spirit but not the grammar of the Latin original. In the phrase *"intaminatis fulget honoribus"*, *"intaminatis"* modifies *"honoribus."* The three words of the motto do not specify the subject of the sentence. The "she" in the original is Virtue, the personification of strength, courage, excellence, vigor.

—*Chris Strauber and Phillip Stone '94*

Wofford

Shining with Untarnished Honor

1854-2004

edited by

Doyle Boggs
JoAnn Mitchell Brasington
Phillip Stone

SPARTANBURG • 2005

First printing, December 2005

Printed in China

Library of Congress Cataloging-in-Publication Data

Wofford : shining with untarnished honor / edited by Doyle Boggs.
    p. cm.
 ISBN 1-891885-40-5 (hard cover : alk. paper)
1. Wofford College (Spartanburg, S.C.)—History. I. Boggs, Doyle Willard, 1948-
LD6201.W32W64 2005
378.757'29—dc22
                                   2004030102

Hub City Writers Project
Post Office Box 8421
Spartanburg, South Carolina 29305
(864) 577-9349 • fax (864) 577-0188 • www.hubcity.org

~In Memoriam~

James Anthony Trentini, Class of 1959
May 24, 1936 – September 11, 2001

Andrew Carl Shields, Class of 2001
August 17, 1979 – December 9, 2004

TABLE OF CONTENTS

From the late '40s into the '90s, Wofford graduates treasured their commencement Bibles signed by Lewis Jones.

DEDICATION

When members of the Wofford College community think about Dr. Lewis Pinckney Jones '38, many images come to mind. Some think of the soft-spoken professor whose wit was interspersed throughout his lectures in such a way that you listened closely for fear of missing a zinger (and frequently you learned more history than you had intended). Some recall the treasured moment when they were invited into the basement on Rivermont Drive to see Dr. Jones' trains. Others recall his consternation as he puzzled over how to preserve and what to do with Dunc's Globe.

Many remember impeccably planned excursions from Wofford to local historical sites. Those who were fortunate enough to participate in one of his two "Orbiting Seminars of South Carolina" interims have irreplaceable memories of journeying across South Carolina (decked out in sport coats and ties) and being introduced to the wonders of the state through the eyes of one of its most ardent advocates.

L.P. ("Long Playing") Jones spoke in class with a soft voice and a dry wit, but students quickly found that he had a lot to say.

But the one image that pervades each of these and many more is that of a true Southern gentleman, passionate about history, his students and Wofford College.

This anthology highlights six generations of Wofford students. Dr. Jones' presence on the campus has influenced four of those six generations, beginning with his enrollment as a student in 1934, and continuing even after his retirement in 1987. As a student he was a member of Sigma Alpha Epsilon fraternity, president of the Calhoun Literary Society and editor of the *Old Gold & Black*.

After serving as a captain of sub chasers and landing ships in the Navy during World War II, Dr. Jones returned to Wofford and joined the faculty in 1946, taking time out only briefly to earn a doctorate. at the University of North Carolina-Chapel Hill. During the next 41 years, he was a cornerstone of the faculty, serving as the secretary of the faculty from 1958 until 1987, and as chair of the history department from 1962 until 1987.

Members of the Board of Trustees, administration and faculty frequented Dr. Jones' office in Old Main seeking his counsel. Dr. Jones' advice was highly valued, and despite his quiet manner, he played a significant role in framing the direction for Wofford. As the secretary of the faculty, Dr. Jones authored minutes that were not only accurate and thoughtful, but also contained morsels of his wit. Because of his attention to his role as secretary, Dr. Jones spoke infrequently at faculty meetings, but when he spoke, his quiet, confident voice and carefully chosen words were incisive and persuasive.

Dr. Jones and his son, Charles, enjoyed the legendary electric train layout in his basement (and Wofford students did, too).

During the turmoil of the Vietnam era, Wofford's leadership was frequently confronted with difficult decisions. Dr. Jones realized early the divisive issues facing the country, and he frequently posed the difficult questions others were hesitant to ask.

In his role as chair of the history department, Dr. Jones provided leadership by example. Even though he taught freshman history hundreds of times, he nonetheless frequently left the campus with a stack of books to consult so he could improve on previous lectures. He gently mentored new history faculty members by handing them a sheet of paper with the comment, "Here is a test I recently gave."

Dr. Jones was a public historian from two different perspectives. First, he endeavored to make history interesting for everyone. He believed "If you get people interested in history they'll teach themselves." His *Synoptic History of South Carolina*, first produced as a serial in *Sandlapper* magazine in 1971, was the first history of the state written for a popular audience. It is still in print and enjoyed more than 30 years later. *South Carolina: One of the Fifty States* (1985), written as an eighth-grade textbook, not only features the state's history illustrated by hundreds of photographs, but also contains informative sidebars introducing students to primary documents, providing an editorial comment or explaining how the historian works.

Second, Dr. Jones has been an ardent advocate of state and local history and the importance of preserving historic sites and related artifacts. He considered a field trip to local historic sites an integral part of understanding the past. He spent countless hours traversing the back roads of the state searching for historic sites and photographing them. The South Carolina slide collection he amassed, organized and carefully indexed over 30-plus years is a monumental resource for historians, both current and future. His articles featuring state and local history topics in numerous magazines and journals highlight the importance of learning about one's

Two masterful teachers, Dr. Jones with Rudy Mancke '67, are equally at home teaching in the classroom and at off-campus locations.

own community. For many years participants in Leadership Spartanburg were treated to a bus tour of the county's historic resources as could only be seen through Dr. Jones' eyes. His efforts on behalf of the Spartanburg County Historical Association assisted in the preservation of local historic sites and the development and expansion of the Spartanburg County Regional Museum. In recognition of his many years of dedication and leadership, the Spartanburg County Historical

Association has a special donor category, the Lewis P. Jones Society.

During Dr. Jones' tenure as chair, the history department graduated 430 majors who have succeeded in a wide variety of careers. From attorneys to physicians, from elementary to university teachers, from ministers to career military officers, from business leaders to professional historians, Dr. Jones' students used the lessons they learned under his tutelage in their professional lives. One former student credits Dr. Jones for his success, noting that in his classes you were exposed to a broad range of historical literature, challenged to develop analytical thinking skills and encouraged to hone writing skills. Often students came to Wofford with clear career goals, but Dr. Jones' ability to bring history alive and make it relevant enticed many into becoming professional historians. One former student who planned to be the next Perry Mason blames Dr. Jones for his becoming a poor (monetarily speaking) historian instead of a prosperous attorney.

Dr. Jones has left Wofford many legacies, but the greatest of these is the Wofford students who departed the college with a genuine interest in history, especially a love for the history of their communities and South Carolina. In addition to the many professional historians he mentored, there are many avid history advocates whose fascination with the past was spawned in one of Dr. Jones' classes or on a field trip. These history ambassadors provide leadership to historical organizations as both professional and volunteer leaders, ensuring the ongoing study and appreciation of the state's past.

It is altogether fitting that this anthology of Wofford's history should be dedicated to Dr. Lewis P. Jones '38. In both his personal and professional life, he embodies the qualities of integrity, intellect and scholarship that provide the nucleus of the liberal arts experience and a Wofford education. All whose lives he influenced are not only better historians, but also better people.

—Rodger E. Stroup '68

Dr. Jones receives the Alumni Distinguished Service Award from David Clark '65 and President Lesesne.

INTRODUCTION

This Wofford Sesquicentennial Anthology is not just a picture book, although it is filled with marvelous pictures of the handsome and homely, dignified and dilapidated people and places that best illustrate the history of Wofford. But it is not just a history either, although it is filled with fascinating essays, vignettes and historical documents. This collaboration between Wofford and the Hub City Writers Project is also a testament to the shared values and visions of a college and its community.

Dr. Deno Trakas

Since 1854, Wofford has been an important part of the identity of Spartanburg. One hundred and fifty years ago, Spartanburg became a college town because of Wofford, and today, with six colleges and more than 10,000 college students, Spartanburg still rightly and proudly claims itself a college town. In Spartanburg, the term doesn't primarily imply only football games (although, in our 150th year, we were the Southern Conference champions), T-shirt shops (we don't have many), and bars (we have plenty); instead, it speaks primarily of a dedication to higher learning and culture.

The college's dedication to higher learning and culture is founded on a literary tradition. Wofford professors have written poetry, fiction, scholarly essays and books, and seminal histories of Spartanburg and South Carolina. Wofford administrators, faculty and students have written for the Spartanburg newspaper for 150 years. Wofford's literary magazine, *The Journal*, has been published since 1889. And in the past 10 years, Wofford has solidified its literary identity. In addition to its publications—*The Journal*, *Bohemian* and *Old Gold and Black*—and its highly respected Writers Series, Wofford now offers a concentration in creative writing, the Novel Experience for first-year students, and a Benjamin Wofford Prize (which includes publication) for the best book-length work of fiction or nonfiction by a current student.

Spartanburg has a unique literary identity beyond the Wofford campus. At least 15 of the contemporary writers listed in *Literary South Carolina* are current residents of Spartanburg. That important research book was produced by the Hub City Writers Project, which was founded in 1995 by a

group of local writers (including a Wofford professor). From their first meeting in a coffee shop on Morgan Square, they conceived of Hub City as a project to connect local artists with their hometown, to encourage them to remember their local history, to record it, to preserve its character and to make it new. Its first book, The Hub City Anthology, (featuring a Wofford administrator, three faculty members, and three alumni) sold out within six months and was reprinted, evidence of the community's need for this connection that is the heart of the Hub City mission. Since then, Hub City has published 22 books, including the work of nearly 200 South Carolina writers. Together they have made Spartanburg a center for literary arts.

Many writers have said that they write in order to know what they think. In an important sense, Wofford and Spartanburg wouldn't know what they are without their writers and other artists. This anthology is a part of that proud tradition. It will help us to know who we are, which is essential to know before we can decide who we want to be.

—*Deno P. Trakas*

First
Generation
1854-1875

THE HILLTOP COLLEGE AND THE CIVIL WAR

by Tracy J. Revels

Wofford College was very much a product of its time, born of republican ideology, religious fervor, intellectual curiosity and economic optimism. Its founder, Benjamin Wofford, was a Methodist minister as familiar with his ledger as his Bible, a homely yet remarkable man who turned a marriage dowry into a substantial fortune, dabbling in textiles before investing in banks and real estate. To all observers, he was a South Carolina success story, a man of humble origins who was devout, patriotic and wealthy, the master of bonds, acres and slaves. Yet the Reverend Mr. Wofford was far deeper than his peers suspected, as he proved in his remarkable legacy.

Benjamin Wofford, like many religious men of the antebellum period, was concerned with his legacy. His life had been shaped in large part by the forces of the Second Great Awakening and the reform impulse that sought to improve and purify America during the Jacksonian era. Wofford's initial plan was to leave a substantial sum to an array of Methodist charities, but a friend (probably the Rev. H.A.C. Walker) persuaded him to keep the fortune intact and endow a college instead. This fit within the framework of the changing times, as reformers held that advanced educational opportunities would create not only better Christians, but the type of citizens and leaders necessary to the continued survival of the young nation. Religion and education were seen as complementary, and Wofford's gift of $100,000 for "the purpose of establishing and endowing a college for literary, classical, and scientific education" was not novel. It was, however, a staggering sum for the time, and an important moment in the history of Spartanburg. After minor debates, the trustees of Wofford's will agreed that the best place to establish Wofford College would be in its founder's hometown, the little burg named for the legendary city-state of ancient Greece.

Wofford College soon became a reality on

Founder of the college Benjamin Wofford sat for this honest portrait by the itinerant artist William Barclay in the late 1840s. As of 2005, it hangs in the DuPré Administration Building. Wofford habitually wore green glasses to shield his eyes, painfully injured after an accident in a blacksmith shop.

(preceding pages) This daguerreotype of "The College" from 1856 is believed to be the oldest surviving photograph made in Spartanburg County. Harvey S. Teal, in his book, Partners With the Sun, speculates it may be the work of Charles H. Lanneau, an artist-turned-photographer who lived in Greenville and traveled extensively around the world.

Until well into the 20th century, Wofford diplomas were written in Latin and individually signed by college officials. Wofford Archives has a nice collection of diplomas through the years, including the one presented to its first graduate, Samuel Dibble (class of 1856).

the city's northern border. The cornerstone was laid with imposing Masonic rites on July 4, 1851. Some 4,000 people, including the famous hymnbook author "Singing Billy" Walker, gathered on the courthouse square and marched to the site. The Rev. William M. Wightman, the first president of the college, promised that the institution would "combine Temple and Academy: will be sacred at once to religion and letters." This main building was not complete when the first session opened in August 1854. Three professors tutored seven students, but the numbers quickly rose and, by 1855, the addition of a preparatory department ensured future pupils. Commencement exercises were held even before diplomas were issued, and the college immediately became a partner with the town, inviting residents to hear the speeches and debates considered an essential part of a classical education.

The college's growth mirrored that of the community. Spartanburg was prospering in the 1850s; one student's letter home mentions the opening of the railroad connection with Columbia and the community celebration the event generated. Other educational institutions, including schools for women and the handicapped, had opened and their activities added to the town's culture and entertainment. Camp meetings and markets also drew in crowds of farmers to what was still a rural center rather than an urban environ-ment. Industry was just beginning to sprout in the county, with ironworks and small textile mills being the most notable economic innovations. For the parents of a prospective student, Spartanburg and Wofford College had much to offer, a small but thriving community with enough culture to enlighten, but little in the way of vice to tempt their young scholar to neglect his studies.

The curriculum of the 1850s would seem daunting to a modern student; the admission examinations were given in Latin, and young men were expected to be familiar with the works of Caesar, Cicero and Xenophon before they reached their junior year. Classes in chemistry, moral and natural philosophy, geology and political economy challenged upper-level students. The goal was not to prepare men for any particular career, but to instill in them moral values and a familiarity with the intellectual world of the mid 19th century. Furthermore, they were expected to be gentlemen, Southern style, avoiding intemperate language and drunkenness. Promoters of the town argued that having a

Only a few buildings still standing in 2005 would have been familiar to students in Spartanburg in the 1850s. These photographs show exceptions: the Seay House on Crescent Avenue on the city's south side and Shiloh Methodist Church near Inman. The third photograph shows Anderson's Mill on the Tyger River a few years ago; it still stands, but in a deteriorated condition.

college raised the moral meter of the upcountry. Students were required to attend chapel, and numerous rules regulated their interactions with the townsfolk. Then as now, rules were broken, pranks were played, but in general town and gown coexisted peacefully. For its first six years, Wofford College led a charmed life, its young men more focused on the ancient past than the turbulent present.

The college's second president, the Reverend Albert Shipp, took office at the breaking of the storm. By 1860, students were riled by national events. Many of them joined a military company and used a third-floor room in Main Building as an arsenal. Following the attack on Fort Sumter, Wofford men eagerly volunteered their services to South Carolina's governor, who urged them to remain at their books. Most did not listen. More than half of the 33 men who remained in classes when the college opened on October 1, 1861, departed before the end of the term. At the 1862 commencement, only eight students, none of them seniors, remained. Meanwhile, Wofford College trustees invested heavily in Confederate bonds, an error seen only in hindsight. Virtually the entire endowment of the school was eradicated as the Confederacy collapsed. Faculty members temporarily scattered and the college limped along with only a handful of students. Unlike many other Southern institutions of higher learning, it did not close. Wofford experienced one moment of wartime excitement in 1865 when a Union cavalry brigade, in pursuit of Jefferson Davis, occupied Spartanburg. The dreaded Yankees made off with Dr. Shipp's horse and a number of books from the library. In all, 35 Wofford alumni died in the Confederate service, and the economic vicissitudes of the war seemed to sound the death knell of the college as well.

Wofford survived the lean years of Reconstruction due, in large measure, to the dedication of its tiny faculty. Living on campus, these men were committed to the city and the institution. In the memorable phrase of

The portrait of President Shipp *(above)*, which hangs in Leonard Auditorium, is the work of Albert Capers Guerry. The H.A.C. Walker *(top right)* and William Wightman *(opposite page)* portraits were painted by Thomas Wightman, Willliam's brother. He was a young man practicing on family members when he did these paintings in Spartanburg, but he later became one of the leading American artists of his generation.

The Rev. H.A.C. Walker

Hugh Andrew Crawford Walker was born in County Antrim, near Belfast, Ireland in 1809. His parents moved to South Carolina in his childhood. He was admitted to membership in the South Carolina Conference of the Methodist Episcopal Church in 1831. He was a presiding elder (now known as a district superintendent) of six different districts on six different occasions, for a total of 21 years. Additionally, he was elected to 10 Methodist General Conferences, including the Louisville Conference where the Methodist Episcopal Church, South was organized.

Walker was named in Benjamin Wofford's will as an original trustee. The Annual Conference subsequently elected him as a trustee in 1851, and he served until 1866. When the first chairman of the Board of Trustees, William M. Wightman, became the college's first president, Walker succeeded him as chairman of the board. Walker married Sarah Elizabeth Matilda Wightman, a sister of President Wightman, becoming the first president's brother-in-law.

Walker died in Marion, South Carolina, on May 22, 1886. The college archives have some of his papers and artifacts, including two scrapbooks, a collection of letters and a small book given by him to his daughter. There are also two account books with some of the records that he kept as Wofford's financial agent.

—Phillip Stone '94

Bishop William Wightman

The Rev. William May Wightman was born in Charleston on January 29, 1808, to William and Matilda Wightman. His parents were active Methodists, and his mother is reputed to have sat in the lap of John Wesley more than once as a small child in England.

After graduating from the College of Charleston, Wightman joined the South Carolina Annual Conference of the Methodist Episcopal Church in 1828. He served for several years as a financial agent for Randolph-Macon College in Virginia, the oldest Methodist college in the South. For 10 years, he edited an important denominational newspaper, the *Southern Christian Advocate*.

Benjamin Wofford's will appointed Wightman to the Board of Trustees of the new college, and in November 1853 he was elected as the college's first president. He and two faculty colleagues were present to welcome the first seven students the following fall. Wofford's first president traveled widely in the state to raise funds to increase the endowment.

Wightman left Wofford in 1859 to become chancellor of Southern University in Greensboro, Alabama. He subsequently was elected a bishop by the 1866 General Conference. He returned to Charleston, where he established his headquarters and died in 1882. The bells of St. Michael's were tolled for the Methodist bishop, a rare honor the Episcopalians conferred upon him.

—Phillip Stone '94

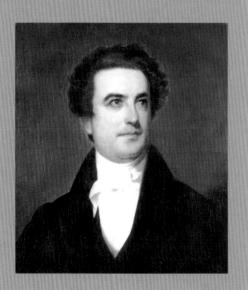

historian David Duncan Wallace, "the axe had to be wielded by hands more accustomed to the book or the pen." The professors also began to teach classes in the preparatory school and received meager financial assistance from the Methodist Conference for their families. A new spirit of maturity seemed to buoy the young men who returned to their studies after having worn Confederate uniforms, but a seismic shift had taken place, and the truly "classical" education was on the decline as fewer students were able to master Greek and Latin. But even as certain antebellum standards declined, the immediate postwar years saw innovation as well. Greek letter fraternities were introduced, the debating clubs became increasingly important,

and the college acquired its first telescope. Wofford's faculty remained underpaid and the facilities were increasingly dilapidated, but pledges of support were made and the endowment was steadily rebuilt as prosperity began to return.

Reconstruction was a stressful time for the town of Spartanburg as well as the school. Those who had invested in the Confederacy lost virtually everything. Mills halted production as demand vanished along with ready cash. Former masters feared that newly freed slaves would not work, or that racial conflict would erupt. Once-wealthy women were reduced to begging for jobs as seamstresses. By 1870, the illicit activities of the Ku Klux Klan were drawing national attention to the area. In 1871 Spartanburg, along with York and Union counties, had the writ of habeas corpus suspended under the

The Wofford faculty of 1867: Whitefoord Smith, English; James H. Carlisle, mathematics; David Duncan, ancient languages; A.H. Lester, history and biblical literature; Warren DuPré, natural sciences; and A.M. Shipp, mental and moral philosophy.

Dollars and Cents

In 2005 Wofford College still had in its vault almost $90,000 in Confederate currency and bonds. The bills range in value from $1 to $100, with the large bills drawing interest of 2 percent. The war bonds range in value from $250 to $10,000, and drew from 6 to 10 percent interest. That comparatively worthless paper represents all that is left of Benjamin Wofford's bequest and the original endowment of the college.

It is interesting to speculate what might have happened if the trustees had found a way to shelter the endowment from the economic upheaval of the Civil War. Benjamin Wofford's bequest represented $100,000 in 1850 dollars. One method of comparing the purchasing power after inflation over the years produces a 2003 equivalent of $2,341,000. Another method, based on the amount of gold a dollar could purchase, yields a sum slightly over $1.2 million.

Simply trying to compute the impact of inflation tells only part of the story. While some of the dividend income of the endowment surely would have been spent in hard times, trustees also would have reinvested some of the income for growth. Based on the history of conservative blue chip investments, the original endowment accounts might now total $50 million or more.

—*Doyle Boggs '70*

Force Acts, which were designed to curb Klan atrocities. By the early 1870s, however, most violence had sputtered out, and people were increasingly more interested in markets, railroads and renovations than in holding grudges about the war. Public lectures, commencements and even a "Ladies' Bazaar" fundraiser to garner money to fix the front steps of Wofford's Main Building kept the town connected to its most famous educational institution.

In 1875, Dr. Shipp retired as president and relocated to Nashville to become a professor at the newly opened Vanderbilt University. A tiff with his successor, Dr. James H. Carlisle, led to the story that Shipp would not even wave farewell to Carlisle as his buggy took him away from Wofford forever. His chilly dignity perhaps symbolized the turning of the era. He could not look back, but Wofford was forging ahead. The old standards of the antebellum education soon would be abandoned in favor of more progressive ideals, as demonstrated by Carlisle's first commencement address, which was delivered in English rather than Latin. A new generation of faculty members was hired, infusing the school with fresh faces and ideas. The town of Spartanburg, which had been battered by Ku Klux Klan scandals and Reconstruction woes, now stood poised to become a standard-bearer of the New South, ascribing to the creed of industry. The sleepy village was ready to put the past behind and become a true hub city; the hilltop school was ready to mature along with it.

Presidents Wightman and Shipp lived and entertained official guests in this mansion, once located at the east end of the campus promenade. (In 2004, Russell C. King Field was built near the site.) Of the six original campus structures, the President's home is the only one no longer standing at the end of the college's first 150 years. The architectural style, designed to protect the occupants from mosquitoes, was more typically found in the antebellum Lowcountry than in the more temperate Piedmont.

Commencement Traditions

Wofford's first commencement was held on Sunday, June 24, 1855, even though Main Building had not been fully completed and none of the 24 students was ready to graduate. President William Wightman delivered the first commencement address, an eloquent sermon based on the first verse of Psalm 80, *Give ear, O Shepherd of Israel. Thou that leadest Joseph like a flock, thou that dwellest between the cherubim, shine forth.* The following year, Wofford conferred its first bachelor's degree, honoring a transfer student named Samuel Dibble, who later went on to become a member of the United States House of Representatives.

Those first two commencements set the precedent for Wofford's impressive 19th century exercises, which were the highlight of Spartanburg's social calendar. Often lasting for four or five days, they featured gymnastic exhibitions, oratorical contests, debates, speeches and sermons. Until 1875, most of the speeches were made in Latin. After the use of English came into vogue, the state's newspapers often printed the sermons, addresses and student orations verbatim.

Much has changed since those early commencements, but several century-old traditions have been preserved. An academic procession has been part of graduation at Wofford since the 1850s. In the early days, the faculty and students formed at the corner of Church and Main streets in Morgan Square and marched all the way to the college. Each graduating senior receives a King James translation of the Bible, signed by each member of Wofford's faculty and staff. Autographing the Bibles has been not only a meaningful activity for members of the college community, but also an enjoyable social occasion. The traditional Wofford commencement hymn, "From All That Dwell Below the Skies," is also a special legacy from the 1800s.

Missing from 19th century commencements at Wofford and at many other Southern colleges were the distinctive caps, gowns and hoods that have become the universal graduation outfit down to elementary school level. Regalia in the United States was not standardized until 1895, and the Wofford faculty and degree candidates did not wear it, even at commencement, until well into the 1900s.

—*Doyle Boggs '70*

Benjamin Wofford *and* His Times

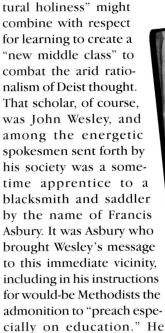

In October 1780, in the red hills of the South Carolina Upstate, where fratricidal conflict was underway and the outcome of a revolution very much in doubt, fall came early and a chill was in the air. It was less than two weeks after the Battle of Kings Mountain and several months before the decisive Battle of Cowpens.

A Whig [or Patriot] partisan, having visited his pregnant wife, had just been apprehended by his Tory [or Loyalist] neighbors who were preparing to hang him summarily. But his wife intervened with desperate pleas, warning that her life and that of her unborn child would also be forfeited. Unnerved, the Tory posse relented and let her husband live. And early on October 19, 1780, Benjamin Wofford was born into a world that, even after the war had ended, continued to be marked by violence and uncertainty.

This area of the Piedmont, stretching from Georgia through the Carolinas, remained a frontier culture for some years to come—as it had been a half-century before. In those years the state was visited by an Oxford scholar whose heart had been "strangely warmed," leading him to found a society in which "scrip-

Books and other items that were once owned or used by the college's founder—an ornate pocket watch; a personal Bible; a cash box; and a grandfather clock—are on display in the college archives in the Sandor Teszler Library.

tural holiness" might combine with respect for learning to create a "new middle class" to combat the arid rationalism of Deist thought. That scholar, of course, was John Wesley, and among the energetic spokesmen sent forth by his society was a sometime apprentice to a blacksmith and saddler by the name of Francis Asbury. It was Asbury who brought Wesley's message to this immediate vicinity, including in his instructions for would-be Methodists the admonition to "preach especially on education." He posed for them a question that would become with time increasingly difficult to answer. "What can be done," he demanded, "in order to instruct poor children, white and black … to teach them learning and piety?"

Among those who responded to Asbury's call was a circuit rider out of Georgia, George Dougherty, who was said to be both a self-taught sage and a mesmerizing preacher. In 1802, the young Ben Wofford, having heard Dougherty preach, was converted and called to the ministry.

His subsequent career has been memorably summarized by Henry Nelson Snyder: "Retiring from the active work of the ministry, he settled down in Spartanburg County for the next 34 years of his life to acquire the reputation of a skinflint and miser on account of his talent for making and keeping money. Traditions of miserliness grew around this lean, gaunt man, six feet two inches tall, Lincolnesque in face and figure—his careful picking up of pins and nails, sweeping of every single grain of tobacco into his pipe, letting his candles burn down to the last gasp of light, using of the torn margins of newspapers for keeping his accounts."

Yet, nearing the end of his life and contemplating eternity, Ben Wofford apparently recalled the exhortations of Wesley, Asbury and Dougherty, whom in his youthful enthusiasm he had so much admired. And, amid the founding of institutions throughout the South such as Davidson, Furman, Randolph-Macon,

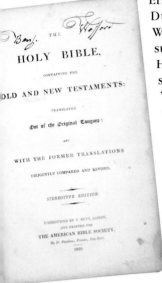

Erskine and Trinity (later Duke University), Ben Wofford responded to the suggestion of his friend, H.A.C. Walker, that he should found a college—"spreading, working, increasing in power and goodness through the ages as they come"—with one of the largest bequests ever made for that purpose. The college that would bear his name was to educate both mind and spirit, to instruct the youth of the South not merely in what was profitable but in what was right and decent, pursuing an ideal later to be enshrined in the motto of the school that it should continue "to shine with untarnished honor."

—*Benjamin Dunlap*
From his inaugural address, 2001

A monument marks the birthplace of Benjamin Wofford on the Tyger River in southern Spartanburg County. Dr. Lewis P. Jones '38 (right) enjoyed a pilgrimage to the site with members of Pi Kappa Alpha fraternity on an autumn afternoon in the mid-1980s.

Anna Todd Wofford
and Maria Barron Wofford

Though it was Benjamin Wofford's will that provided for the founding of Wofford College, without the two women who were his wives, there would have been no funds for a bequest.

The only child of Thomas and Ann Todd, Anna Todd was born on July 23, 1784. Thomas Todd was one of the largest landowners in

The old Todd farmhouse in southern Spartanburg County looked this way in the late 19th century.

southern Spartanburg County and thus one of the wealthiest men in the backcountry. Anna met Benjamin Wofford, probably at the church on her father's property, in the early 1800s, and they were married on July 30, 1807. Thomas Todd built the young couple a house near his home, which became known in the family as the "red house."

When Thomas Todd died in July 1809, Ben and Anna moved to the Todd house to be closer to Anna's mother. Benjamin Wofford was the executor of the Todd estate. Beginning in 1816, Ben served first as the minister of the Enoree Circuit, then of the Reedy River Circuit. When Mrs. Todd died in 1818, Anna and Ben continued to live in the home, and Anna inherited all of Thomas Todd's estate. The laws of the day gave Benjamin Wofford the ownership of all of his wife's personal

property, and management (but not ownership) of her real estate. This inheritance allowed Ben and Anna Todd Wofford to live comfortably but not lavishly, and the additional income allowed Ben to become an investor, mostly in bank stocks. Perhaps these responsibilities, along with the uncertainties of serving as an itinerant Methodist minister in the early 1800s, led Ben to leave the active ministry in 1820.

By all accounts, Anna Todd Wofford was a generous woman, known for many kind deeds. Wofford family tradition credits Anna with planting in his mind the idea of supporting education. President James H. Carlisle wrote in the winters that Ben and Anna lived in Columbia, they were associated with Rev. William Wightman, then the agent for Randolph-Macon College, the only Methodist college in the South at the time, and through him, with its president, Dr. Stephen Olin. Carlisle wrote, "These influences, no doubt, helped to enlarge the plans of benevolence which Mr. Wofford and his wife had begun very early to devise."

As they had no children, Ben invited his niece, Nancy Tucker, to come to live with him and Anna. Around 1830, when Nancy married, Ben sold the property to her husband and moved to a new home a few miles south of the Todd plantation. The only stipulation made in the property transaction was that Ben reserved a small area of land around the graves of Thomas and Ann Todd for his and Anna's burial. When Anna Todd Wofford died in October 1835, her funeral overflowed the nearby Grace Chapel that Ben Wofford had built.

After Anna's death, Ben traveled, and while in either Virginia or East Tennessee, he met Maria Scott Barron. She was the daughter of Dr. Hendley Barron, a native of Maryland who, with his wife, Margery Cox Barron, moved to an area south of Alexandria, Virginia, after their marriage. Maria Barron was one of 10 children, all of whom were educated beyond what would have been considered average for the day. One of her sisters married a distant cousin of George Washington, and a brother married a granddaughter of George Mason. Maria and Ben were married in September 1836 in Greene County, Tennessee, where Maria's sister, Ann Barron Wells, lived. He was 56; she was 33. D. D. Wallace wrote in the *History of Wofford College*, "In both his marriages Wofford illustrated that common occurrence of a man of ability out-marrying himself socially."

Benjamin and Maria Barron Wofford returned to his home in southern Spartanburg County, but after a few years, Maria grew tired of rural life. They moved into the village of Spartanburg in 1840, living in a home on the courthouse square. As the couple had no children, they busied themselves with visiting friends and family, attending church events and occasional travel. Maria must have known of Ben's interest in education, for he nearly bought a plot of land near Limestone Springs in 1844 to give to the Annual Conference for a school or college. She also had learned a few things about Ben's gifts for making money. Maria wrote her sister in 1847 that she would rather have money than slaves from her mother's estate, for "I could loan it out and it would do me more good."

After the death of her husband on December 2, 1850, Maria Wofford was not particularly happy to see so much of her husband's estate given to other people. However, Ben had provided for his wife, leaving her their home and furnishings, carriage and livestock, $10,000, and 50 acres of land. Still, she did not contest the will. Gradually, Maria came to see herself as a co-founder of the college. She was present at the laying of the cornerstone of Main Building in 1851, and a lock of her hair went into the cornerstone. Dr. Carlisle writes that the college treated her as a co-founder by giving her an honored place at ceremonies and commencements. Perhaps relieved that she did not challenge the will, the trustees granted her a scholarship permitting her to send a student to the college tuition free.

While Barron family tradition says that all seven of her favorite sister's sons were to have a free education at Wofford, only two of her nephews, Benjamin Wofford Wells and Gustavus Barron Wells, ever enrolled in the college or the fitting school. The founder's namesake enrolled in 1858 and attended through his junior year in 1861. He died in Confederate service at Richmond on October 29, 1862. A third nephew became a Methodist minister in South Carolina. At the same time, Maria's niece, Maria Wells, came to live with her in Spartanburg. When young Maria Wells married, Maria Wofford moved to New York with her. Eventually, Maria Wells Agnew and her family found their way to North Hudson,

Displayed in an elaborate case against a dark background, this ambrotype image of Maria Barron Wofford actually is fixed on the back side of the polished glass plate. No likeness exists of Anna Todd Wofford, Benjamin Wofford's first wife.

Wisconsin. Maria Wofford maintained contact with the college, and it was her wish that the portraits of her and of her husband be presented to the college after her death on January 13, 1883. Those portraits hang in the DuPré Administration Building, side by side, to this day.

In 1920, on Founder's Day, the graves of Benjamin and Anna Todd Wofford were moved to the campus. Today, they lie side by side, 70 yards in front of a building neither lived to see constructed, under a monument bearing the words, translated, "if his monument you seek, look around."

—*Phillip Stone '94*

In 1920, on Founder's Day, the graves of Benjamin and Anna Wofford were moved to the campus from the Todd family cemetery.

Edward C. Jones *and a* Classical Tradition

Edward C. Jones, the man chosen by Wofford's original Board of Trustees to design the Main Building, was one of South Carolina's leading architects in the 1850s. A native of Charleston, Jones was best known for designing public buildings in the Italianate style, which was quite popular in South Carolina during the 1850s.

Jones first became active in Charleston in the late 1840s, when he designed the Westminster Presbyterian Church (now Trinity United Methodist Church). He soon found his talents much sought after in and around the Holy City, and in 1850, his plans were selected as the design for Roper Hospital. He became the surveyor and architect for the city's Magnolia Cemetery. Later that year, Jones designed the Church of the Holy Cross in Stateburg, South Carolina. Perhaps his most unusual building, the cruciform church was built of pisé de terre and was in the Ecclesiological style. In the following years, he designed the Bank of Augusta in Augusta, Georgia; a courthouse in Bennettsville, South Carolina; and Furman's Richard Furman Hall.

By the time Wofford's trustees held their organizational meeting in Spartanburg in April 1851, their chairman, the Rev. William M. Wightman, almost certainly would have been familiar with Jones' work. That summer, the future Wofford president described Jones' proposed design for the Main Building in the newspaper he edited, the *Southern Christian Advocate*.

Jones entered a partnership with Francis D. Lee, his former student, in 1852. Over the next five years, they designed numerous buildings in Charleston, including the Citadel Square Baptist Church, the State Bank Building at 1 Broad Street and the building at 2 Broad Street that for many years housed the offices of printers Walker, Evans and Cogswell. Other works included the Farmers' and Exchange Bank on East Bay Street, jails in Walterboro and Orangeburg, and the main building of the South Carolina School for the Deaf and the Blind in Spartanburg. This structure is now called Walker Hall and has been beautifully restored.

Jones designed a number of homes around the state as well, including Kensington in lower Richland County, a Renaissance Revival mansion that was built in 1854. In Charleston, he designed the Col. Algernon S. Ashe house at 26 South Battery, noted for its two-tiered arcaded porches.

After the Civil War, he moved to Memphis, Tennessee, where he resumed his work as an architect. Partnering with Mathias Harvey Baldwin, Jones first came to the attention of the Memphis community in 1868 when he coordinated the design of the block of commercial buildings that included the original Peabody Hotel on Monroe Avenue. Jones was regarded as one of the most accomplished architects in Memphis, known for the symmetry in design and tasteful ornamentation of his buildings. A number of the homes he designed are in Italianate or French Victorian style.

Jones' last major project was the design of the 1895 Porter Building, a 12-story building that was the first steel skyscraper built south of the Ohio River. The building, with a Renaissance palazzo effect on its top two floors, was something of a tourist attraction. Visitors paid ten cents to ride the elevator to the top floor to view the city.

Jones retired in 1897. One of his retirement projects was the creation of a chart of the history of the world along religious lines. He died in 1902, at age 80, having contributed to the architectural style both of antebellum Charleston and the late 19th century building boom in Memphis.

—*Phillip Stone '94*

These are three examples of the work of Edward Jones. On top, he chose the Italianate style for Kensington Mansion, which was completed in 1854 as a plantation residence for Matthew Richard Singleton. In the middle, the Gothic Church of the Holy Cross (Episcopal) at Stateburg was built in 1850. The exterior walls are made of earthquake-proof pisé de terre (rammed earth). At bottom, Furman Hall, on the old campus of the university in downtown Greenville, was erected in 1851 and demolished in the 1960s.

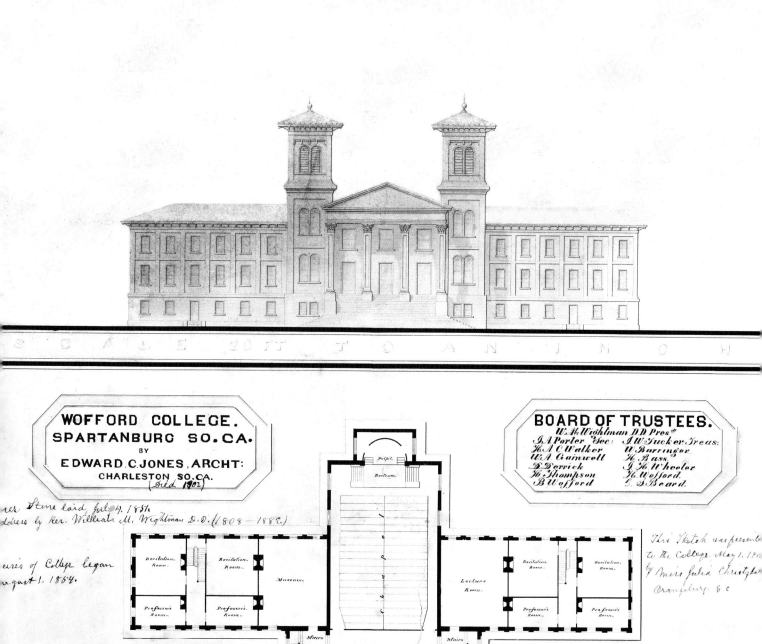

SCALE 20 FT TO AN INCH

WOFFORD COLLEGE.
SPARTANBURG SO. CA.
BY
EDWARD. C. JONES, ARCHT:
CHARLESTON SO. CA.
(died 1902)

ner Stone laid Jul 4. 1851.
ddress by Rev. William M. Wightman D.D. (1808 – 1882.)

cises of College began
ugust 1. 1854.

This Sketch was presented
to the College May 1, 19
by Miss Julia Chreitzb
Orangeburg S C

Recitation Room.   Recitation Room.   Museum.   Pulpit.   Rostrum.   Lecture Room.   Recitation Room.   Recitation Room.

Professor's Room.   Professor's Room.   Chapel   Professor's Room.   Professor's Room.

Stairs   Stairs

Portico.

COLLEGE APARTMENTS.
- Chapel   48.80.   11. Recitation Rooms 22.24.
- Museum   30.37.   12. Professors Rooms 12.22.
- Library   30.37.   Chemical Lecture R. 30.37.
- 2 Society Rooms 30.37.   2 Study Rooms 30.50.

Main Building stands as one of the most ambitious projects ever built in the classical Italianate style, gradually becoming popular throughout the South for academic and other public buildings during the mid 19th century. The college is fortunate to possess Edward C. Jones' original drawings, presented in 1902 by Julia Chreitzberg.

Duncans and DuPrés—the second generation.
Methodist Bishop William Wallace Duncan was a son of
Professor David Duncan and a member of the Wofford Class of
1858. He also served the college as a faculty member and later
as a trustee. He appears to be the model of a Victorian family
man in the photograph, made in 1893 or 1894 in the study of
his stylish home on North Church Street. One of the bishop's
daughters (Caroline) married Warren DuPré, grandson of the
Wofford professor of the same name; the couple stands behind
the bishop in this picture. Another daughter was the wife of
Professor A.G. Rembert. The house was moved to Howard Street
in 1999 to make room for the Spartanburg Marriott at Renaissance Park. ~Courtesy of Wallace DuPré.

Duncans and DuPrés—the third generation.
Mary ("Mamie") Sydnor DuPré was the college librarian for
48 years; Dr. David Duncan Wallace was professor of
history and economics from 1899 through 1947.

Duncan and DuPré: Wofford College's First Families

They say if you walk the Wofford historic district on a quiet summer evening just after commencement, when the students have all gone home and the professors are on vacation, you can still feel the benevolent presence of first faculty families: you can hear the lively debates in rocking chairs on white-columned porches, see the gracious dinners by flickering gaslight, or hear some ghost from the past reading aloud from a letter or practicing a speech.

Dr. Lewis P. Jones '38 likens Wofford's first families (particularly the Duncan and DuPré families) to European dynasties. Wofford's first faculty not only taught the classics, they held administrative posts at the college and were active in the Methodist Church.

David Duncan, a member of the original faculty, studied Latin at the University of Glasgow in Scotland before serving for three years in the British navy. Family members are not quite sure why he jumped ship in Virginia, but descendant Wallace DuPré's theory is that he had been pressed into service and left the ship at the first opportunity. He taught at Randolph-Macon before coming to Wofford with William Wightman, Wofford's first president.

Duncan was the first occupant of the faculty home nearest the present Russell C. King baseball field, taught on the third floor of Main Building and served the college as treasurer, according to Jones, "a skill he had acquired while a British purser." He had five sons: James A. Duncan, who became president of Randolph-Macon; William Wallace Duncan (Class of 1858), who served as chaplain in Lee's Confederate army, joined the faculty in 1875, was elected a Methodist bishop in 1886 and served as chairman of the Wofford Board of Trustees for 19 years; Major D.R. Duncan, a lawyer, politician and railroad president for whom Duncan Park in Spartanburg is named; Col. D'Arcy P. Duncan, a state leader in agriculture and textiles; and Thomas Carey Duncan (Class of 1860), who was killed in the Civil War.

A granddaughter of David Duncan, Alice Amanda Lomax, and her husband, William Henry Wallace (Class of 1871), were the parents of another important figure in college history, David Duncan Wallace. Born in 1874, he completed a degree at Wofford in 1894 and continued in graduate studies at Vanderbilt, where he became the first to earn a doctorate in history at the Nashville university. He came back to Wofford in 1899 as head of the department of history and economics. Except for a few years on leave to do research and to write, he served continuously until he retired in 1947. Dr. Wallace had no peer among South Carolina historians of his generation. His straightforward and thorough works on the state's constitutional and political history have stood the test of time. He is also remembered today by generations of alumni for Dunc's Globe, which was first displayed in his classroom and later in a large lecture room on the first floor of Main Building's west wing. Convinced that political structures are temporary at best, Dunc declined to change the world's political boundaries after World War I and World War II and insisted on maintaining the boundaries of 1914. Legend also has it that students sometimes used the globe as a giant roulette wheel, spinning the globe and betting on which latitude it would stop.

Also on the college's first faculty was Warren DuPré, professor of science. He and his family moved into the house that stands to the left of Main Building (and is the only original

By the opening of the fall term of 1855, the Duncan and DuPré families had moved into two of the four original faculty homes, which are still in daily use. ~Courtesy of Cynthia and Carlos Mosley.

The 50th anniversary portrait of Professor and Mrs. Dan DuPré. ~Courtesy of Cynthia and Carlos Moseley.

house in this row of three). Five generations of Warren DuPré's family lived in the house: his father, Daniel DuPré (a Huguenot from Charleston who pronounced the name *dewPRAY*) lived on Wofford's campus for a year following the Civil War. Warren DuPré's son, also named Daniel, later lived in the house with his children and grandchildren. After Daniel's death, Dean A. Mason DuPré, a distant cousin, moved into the DuPré house. After that, it was converted into administrative offices.

When Warren left the college to become president of Martha Washington College in 1876, his son Daniel replaced him as Wofford's professor of natural sciences. Daniel held the position for more than 50 years, also serving as treasurer and superintendent of buildings and grounds. According to Daniel DuPré's daughter, Helen DuPré Moseley, her father "was a little boy 6 years old when the family came to Spartanburg, but he remembered riding in a stage coach … with the servants and furniture following in covered wagons."

Warren and Mary Ann Sydnor DuPré must have been covered in dust, stiff from the rough ride and completely wilted by the heat when they arrived on campus with sons, Sydnor (9) and Daniel (6), and daughters, Sarah (13), Mary Ann (4) and Lucy Palmer (a baby). Sadly, tragedy struck the family three weeks after arriving at Wofford. Sydnor died of typhoid fever, followed exactly a year later by Lucy. In the meantime, the DuPrés had two other children, Warren and Anna Leland. In later years Gertrude and William Beverly were born.

"The campus was rather stark in those days," Mrs. Moseley describes, "and there was no planting around the house, but Warren DuPré, with his great love of nature planted the older trees in the yard … as well as many of those on the campus … this love descended to his son Daniel, who planted the majority of oaks and elms of a later period."

She remembers that the rooms were heated by fireplaces, and in winter they were kept blazing with fires. In the living room "a semicircle of rocking chairs put some sitters farther away from the fire than others, so a frequent swapping of chairs took place, and sometimes if men were not present, a skirt might be lifted gently and one's backsides thoroughly warmed.

"On long winter evenings when we all sat around the fire, we loved to hear Papa [Daniel DuPré] talk of the past and the people he knew, and it is hard for me to realize that I did not also know 'Wightman' and 'Shipp' and 'Tilla Lomax' and 'Dr. David Duncan.' I do faintly remember Dr. Whitefoord Smith and his family."

Helen, an artist and postmaster of Spartanburg for 21 years, was born in the DuPré house on campus. Also born there were her sisters Mary Sydnor "Mamie" DuPré, who served as librarian of the college for 48 years, and Grace, a nationally recognized portrait artist. Her subjects included Harry Truman and his mother (a painting she never liked, but felt compelled to complete at the request of the president). A brother, Fayssoux DuPré, a baseball standout at Wofford, was born in Charleston.

After Helen's husband, Carlos Roland Moseley, died, she and her children came to live on campus. A son, Carlos Moseley Jr. (retired managing director, president and chairman of the New York Philharmonic), recalls the taste of the fruit of the trees behind the house—peaches, plums, apricots and persimmons "with their attendant honey bees, plus the plentiful bushes of Himalaya Blackberries and raspberries, scuppernong and grape vines and strawberry beds." His sister, Cynthia Moseley (a historian who has edited several volumes of family letters), also remembers a "large vegetable garden that stretched to Evins Street" and the cow, "which tempted students to play tricks."

May the echoes of Wofford's first families never cease to resonate through the halls of Wofford's buildings and the hearts of graduates.

—*JoAnn Mitchell Brasington '89*

Warren DuPré's Earthquake

I n February 1874 a series of small earthquakes shook Stone Mountain, North Carolina, just 40 miles north of the Wofford campus. A telegram printed in *The New York Herald* described the event in cataclysmic terms:

"Last night there was a succession of terrible shocks on the sides of Bald Mountain, accompanied by a sharp thunder storm. Simultaneously with the thunder, quick and loud reports could be heard from the mountain sides. The shaking of the earth was quite perceptible, and it was almost impossible to sleep. As yet no one has been able to give any definite account of the source of the convulsion. ... A party of students from Spartanburg, accompanied by a professor of geology arrived at Rutherford last evening, and will make a scientific examination."

Wofford Professor Warren DuPré was the leader of the scientific team mentioned in the dispatch, which was reprinted, closer to home, in Charleston's *News and Courier* newspaper March 25, 1874. DuPré subsequently wrote this letter to his father, Daniel DuPré, a planter, of Palmetto Plantation, St. James, Santee. At the time the letter was written Professor Warren DuPré was 58 years old; his father was 81.

—special thanks to Terry Ferguson '75

My Dear Father,

Our trip to the mountains was quite amusing, although it was cold and raining most of the time. We had altogether six buggies and five saddle horses—making quite a cavalcade along the road. ... After supper, furnished and cooked by the students, we gathered around a big fire and laughed until our sides ached at the accounts of the earthquake by our hosts, Mr. and Mrs. Elliott. You would suppose the mountain had a big bellyache, and that their house was rocked by the contortions of the entrails. Before going to bed, I took occasion to explain the different theories of earthquakes, to which Elliott and wife seemed to listen with great interest. Next morning Elliott said to Carson, one of the seniors, "Ain't that old man in there a very smart codger? He must have read a dozen books!"

The people about the mountains took up the notion that I had the power of stopping the commotion, or of abating its effects. They followed me everywhere, offered their services to do anything I wanted, and begged me not to leave them. They would feed us all with our horses, for nothing, if we would only stay with them a week. For two weeks they had prayer meetings day and night. ... They met at some house, 50 or 60 together, and everyone just knuckled down on the floor and each one prayed for himself as loud as he could, all at the same time. You can thus form some idea of their fright and the excitement.

After ascending to the highest point of Stone Mountain, we met the reporters of the New York Herald & Tribune. After promising to give them an interview next day, our party went on to Hickory Nut Gap. The water of the falls seemed to descend from the clouds as we looked in showers of pearls mingled with white foam, that dashed upon the platform where we stood, then leaped and bounded from rock to rock down the mountain gorge for a thousand feet below us ...

If the commotions continue until July, I will make a more thorough exploration during my vacation. In two days I had not time to observe much, and it will require weeks of observation and exploration to get sufficient facts upon which to base a decided opinion.

Your afft son,
W. DuPré

From the very beginning of the college, geology has been taught in the field. This photograph was made early in the 20th century, when students were expected to come to class in coats, ties and hats.

FROM A LOST GENERATION, HAUNTING WORDS AND FACES

To be a student at Wofford in the 1850s meant encountering new ideas and meeting new people in a pleasant, if quiet, small-town atmosphere. The young men (boys, really) were excited about being away from home for the first time, but they were also in close emotional touch with their families and friends. They dreamed big dreams about their futures, which some of them had begun to hope would be lived out in an independent Southern Confederacy.

Many of these thoughts were articulately written and mailed. In keeping with the culture of the time, the recipients put the letters away carefully and saved them, and they became special family treasures after the Civil War decimated the ranks of these young alumni. The letters here are just a sampler. Additional letters written by Wofford students and alumni before and during the Civil War may be found in the college archives and at the South Caroliniana Library.

—Texts chosen and edited by Karla Parris '04

Spartanburg Courthouse

October 6, 1855

My dear Brother,

I take my pen in hand to write a hasty line or two this morning. I wrote yesterday a letter to Aunt C—. Tell her I was very unlucky about that letter, for I did not hear the college bell, and therefore was late at college.

It is just clearing off from a rain, which commenced yesterday afternoon and continued through the night; and it is a windy day. Several persons in the [boarding] house have colds, but so far I am clear and will try and keep so. Mr. Fripp and myself have a comfortable room, with the additional comfort of a fireplace. I am gradually getting over being foolishly homesick and am tolerably well satisfied with my situation.

I spoke in the chapel of the college on Thursday last. It is the custom to speak selected pieces. I gave them "The Future." Mr. Fripp gave them "Destiny of Mind" the next day, and spoke admirably well. I am getting used to the college, and like it very well, if they would only have regularity in ringing the bells. But they vary from 10 minutes before to about 10 minutes after the proper hour in ringing the first time, and then ring the second at the right time, thus creating great confusion.

I saw the first Charleston paper I have seen since I left Charleston this morning. The papers here have hardly any news at all, and what they have very uninteresting. I wish you would send me some paper with interesting news about once a week, at least. Some Tuesday, Thursday, or Saturday paper, as they will give the latest news in shortest time; or if others are more interesting, send others.

I am very sorry to hear of Miss Hannah's illness, and hope she is better ere this. I received a letter this morning from Mr. Turner, which stated that Father was in church Sunday looking very much improved by his trip to the North.

But I must close. I am going to do some studying today, and have not any more time to write. Give my love to Father, Mother, Aunts, Fanny, Freddy, and kiss the children. Howdy to Mary. Goodbye. Accept the love of

Your Affectionate Brother
Sam'l Dibble

Samuel Dibble of Orangeburg, who left the College of Charleston after participating in a student "rebellion," entered Wofford as a junior. He was thus the only member of the first graduating class of 1856. He returned to his hometown, where he ultimately enlisted as a private in a local Confederate company, the Edisto Rifles, in July 1861. Dibble was mentioned in an official report for his heroism during the Battle of Secessionville. After being promoted to first lieutenant, he was captured on Morris Island on July 10, 1863, and spent more than a year as a prisoner of war. He was exchanged in October 1864, but was taken prisoner again during the Siege of Petersburg. Samuel Dibble survived the war and became an attorney and businessman in Orangeburg. He served five terms in the U.S. House of Representatives. He is credited with improving the port of Charleston and also played a key role in the establishment of South Carolina State College.

Samuel Dibble with his wife and daughter posed for this picture after the Civil War, perhaps during his service in Congress. Dibble's gray frock coat suggests that the photograph may have been made at a reunion of Confederate officers. ~Courtesy of Caroline Emanuel

Wofford College

October 16, 1858

My dear Aunt,

Since my arrival I have enjoyed myself finely. I spent the night with Cousin John Wright and have become acquainted with most of the "Big Bugs." All kindly invite me to call on them. Of course I promised. And when I become better acquainted with them, I expect to make good my promise.

I am perfectly delighted with the faculty, students and citizens in general. If you wish to send Harry to a place noted for its morality, Wofford College is the place. I suppose we have the ablest faculty South, or as able as any. Mr. Carlisle, the professor of mathematics, will deservedly be called the eighth wonder of the world. We are doing very well as to the collegiate course and find that it takes harder studying than we anticipated.

I went to the Ladies Fair the other night and saw some of the prettiest work I ever saw. The things are so numerous I can't mention half of them. But suffice to say they far surpassed the Pendleton ladies in their exhibitions. A good many of the students were out and we had so much fun that whilst participating it brought the pleasant times I have had in Pendleton so vividly before me that I had to go off and think alone. Oh how delightful the sweet reminiscences of home!

No news of importance having occurred, except a little scrape in town between Young Walker (that good for nothing chap that was in Pendleton some time ago and was taken up by Hanby Campbell and John Sloan for debt) and another of the citizens. What the fuss was about I don't know, but it went so far that Walker pulled out a pistol, fired twice in his opponent's face; one ball took effect. Shattered his upper jaw and passed under the skin near his eye where it lies yet. Walker is in jail and the wounded in quite a critical condition.

Tell Carrie, Bessie and Harry and all to write me a letter. For nothing would so fill me with pleasure as to receive news from their little hands.

Write soon dear Aunt.
And ever believe me your devoted nephew
T.N. Simpson

Taliaferro (Tally) and Dick Simpson, who both attended Wofford, were the sons of South Carolina Congressman Richard F. Simpson of Pendleton. During the Fort Sumter crisis, Tally went to Columbia and offered the student Southern Guards rifle company to the governor, but was turned down, because the governor wanted them to at least finish the 1860-61 term. Dick and Tally ignored that advice and went to Laurens to join the Third South Carolina volunteers, where a number of their cousins and family friends had enlisted. Their first company commander was Conway Garlington, who soon was named the regiment's lieutenant colonel but was killed at Savage Station during the Seven Days Battles. Dick Simpson married Maria L. Garlington, Conway's sister, in February 1863. She had diphtheria on her wedding day, but Dick's health was so precarious (he had to be discharged from the Confederate Army in July 1862 because of chronic dysentery, a complication of an earlier bout with the measles) that they got married anyway. It turned out that they almost made it to a Golden Anniversary (47 years). Tally served in the ranks of this company until he was killed at the Battle of Chickamauga in 1863.

Tally Simpson in the uniform of the Southern Guards at Wofford. ~Courtesy of Ed Simpson

February 16, 1860

Dear Brother,

I received your kind letter a short time since, and now I have just returned from college and shall endeavor to answer it. We have had some very inclement weather for the last few days, but it has cleared away now, and we have some very pleasant weather with the exception of the wind, which blows very hard.

I attended a hot supper about five weeks ago given by the ladies of the Presbyterian Church, at which I enjoyed myself very much. There was also another party last Monday night, but I did not attend it, for one dollar was too much to throw away, so I remained at home. Last night, I heard a temperance lecture from Professor Carlisle. It was an excellent address, the best I've heard in some time. I think I shall join the Sons of Temperance next Wednesday night.

I suppose you have heard that Mr. [George] Cofield was elected tutor in College. I like him very much, as he and Professor [Warren] DuPré are the only ones in the faculty who show any justice at all. But I shall be satisfied with even that, for we do not recite to any of the others regularly except Professor [David] Duncan, and as for him, he seems to be more childish every day. And if he happens to take a liking to anyone, he will do all he can for him, but he is just as bad on the opposite side, and I think I am one who he did not exactly take a liking to. However, I can do very well without his love, and it is only that of a Scotchman anyway. But enough of this matter.

You must try to persuade Patrick and Edwin to come up to College. I think Pat could be persuaded to come up in October. He would then enter the sophomore class, the same one with myself. I hope he will come. We want as many as possible. We have 23. One of them quit because his father would not pay his way through, but our class had a meeting and agreed to pay his way ourselves, and he has concluded to stay. It will be about six dollars a year. I think he will not take a thorough course, but I do not know. I expect that we will have about 100 students next year.

Well, I have nothing more to write now, very dull times now about Spartanburg. They have a railroad meeting occasionally in order to carry on the present railroad up into North Carolina. I suppose they will eventually succeed, but not for a very long time.
Give my love to all the family, Miss Willie and Mary.

Your affectionate servant,
Sumter W. Tarrant

These typical Wofford students of the late 1850s lived at Mrs. Dean's boarding house in the courthouse village.

R. Benson Tarrant and Sumter W. Tarrant were sons of John Robert Tarrant of the Mink Trap section of Abbeville District. While his older brother was an excellent scholar, Sumter Tarrant's spelling and grammar left much to be desired, and he was quite the unhappy student. He rushed to the colors in time to fight at First Manassas. After this battle, he wrote in a 13-page letter home that he had heard that to fight in a battle offers a kind of sublimity, but "I don't wish to feel sublime very often." That fall, he died of disease in an army hospital. R.B. was the first honor graduate of the class of 1858. He was admitted to the South Carolina Conference of the Methodist Church and was assigned to the Orangeburg circuit when the incumbent minister became a Confederate chaplain. For a while, he solely was responsible for 18 churches located within a 40-mile radius of Orangeburg. When Sherman reached South Carolina early in 1865, R.B. joined the Confederate Army as a quartermaster, but he was soon captured. He was offered the opportunity to serve as a chaplain in the Union Army rather than become a prisoner of war, but he declined, finally making his way home in December 1865. After the war, he was a preacher, teacher, legislator and later the postmaster in Springfield, South Carolina. He died in 1922.

How Zach Came to College

For two decades, the canteen in the Campus Life Building—Zach's—has been a part of everyday Wofford life. Many customers never stop to consider the namesake of the frequented spot. In fact, the story is quite intriguing and perpetuates the legend of a first-generation Wofford student.

Dr. John G. Clinkscales graduated from Wofford in 1876 and returned to the college in 1899 as a faculty member. One of his principal duties was to recruit students and solicit funds in South Carolina communities and Methodist churches. In such assemblies, he loved to tell the story of Zachary Taylor Whiteside of the class of 1877, a mountaineer from the Green River Valley of North Carolina. In 1904, Clink recorded this story in a novelette, and in this passage he paints a memorable picture of the day Zach decided to go to college.

One warm, lazy June day in the early 1870s, there stood in a store door in Spartanburg two men—one, the proprietor, Maj. John A. Lee, the other, a young mountaineer … Stroking his heavy boots with one end of his long whip handle, the young man raised his brown eyes till they met those of his friend, and then said, with some hesitation:

"Major, whut's that?"

"That's a bell, the College bell; they are having Commencement over there today," replied the gentle, sympathetic merchant.

"Whut is Commencement, Major, and whut is a college?" asked the lad, this time an expression of intense interest spreading over his face.

The kind-hearted business man consumed several minutes endeavoring to convey to the mind of the young man some idea of what a college is supposed to be and do, and of what is meant by the word commencement when used in this way, and then said:

The Wofford bell, "From Meneely's, West Troy, NY, 1854," weighs approximately 700 pounds and is 33 inches in diameter. Recently restored and enhanced by 21st century technology, it has served as the "voice" of Wofford for 150 years.

"I am going over to attend the exercises, won't you go along with me?"

"Don't keer if I do," was the quick reply, and the mountaineer shambled off to his cart to get his coat with the apparent delight of one who has just received a new view of the possibilities of life.

The dazed mountaineer watched with intense interest the long line of students file into the hall and the fifteen members of the Senior Class take their seats on the rostrum preparatory to delivering their graduating speeches.

After one particularly patriotic address in which the young orator spoke of the "Lost Cause, the Blood of Southern Boys" and "The Graves of the Gallant Confederate Dead," the band played Dixie, and the audience "went wild."

When the applause subsided, our mountaineer leaned over and whispered to his friend, the merchant: "Major, I'll speak up thar one o' these days…"

The students repaired to their homes and boarding houses—the mountaineer to his cart. On the walk from the college, he spoke but few words. He was thoughtful. That day, a purpose was born in him. He became another man.

Zach, along with his brother, Zeb, did in fact leave home in the Green River Gorge in North Carolina to attend Wofford. During their college careers, the two recognized the problem of the expense of room and board in town, as it was not provided on campus. A small group of less affluent students were being allowed to camp out in unused classrooms, and the Whitesides organized them into a co-op to purchase food and cook a traditional Southern noon-time dinner. Zach's lasted for several years until college officials, probably concerned about the dangers of fire, began operating a dining room called Wightman Hall on the first floor of Main Building.

According to college historian David Duncan Wallace, Zach went on to become a Baptist preacher, and Zeb "a good citizen farmer in their native valleys."

— *Kristin Sams '05*

Culler Family: Present at the Creation

Five generations of Orangeburg's Culler family have studied at Wofford College, starting with Hayne Leonidas Culler, who attended before the Civil War. There were Cullers at Wofford when McKinley was shot, when the stock market crashed, and during the Vietnam War. As the college prepared to celebrate its Sesquicentennial in 2004, at least a dozen family names representing five generations of Cullers were on the alumni roll books, including Katherine Wilkinson '05.

The story of the Culler family in South Carolina actually began more than a century before the founding of Wofford College. Benedict Koller (as the name was originally spelled) arrived in Charleston from Pomaria in 1735. He had received a substantial land grant in the Orangeburgh Township, part of a plan to attract settlers to the backcountry. Their holdings, which eventually acquired the name Millwood Farms Inc., always have been among the most prosperous agriculture businesses in the state.

Why the first Culler came to Wofford is not known, but it's possible his family knew Wofford's first graduate, Samuel Dibble of Orangeburg, or there may have been a Methodist Church connection. In any case, the official records of the college show that in January 1857, Hayne Culler, son of Jacob Culler of Orangeburg, enrolled with sophomore standing. A family emergency, and then the Civil War, interrupted Culler's studies, and he was not able to complete a degree.

His son, Edgar Leonidas Culler, graduated from Wofford in 1897, and Edgar's son, Woodward "Woody" Durham Culler, graduated in 1928. Two of Woody's brothers also graduated from Wofford: Edgar L. Culler '29 and Dr. O.Z. Culler Sr. '30. Representing the fourth generation, Woody's son, Hayne Culler, graduated in 1966. "My brother and at least five cousins graduated in the 1960s," Hayne Culler says. "Wofford means everything to me. I'm in love with the institution."

Stewart Culler '96, Hayne's daughter, represented a fifth-generation Wofford legacy. She recalls that when she was only 6 or 7 years old, the Culler family passed near Spartanburg on the way home from a mountain vacation. Her grandfather requested a stop on the campus to have a photograph taken in front of Main Building with all of his grandchildren. She remembered thinking at the time that "Old Main" must have more steps than any building in the world.

"I made wonderful, lasting relationships at Wofford College," Stewart Culler says warmly, when reminiscing about her college years. "I loved the fact that I didn't have to go out to meet people. All my best friends were right on campus."

—*Beth Varner Broadwell '90*
and David H. LaBorde '07

Hayne L. Culler, shown here in his Confederate uniform, studied at Wofford from January 1857 through June 1858.

Edgar Leonidas Culler (class of 1897) posed for this graduation portrait in the regalia of a literary society president. Both illustrations courtesy of J. Hayne Culler '66.

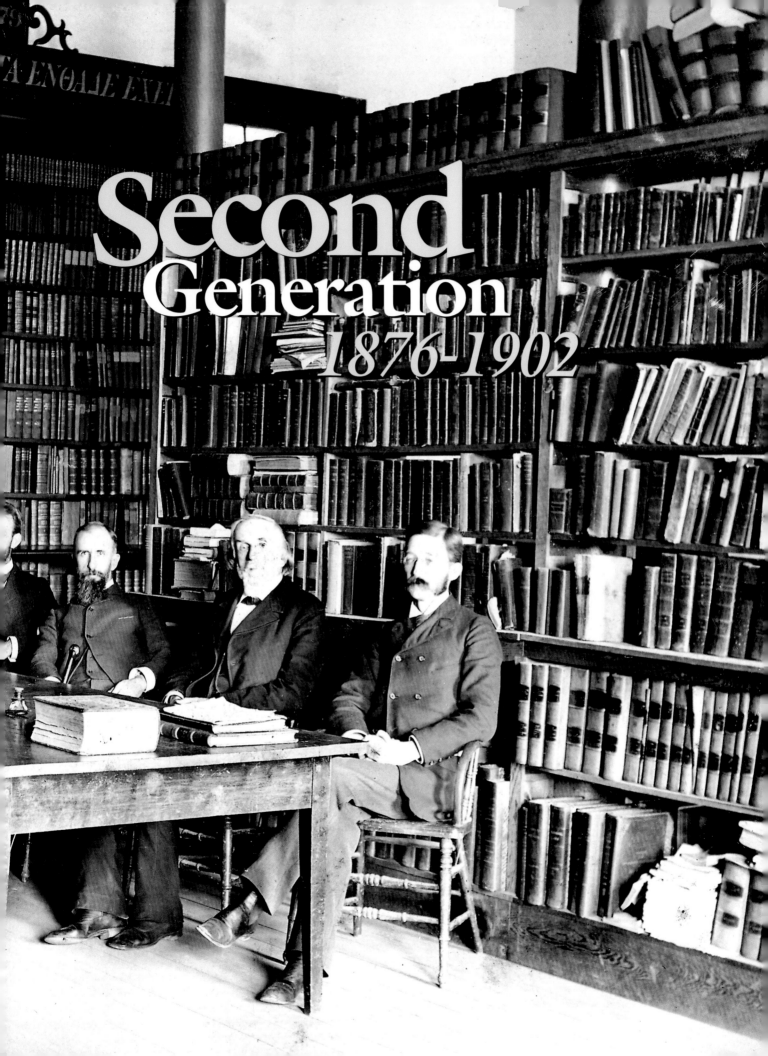

Second
Generation
1876-1902

ETHICAL LEADERS FOR A NEW SOUTH

by Philip N. Racine

This unusual bird's-eye view looking south shows the Spartanburg legal and business district. Church Street recently had been rerouted to bypass the campus, and the Spartan Mill village had displaced the residential area west of the campus. ~Courtesy of the Spartanburg County Historical Association

In 1876, one year after his election as president of Wofford College, James H. Carlisle wrote in his report to the college Board of Trustees: "We have been at times rendered anxious about the morals of some of the students, from causes rendered necessary perhaps by the change which our town is passing through in its growth from a retired village to a thoroughfare on two lines of daily railroads."

Carlisle here reflected a truism that marked

These public improvements complemented a new courthouse on Magnolia Street that stood across the way from the Cleveland Law Range, a stately new office building. The wealth being created in the area built not only public and commercial office buildings but also many magnificent Victorian homes on Magnolia, Main, Church and Pine streets. These improvements added to the aura of prosperity in Morgan Square given off by the Spartan Inn and the Palmetto House (both

(preceding pages) The faculty gathered in the library of Main Building for this picture on February 25, 1894. Shown are A.G. Rembert, J.B. Thomas, D.B. Easter, John C. Kilgo, Henry Nelson Snyder, James A. Gamewell, James H. Carlisle and Daniel A. DuPré. Note the Greek inscription on the bookshelf and the gaslight fixture (Main Building did not become electrified until after 1900).

Spartanburg throughout his presidency, which ended in 1902. The town grew at an amazing pace (a threefold increase during the 1870s alone). As the population increased, investors moved headlong into the Industrial Age. They built cotton mills and their accompanying villages at an incredible rate (29 mills built between 1881 and 1902) and attracted railroads that connected Spartanburg to the rest of the country. In 1881, city leaders placed a statue of Daniel Morgan in the city center to commemorate the centennial of the Battle of Cowpens. They erected gas lamps in what had become known as Morgan Square, followed eight years later by electric lights, a sewage disposal system, a public water supply, a fire department and, by 1892, a streetcar system.

hotels), the Opera House (a public theater and administrative building), and the First National Bank, all of which generated that feeling of dynamism and spirit of modernization alluded to in Carlisle's prescient remark to his board. Indeed, this activity epitomized the late 1880s phrase, "the New South," coined by Henry Grady, the editor of Atlanta's newspaper, *The Constitution*. This New South spirit needed to be nurtured and given direction, and what better source of inspiration than a Christian, liberal arts institution such as Spartanburg's own Wofford College?

Located auspiciously on the city's northern border, Wofford's geographical orientation symbolized its leadership potential. Unlike some communities in the South in the last

On January 25, 1837, Benjamin Wofford and eight others constituted Central Methodist Church, creating the first congregation in the courthouse village. Over the years, the connection between this church and the college has been exceptionally close. This handsome building, the third to serve the congregation, dates from 1885-1886. ~From the postcard collection of Steve Garris

quarter of the 19th century, Spartanburg supported its all-men's liberal arts college as a necessary component of its progress. Just as the South, and Spartanburg in particular, was adopting Northern industrialization with a Southern twist, so might Wofford College learn from Northern educational experience. In the 1870s, Wofford acquired a new president, James H. Carlisle, and hired several new faculty members who were determined to bring about changes in the curriculum intended to develop stronger and better leadership for the newly industrializing South.

These changes actually came in two installments, the first in the 1870s and 1880s, and the second in the 1890s. In the 1870s, the trustees hired two new faculty members, Charles Forster Smith (class of 1872) and W. M. Baskervill. Within a few years, the college faculty substituted written tests for oral examinations and offered a Bachelor of Science degree that allowed students to substitute modern languages for the classical languages required for the B.A. degree. This action reflected a national trend to emphasize the study of English language and literature, placing it on par with classical languages. Finally, the faculty required more science courses, again following a trend in American higher education that favored the study of science over any other discipline. At Wofford, though, that emphasis was not as strong as in other schools where science reigned supreme as the ultimate source of the soundest knowledge. Simultaneously, the doctoral degree, a research degree at the heart of

Main Building sprouted a third tower in 1876 for a U.S. Coastal Survey. The mapping crew triangulated the precise latitude and longitude by observing signal lights on King's and Hogback mountains. The roof over the chapel was found to be 878.8 feet above sea level, the tallest structure in Spartanburg at the time. ~Courtesy of Cynthia and Carlos Moseley

These photographs are from Wofford's first pictorial admissions prospectus, dating from 1898. At the top is Daniel DuPré's natural science laboratory and museum in Main Building. Both the exterior and interior of the Wilbur E. Burnett Gymnasium are shown. Opened in 1897 and demolished after World War II, this facility stood on a site later used for parking by the Spartanburg Memorial Auditorium.

German education, became the benchmark for quality in American higher education. Both Smith and Baskervill went on leave from Wofford to earn their doctorates in Germany, and Baskervill became the first Wofford faculty member to possess the coveted distinction.

The second wave of changes occurred in the 1890s when the number of new hires composed a majority of the faculty. Among these were Henry Nelson Snyder, S.R. Pritchard, J.C. Kilgo and David Duncan Wallace, all of whom were intent on curriculum reform. Of these, Kilgo was the most outspoken and the most willing to lead the rest of the faculty to improve both the curriculum and the quality of the student body. Curriculum changes further eroded the influence of the classical languages, introduced even more science courses, and strengthened the master's degree. They also caused disagreement between the newer and older faculty, but the real tension was between the faculty and the Board of Trustees. Many trustees had held their positions for decades, and they resented what they considered the brashness of the young and new faculty. Also, they saw the changes advocated by the new faculty as devaluing character education, although President Carlisle's presence proved an important counterweight to that impression. Yet, modernization would not be denied, and reform, curricular and otherwise, did take place.

The most manifest of these changes began in 1887 when the board founded the Wofford Fitting School (a high school for future Wofford students) adjacent to the campus. The board took this action as a result of what President Carlisle had told them in 1885:

We have tried to meet as fully as we could, the difficulties that arise from the insufficient preparation of those who join our Introductory Class. Only those in the actual work can appreciate the embarrassments under which the colleges of our State have labored because of the want of good schools.

The problem of an inadequate public school system in South Carolina continued. In 1891 the trustees decided to create more fitting schools, which they called Training Schools for Wofford College, throughout the state, although the first of these, founded in Bamberg County in 1892, was also the last.

Who were these young men who the faculty and Board of Trustees were trying to educate? Not surprisingly they were not much

different from contemporary students. In 1880 there were 125 of them, and in 1890-91 there were 258. Their tuition ranged from $226 to $370. Many of them, in an effort to keep their costs down, ate their meals in a student-initiated and student-run cafeteria located in the Main Building. They were from all over South Carolina. After 1886, they enjoyed organized athletics, especially tennis and baseball. In 1896, the Board of Trustees, in step with other Southern colleges and universities, denounced football as brutal and a hindrance to intellectual pursuits and banned intercollegiate play from the campus. That sport had been imported from the Northeast, but it was one Yankee innovation that proved unwelcome until reinstated in 1900. Intercollegiate play did not resume until 1914.

Social activities included an avid interest in Spartanburg's young women, especially those at Converse College, founded in 1889. Wofford men had women on campus from 1897 to 1904 when the college had a fleeting period

of coeducation, but the experiment was abandoned. Many students joined social fraternities, which in 1898 began occupying cottages on campus, and the college required all students to join either the Preston or Calhoun Literary societies that existed for "improvement in Declamation, Composition and Debate."

Wofford is fortunate to have a journal (ably edited by Maureen Ward Shealy '87) kept by a student, Henry Felder Jennings, in the spring of his junior year and throughout his senior year of 1890-91. Jennings' journal gives significant attention to classes and an appreciation for the new professors, especially Kilgo and Snyder, whose departments he thinks "will become interesting." He was fiercely loyal to his fraternity, Chi Phi. In addition, drinking and other activities, to which Carlisle frequently alluded in his annual report to the trustees, seem to have been widespread. On a Wednesday, Jennings refereed a tennis match but was too drunk to do it well—he also admitted to not knowing

The brothers of Chi Phi fraternity posed for this picture in 1896. Joining the students were Professor Henry Nelson Snyder (center) and a local physician, Dr. J.E. Edwards.

the rules—and on his way back from the courts, "I drank more after leaving the court but on my way home met Rankin beastly drunk. I sobered up sufficiently to take care of him until bedtime." This in the middle of the week!

Although Jennings's behavior sometimes seemed outrageous, he was concerned about behavior on campus and hopeful for a better atmosphere:

At present there are such practices and certain faults which students have, that are dangerous to the college community. There was a time in the history of Wofford when, for the sake of mischief and a desire to be considered bad, the students were constantly playing tricks, drinking, gambling and to some extent visiting houses of prostitution. I mean there were a certain bad [element] around that did this. … But what a different sight we behold now! Earnest, honest, hopeful, the ministerial students worked these vices almost completely out. But reaction came in the form of underhanded rascality which now threatens seriously, painfully the high tone which has pervaded our campus and greeted newcomers.

Jennings knew that he was not one of Wofford's finest students; indeed, his academic achievements were marginal at best. When he was called in to see President Carlisle he recorded Carlisle telling him, "It is a painful doubt whether you should come back next year. Do you think it best for you that you come back?" Jennings commented: "I was well shocked by the question[,] and its abruptness was beneficial in setting me to thinking." The respect that President Carlisle commanded among students, faculty and the state as a whole is well illustrated by Jennings' decision not only to return for his senior year but also to markedly improve his performance. Evidence of Dr. Carlisle's influence is revealed in Jennings's description of the last months of his senior year:

During the time which has elapsed since I last wrote herein our class has had the privilege of meeting Dr. Carlisle five times a week. It is a precious privilege, seldom justly appreciated, to sit at the feet of one so learned, so scholarly, so able, so delicately just. A fountain ever flowing, his waters of crystal purity, are fresh from veins untouched. That man is low, indeed, who can sit beneath his charge and never feel the inspiration which stirs his noble heart. Besides the vast information which compasses the conduct of our entire future, besides the humility which is the essence of marvelous growth he speaks before our eyes the most tempting morsels of perfect character and Christian piety.

The Misplaced "i"

Dr. Herman Baer graduated from Wofford in 1857. A native of Germany, he stayed on to teach foreign languages for a time, terrorizing students with his demands. Eventually he became a trustee and a successful pharmacist, although he remained—according to the diplomatic college historian—a "direct and blunt old gentleman."

In 1900, Dr. Baer decided that it was time to honor founder Benjamin Wofford and made arrangements to place an impressive bronze plaque in the vestibule of the chapel. He worked for hours on the wording and exact arrangement of the inscription. On commencement day that June, the eccentric old gentleman lovingly traced every word with his index finger. Suddenly his hand stopped. Where he had correctly written "beneficent" was the word "benificent."

"Be-NYE-ficent!" he shouted. Slamming his cane so hard on the floor that it almost broke, he stormed out the front door and down the steps. Such was his anger that he refused to have the plaque recast, leaving it instead to warn students about the dangers of sloppy work.

—*Doyle Boggs '70*

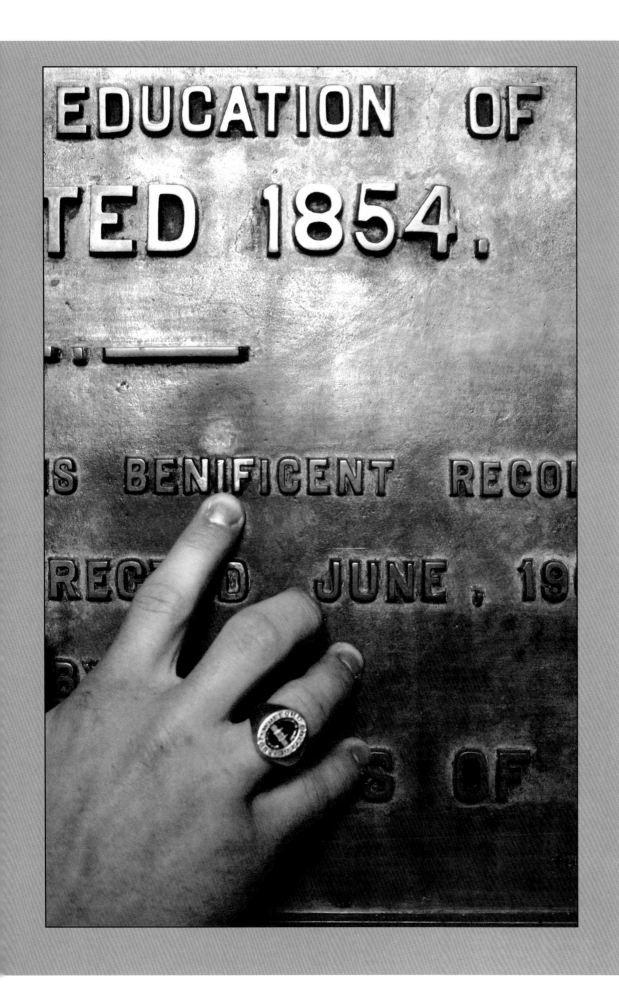

James H. Carlisle: A Firsthand Account

The following description of James H. Carlisle was written by Robert A. Law, Class of 1898, who later became a professor of English at the University of Texas. It was originally published in a faculty newsletter, but was reprinted in a memorial book published shortly after the death of Carlisle in 1909.

James Henry Carlisle was a member of the Wofford College faculty from its foundation, in 1854, to his death, in 1909, and was president of the institution for [27] years. Before he died hundreds of well-informed persons declared him to be the greatest living citizen of his state, and several thousand mourners attended his funeral.

The college seal was included on the tombstone of James H. Carlisle in Spartanburg's Magnolia Cemetery.

If you once heard Dr. Carlisle speak, you caught the secret of his greatness. Almost six feet and a half in height, carrying himself always erect, he had a frame well proportioned to his stature, a full white beard, as I knew him, flowing gray locks, and a countenance of singular strength and benignity, suggesting the Hebrew patriarch. When he spoke it was a clear, resonant tone that fairly thundered over his audience. The pithy diction, the apt illustrative incident, the seasoning of quiet humor, the new angle from which the truth was presented kept the attention of old and young. His exhortations went home. "I could not go to the devil," remarked an old Wofford man who settled in the pioneer West, "because wherever I went I saw Dr. Carlisle's long forefinger pointing at me."

As a teacher it would be unjust not to accord him high rank. Yet, strange as it may appear, he seemed, at least in his later years, not to have the special gift of imparting knowledge. All the students he met once or oftener every week, teaching courses in astronomy, in the English Bible, and in moral science—that is, Butler's "Analogy of Revealed Religion." But in none of these courses were examinations held or written work demanded, and only the more conscientious students ever made them subjects of serious study. The old Doctor was not teaching astronomy; he was teaching men. The teacher's consistent purpose was to learn more about his pupils and to arouse the sluggish from their intellectual or moral lethargy.

I doubt whether Dr. Carlisle's best teaching was done either in the classroom or on the public platform. No Wofford graduate will forget many hours spent, whether in college or years after he left it, in "visiting the Doctor," with or without an invitation. Sometimes he received the caller on his well-shaded front porch, presenting a long vista of tall pine trees. More frequently he was to be seen in his study, which contained little furniture and almost no ornaments, but surrounded on all sides by crowded bookshelves that fairly touched the ceiling. The conversation was apt to be extremely personal, and the visitor usually did his full share of the talking.

Often the talk would flow into a larger channel, as the teacher possessed a keen knowledge of human nature, a remarkable memory for details connected with men or with books, and at the same time a breadth of vision and an unfailing kindliness such as are seldom found in men so dominated by Puritan traits as he was. For example, he had cause to dislike Northerners, "Yankees," the Carolina boy would term them. As a young man he saw rise the full tide of sectional rancor; and in 1860, against his will, he was chosen by the people of Spartanburg County to represent them in the State Secession convention. Over his negative vote the convention resolved to secede from the Union, but his name was signed in bold hand to the Ordinance of Secession [Carlisle's personal copy with original signatures is now in the Wofford College Archives.] In the Confederate War and Reconstruction that followed, he did not actively participate, but the college was practically broken up. He lived through it all without allowing bitterness to enter his soul. Even of General Grant he would speak with a tone of admiration. Moreover, he was an unfailing friend of the freed slaves. He once introduced Booker Washington to a Spartanburg audience. He frequently voiced his disapproval of "Jim Crow" laws [for streetcars and passenger train cars] on the ground of their injustice to the Negro race. His counsel on all such problems breathed a spirit of Christian brotherhood.

This bust of Carlisle, now in the college archives, is the work of Henry Bernhardt, who turned to sculpture after retiring as one of Spartanburg's leading photographers. He is occasionally remembered today for his front yard sculpture garden of nude women on West Main Street, which was featured in LIFE magazine, August 7, 1939.

In Carlisle's own words

"The student ought to be educated not simply or chiefly because he intends to become a farmer, lawyer, or statesman, but because he is a human being—with inlets of joy, with possibilities of effort and action that no trade or calling can satisfy or exhaust."

"Some of the newspapers have been very kind in predicting an increase of attendance for Wofford next year, possibly reaching two hundred. Young gentlemen, when two hundred students enter the front door of Wofford College, I shall walk out of the back door."

"If this country is ever going to ruin, it will not be from the lack of Greek, Latin and mathematics, but from lack of a basis in honest and true character."

"Our Lord knew infinitely more of the good and evil in this world than we, and yet he was no pessimist."

"Scholarship and character are too close together for young people to build up the one and at the same time tear down the other."

"You have been through college, but has college been through you?"

"And who is Dr. Carlisle? A man who went to Wofford College as a teacher of 'astronomy and moral science' in 1854, when it was founded, and who has been there ever since, a part of the time as teacher, a part of the time as president, and again as teacher … It is doubtful whether there be an astronomer or a philosopher at any institution or in any community in our land who has exerted so strong an influence upon the young men who have come in contact with him … throughout the area of the college's influence, men and women say, 'We must send our sons to Wofford College because Dr. Carlisle is there.'"

—Walter Hines Page, in the 1908 commencement address.

In 1791 President George Washington made a southern tour. After spending May 26-27 in Lancaster County, South Carolina, he paused for a breakfast of mush and milk at Nathan Barr's Tavern. He then took a Spanish piece-of-eight, a dollar, sliced it in half with his sword, and gave it to one of the Barr daughters. The family later presented Washington's "four bits" to Dr. Carlisle.

1895: A Graduate Remembers

Dr. Samuel C. Hodges, Class of 1895, lived in Greenwood, South Carolina, where he owned and operated a drug store for many years. He was a South Carolina state senator, president of the state pharmaceutical association and a trustee of the Medical College of South Carolina. He died August 21, 1957, at the age of 83. These remarks were made at the conclusion of a speech during the celebration of Wofford's centennial in 1954. In speaking of the chapel, Dr. Hodges refers to the space now known as Leonard Auditorium in Main Building, as it was configured prior to 1902. The original dimensions were 48 feet by 80 feet, with an apse-like structure extending from the north, or rear, wall. Students sat in rising tiers on straight-backed benches that were beautifully decorated with scroll heads and beaded edges. The rostrum, or pulpit platform, towered at ground level more than four feet above the heads of students.

One of my most vivid recollections is when my turn came for declamation in chapel for the first time. We had to march up what then seemed the longest steps and highest platform ever erected, with seven or eight faculty members seated at the back, and we—young barbarians—were keenly sensible of an unsympathetic atmosphere down in front, a sea of those "angel" faces, the pride of their teachers, who fully expected our downfall. I remembered only my opening sentence and I had a stroke, paralysis of the mind, and like a fish out of water, I retreated to more familiar quarters, and no one seemed the least surprised when I took my seat.

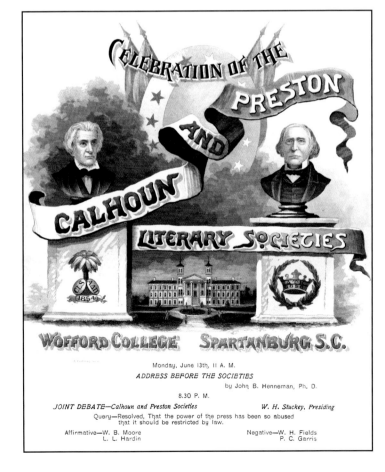

Even more indelibly impressed upon my mind was the similar occasion when Jack Strother, over six feet tall, reached the platform. The sun streaming down from the back window caught his legs in floodlight as they oscillated. Jack never uttered an audible word but he sputtered like a firecracker that wouldn't go off. Then he, too, went up the hill and down again, among a thunderous applause, worthy of a Demosthenes. The outburst caused Dr. Carlisle's face to grow crimson with mortification. Later when "The Doctor" met each class, he faced it, with that index finger pointed in solemn warning, and said, "Young men, I wish to say this to you, that anyone who can face an audience without a certain physical and mental excitement and trepidation is made of pure brass."

Another incident comes forcibly to mind. Professor Snyder in his gifted and enthusiastic manner represented to our class the sheer delight and enriching experience of a special afternoon meeting for a study in Old English Literature. Preston Wells, who later became an outstanding English scholar and Methodist preacher, was one who volunteered, with another, not so prominent, who fell under the spell and joined the class. Unfortunately the baseball season opened at the same time and practice was due. Wells rose in class and confessed to Professor Snyder "owing to conflicting interests and demands upon his time, he would be obliged to discontinue the extra study class."

Professor Snyder expressed regret. As Wells was making his departure, Hodges said to Professor Snyder, "Wells has so perfectly described my own situation and sentiments that I, too, would like to be excused." As he went out of the room, he distinctly heard his teacher's lament: "One by one the dead leaves fall."

A striking thing that I recall was the fact

that in our college days we had so little money and how well we got along without it. I remember that only two boys on the campus had bicycles. Board at Wightman Hall was $6.50, if we furnished our own butter, and that we could buy for 15 cents a pound. Board at the Alumni Hall was $10.00 or $12.00. Our greatest treat was to indulge in a plate of stewed or fried oysters at Becker's, served with a dish of cole slaw, superior to any slaw I've eaten since, at a cost of 25 cents.

But to turn to more serious thoughts for my strongest impulse in writing these reminiscences is to pay a tribute to Dr. Carlisle and my teachers, who for 58 years I have held in honor and kept in tender and grateful memory. But how can this be done in a few brief words?

Any man who spent four years under Dr. Carlisle's Bible teaching, listened to his chapel talks, stood with him and looked at the stars, felt deeply the dignity and nobility of a great human being, the majesty, of his physical, moral and spiritual stature, with a humility that enabled even a child to talk with him without fear.

For one to have experienced the warm friendship of Professor Snyder and the high privilege and inspiration derived from his matchless teaching in English Literature, especially the studies in Shakespeare and Browning, was in my opinion to be half educated.

Professor Gamewell, a great and gentle soul, was a teacher who made Roman history live again.

Professors Rembert and Craighead, men of strong intellect and character, were outstanding teachers in Greek.

Professor Few was earnest and thorough and his success at Wofford no doubt helped to prepare the way for his wider field as president of Duke.

Professor DuPré not only excelled in his department but as a Christian gentleman created an atmosphere of gentility.

Professors Pritchard and Thomas were excellent teachers and it was not counted against them that some of us were allergic to mathematics.

Professor Kilgo, afterwards president of Trinity and a Methodist bishop, was recognized for his superb mind and a magnetic personality, and we felt most grateful for the two years we had with him.

But who can estimate the value of such able teachers, their characters and usefulness? Just as the streams of light which radiate from

radium are inexhaustible, so these things are simply the endless streams of influence that have and still flow from Wofford College: in the development of mind, the molding of character, and the impress of Christian ideals upon the minds and hearts of young manhood. Those who have been so enriched and better prepared for life work feel a deep and abiding gratitude.

And now, last but not least, is the tribute I would pay to my classmates of 1895. No one of my memories is more vital and tender than that of my happy association with that group for whom I formed a genuine affection in college and who became my life-long friends.

Their names are indelible and their faces come before me as plainly as though it were but yesterday that we walked, or "cavorted," side by side those four years. I could fill pages of those years, both serious and comic. I can without partiality testify that my classmates were men of true character, and without exception achieved honorable success in their chosen fields. I know what they were, and I know what they did, for I have followed them through the years with a warm personal interest and have rejoiced in their useful lives. Only God and eternity can reveal the far-reaching good results of their Christian characters and influence.

Oh, Wofford, luminous with a hundred years of service! May your beneficent work continue for untold centuries and your spirit and influence be far-reaching and eternal.

Wofford's African-American Neighbors

With a population of about 3,000, Spartanburg was too small to have distinctively black and white neighborhoods until about 1880—prior to that time, the majority of the county's African

Hattie Belle Penland and Wofford students dedicate a memorial plaque at the entrance to Gibbes Stadium.

Americans continued to grow cotton on the farm. Then a growing number of black families began to make their way into the city. At first, most of the men were artisans, laborers, railroad employees, or construction workers, and most of the women were domestic servants. But the city was expanding rapidly in those days, and a number of distinctive middle-class African-American neighborhoods began to emerge.

Perhaps the earliest of these communities (1867) was Silver Hill, on North Dean Street between St. John Street and the Wofford campus. Like most of the northside black communities, it was built around a Methodist church (this one affiliated with the white churches of that denomination in the North). The church took its name from the fact that silver dollars were put into each of the four cornerstones of the original building. A little later, the Rev. A.W. Cumming, a Northern clergyman, purchased land to the north and east of the Wofford campus and donated lots to working-class African-American newcomers so they could build their own homes. The main thoroughfare in that vicinity, known throughout the 20th century as "Back of the

College," still bears his name, Cumming Street.

Although it certainly would be incorrect to praise 19th century Wofford College as a center of enlightened race relations, a number of leaders in the African-American community in the days of segregation maintained close ties to the college. President A.M. Shipp is said to have tutored Tobe Hartwell in a variety of academic subjects in slavery days and then brought him from Virginia to Spartanburg. After Emancipation and the departure of Shipp to Vanderbilt, Hartwell was employed as a well-respected bank security officer. He worked successfully with Charles Bomar in 1884 to establish public schools for African Americans in the city. His name is memorialized in a complex of the Spartanburg Housing Authority.

Shortly after Emancipation, Millie Penland was born "Back of the College." At the age of 18, she was hired as a domestic worker and cook in the campus home of Professor J.A. Gamewell, a place known for gracious hospitality to visiting speakers in the Wofford Lyceum.

Hattie Belle Penland, her daughter, attended Claflin College and South Carolina State, and became a beloved teacher in the Spartanburg schools. At the age of 93, the late Miss Penland recalled, "From the time I was four years old, I was part of the Gamewell household. The day William Jennings Bryan came to Wofford, Mrs. Gamewell told us to get cleaned up and come to the study. When the Gamewells introduced me, Mr. Bryan reached out for my hand, shook it, and said, 'I'm so glad to meet you, and what a fine little girl you are, Hattie Belle.' I thought Professor Gamewell was the smartest man in the world because he worked at Wofford College. I thought he was the richest man in the world because he had books from the floor to the ceiling."

The success that Spartanburg African Americans attained economically and socially between the Civil War and the solidification of Jim Crow laws around 1900 remains a story largely hidden. Dwain Pruitt '95, who joined the history faculty at Rhodes College in 2001, after graduate studies at Emory University, did much to remedy this injustice by his research and writing under the sponsorship of the City of Spartanburg's Community Relations Office.

—*Doyle Boggs '70*

Women at Wofford: A Road Not Taken

During the 1890s, leaders of women's organizations were in the forefront of a widespread national reform movement. Doors slowly began to open for women in higher education, journalism, social welfare and other professions. While the South lagged behind other sections in its enthusiasm for these developments, Wofford, Erskine and other denominational colleges considered offering their liberal arts degrees to both men and women, albeit with vast differences in student life regulations and restrictions.

The will of Benjamin Wofford prescribed the curriculum (literary, classical and scientific education) and the location of the college in Spartanburg District, but it did not limit the authority of the trustees to determine the most desirable composition of the faculty and student body. In 1894, the board approved the admission of women. A year later the construction of a residence hall for women on the campus was authorized, but nothing was done to provide the funds necessary to move ahead. Nevertheless, three women enrolled as commuting students in 1897, and two of them, Puella M. Littlejohn and Mary Duncan Wannamaker, graduated on schedule in 1901. Six other women students followed, with the last finishing their degrees in 1904.

College historian David Duncan Wallace referred to these Wofford women as excellent students and wrote, "Not the slight untoward incident ever occurred." Yet, the small group of women felt isolated, as is evident in this photograph from 1899, and the male students appear not to have treated them very well.

The board had a more pressing concern as the turn of the century approached. In 1889, D.E. Converse and a group of 13 prominent men, including several Wofford alumni, assembled at John B. Cleveland's law office in Spartanburg and agreed to form a women's college stock company. Converse College opened on October 1, 1890, with Converse's daughter, Marie, attending as a member of the first class. The plan for the new institution was distinctive and ambitious, with much benchmarking of the best contemporary women's colleges in Virginia and the Northeast. Simultaneously, South Carolina became one of several states across the region to open a public normal [teacher-training] institution for women, Winthrop College in Rock Hill. These developments seemed to threaten two existing Methodist institutions for women in the state, Columbia College and Lander College, creating opposition in church circles to the Wofford policy.

So it was that the all-male admissions policy was resumed for another 70 years. While Wofford continued to make great progress after 1900, it is interesting to speculate about what might have happened had the trustees continued down a promising road not taken.

—Doyle Boggs '70

Oct. 26" 1899.

The *Early Fraternities*

White males in the South in the late 19th century lived in a society honeycombed with secret and semi-secret fraternal organizations, some of which were benign and charitable, some highly politicized and violent. They reinforced and perpetuated "Old South" values even as the population moved from the countryside to "New South" towns centered on courthouses, textile mills and railroad depots. Given the background from which young college students came, it is not surprising that a network of social fraternities, many of which had been founded in the North earlier in the century, evolved to help them adjust to being away from home.

At Wofford, the first fraternity to receive a chapter was the Kappa Alpha Order, which was

founded at Washington University (soon to be renamed Washington and Lee) in Virginia. By the late 1860s, this brotherhood had coalesced around its "practical founder," Samuel Zenas Ammen, a master Mason whose background was reflected in the order's secret ritual and constitution. An early initiate on the Lexington, Virginia campus was William Anson Rogers of Bishopville, South Carolina. Bringing with him a letter of recommendation from President Robert E. Lee himself, Rogers transferred to Wofford (Class of 1872) and organized Delta chapter of KA in 1869. Civil War veteran Joseph Augustus Gamewell (Class of 1871), a beloved Wofford professor and loyal KA through the 1930s, was one of the first chapter members.

Although various societies came and went through the years, Wofford went on to establish a typical undergraduate fraternity

system. After Kappa Alpha came chapters of two well-established national brotherhoods from the Northeast that were expanding at the time: Chi Psi (1869) and Chi Phi (1871). Then on October 16, 1885, James C. Jeffries founded South Carolina Gamma of Sigma Alpha Epsilon at Wofford. Wofford represented the 48th charter for this pre-Civil War fraternity that had originated at the University of Alabama, but only about a dozen chapters were active at the time. Pi Kappa Alpha and Kappa Sigma both are included in the Virginia circle, fraternities founded at the University of Virginia in the late 1860s. The Wofford chapters were originally established in 1891 and 1894, respectively.

What were these fraternities like? At any one time, they had only eight to 12 members, and it often took pre-existing kinship or close friendship connections to secure an invitation to join any chapter. While the faculty lived in college-owned housing on the campus, the students were expected to take care of their own room and board, so many fraternity men slept

and ate the midday meal together in their "lodges" along Cleveland Street on the northwest corner of the campus. Fraternity men had a big advantage when they sought to network. Graduate members of a particular society who lived in the city of Spartanburg usually maintained contact with the collegiate chapter and often opened their homes or clubhouses for various functions. There also was considerable interaction with chapters of the fraternity at nearby colleges.

As might be expected at a Methodist-related institution, many Greeks at Wofford did not carouse at all, but there were enough problems to encourage frequent discussions of the need to build and operate orderly residence halls, an issue not totally resolved until the completion of the original Carlisle Hall in 1912.

President Carlisle was quietly skeptical of the value of fraternities, but through the 19th century, most faculty and trustees supported these organizations as a worthwhile part of college life. Problems at Wofford did not become serious until 1900, when there developed across the state a church-based movement critical of all secret societies. By the time it crested, the General Assembly had passed laws banning fraternities at state-supported colleges. Also, most non-Greeks resented the tactics of the fraternities called "cliquing," where various offices and honors on campus secretly were bartered and divided. At Wofford, an organization of 48 independents called the "Philanthropeans" became so powerful and so openly hostile toward fraternity men that they were successful in getting the trustees to ban secret societies (at least officially) in 1906. However, there remained a number of "social clubs" on campus that certainly looked and acted like fraternities; in fact, Pi Kappa Phi's Zeta chapter has a charter dated 1911, when the ban was in effect. Wofford students were sometimes initiated into fraternities on other campuses, and if the faculty discovered such instances, the guilty could expect to be expelled.

The challenges that the college had experienced in managing its 19th century fraternity system are evident in the restrictions that were imposed when the national organizations were allowed to reactivate their chapters in 1915:

(1) There will be no chapter houses, either owned or rented;
(2) The names of all members must be submitted by each fraternity to the faculty;
(3) No student shall be initiated until he has been in college for at least five months;
(4) The place of meeting must be approved by the faculty;

(5) Every fraternity member will sign a pledge that he will act courteously toward all fellow students and that he will abide by college rules governing fraternities.

Interestingly, national Panhellenic organizations for women that came to Wofford after 1970 were created during this period. Rejecting the older concept of the snobbish "ladies' societies," the founders typically were at odds with a fraternity system that seemed to have much to offer but refused to see women as worthy of membership. Kappa Alpha Theta originated in January 1870 at DePauw, a fine Methodist-related liberal arts college that first admitted women in 1867. Sarah Ida Shaw and Eleanor Dorcas Pond, who together wrote the rituals and constitution, organized Delta Delta Delta at Boston University in 1885. Kappa Delta and Zeta Tau Alpha both were founded in the late 1890s at the State Female Normal School in Farmville, Virginia, by middle-class women who intended to teach in public schools.

The two historically African-American fraternities that later established chapters at Wofford, Omega Psi Phi and Kappa Alpha Psi, both were founded in 1911, at Howard University and Indiana University, respectively.

—Doyle Boggs '70

Members of Kappa Alpha invited four alumni members to pose with them during the 1901-1902 academic year. The third man from the left on the first row is the founder of the Wofford chapter, the Rev. W.A. Rogers. To Rogers' immediate right are three members of the faculty, "Uncle Gus" Gamewell, "Dunc" Wallace, and "Mase" Dupré.

The *Alumni Pitch In*

When Wofford College was five years old and had 18 alumni, graduates petitioned the trustees to charter an official alumni association. Accordingly, on July 12, 1859, the young men met in the chapel in Main Building. They adopted a constitution, bylaws and a Greek motto, which freely translated read, "We, the adopted, honor the mother who nourished us." Until an extensive reorganization in 1915, the association held an annual meeting at commencement and one of its members was chosen to make a lengthy address during the ceremonies.

Charles Petty, Class of 1857, had the honor of serving as the first president of the alumni association. Except for a period of service as an officer in the Confederate army and a one-year hiatus in 1870, Petty headed the association through 1874 while farming and teaching in Union County. He eventually moved back to Spartanburg, where he became the proprietor of the *Carolina Spartan* newspaper and also served in the General Assembly. In both capacities, he was a loyal and very valuable supporter of the college throughout the 19th century.

Another noteworthy early president of the alumni association was William Wallace Duncan of the Class of 1858, who served from 1876 through 1887, with a one-year interruption in 1880. Under the leadership of the future Methodist bishop, alumni began organizing chapters and holding meetings in most South Carolina counties. The association had become active in financially supporting the college by 1872, when a $50,000 campaign was organized.

At their meeting during the 1888 commencement, alumni went on to pledge $10,000 to build a four-story dormitory, a portion of which still stands on the campus and is known as the Hugh S. Black Building (the admissions and financial aid office). Most of that pledge was ultimately paid by Edgar L. Archer, Class of 1871.

Alumni Hall as it appeared in the 1890s.

John Bomar Cleveland

Jesse Cleveland moved to Spartanburg to establish a store in 1810, a time when the village had little to offer beyond a courthouse and jail. Several branches of his family have invested in land, banking, industries and railroads and, as of 2005, are still leaders in regional economic development and public service. Wofford College stands on land that was once owned by the Cleveland family

John Bomar Cleveland, born in 1848, was a grandson of Jesse Cleveland. He was one of 15 members of the Wofford Class of 1869, which included several Confederate veterans as well as the future Wofford professor Dan DuPre. It was apparently this college friendship that made Cleveland a particular friend of the sciences at Wofford. When it finally came time to build a separate science hall in 1902, he simply told his classmate to draw up the plans and send him the bills.

Even though he was a lifelong Episcopalian, Cleveland was elected by the Methodist Conference to the Wofford Board of Trustees in 1900 and remained a member through 1914. His beautiful Second Empire mansion, Bon Haven, still stands just a few blocks north of Wofford on Church Street.

~Courtesy of Dexter Cleveland

The *Sweet Sixteen*

Wofford College's class of 1889 had only 16 members, but it was a remarkable group of young men. In college, they launched the Wofford College Journal, one of the oldest continuously published collegiate literary magazines in the country. Most went on to brilliant careers in education and the Methodist ministry. Five achieved national distinction:

William Preston Few received his doctorate in English from Harvard in 1896 and served as co-editor of the *South Atlantic Quarterly* when that publication was leading the Southern literary renaissance. Later, when tiny Trinity College began its transition to Duke University, he was chosen to become Duke's first president. He served in that position from 1910 until his sudden death in 1940, at the age of 71.

Edwin D. Mouzon became a Methodist bishop and was one of the founders of Southern Methodist University in Texas. He was also a leader in the campaign to reunite the Northern and Southern branches of the Methodist Church just before World War II.

E.D. Smith represented South Carolina in the United States Senate for almost 36 years. In his younger days, he was effective and progressive, one of Woodrow Wilson's strongest supporters in Congress. Even though he continued to be very popular in South Carolina long after that time, "Cotton Ed's" national reputation suffered when he resisted the changes brought about by the New Deal.

A.M. Muckenfuss became an organic chemist and distinguished college professor at the University of Florida, doing postgraduate study at Johns Hopkins and in Germany. He was known for his pioneering achievements in the manufacture of paint and varnish compounds.

James M. Workman was president of Henderson-Brown College in Arkansas. After several mergers, this college became part of Hendrix, a fine United Methodist liberal arts college.

The *Literary Societies*

Robert A. Law wrote this description of Wofford's literary societies in the early 1900s. Originally published in a faculty newsletter, it was reprinted in a memorial book in 1909.

Plaque from the Preston Literary Society Room

Every student was required to be a member of either the Calhoun or the Preston Literary Society. Generally speaking, I believe this rule was wise and proper. Each society was run by the students themselves, with almost no suggestion from the faculty, who usually knew what was going on, but very rarely visited the meetings. The society halls were comfortable, carpeted rooms, devoted solely to that purpose, were well lighted and furnished with attractive opera chairs, and their walls were ornamented with many oil paintings of distinguished alumni and professors. The president of the society sat on a high platform under a canopy, and he always wore a black gown of the kind that South Carolina judges still wear on the circuit bench.

Regular meetings were held each Friday night, beginning at seven-thirty o'clock and lasting frequently until midnight or later. Roll was called at the beginning and at the end of each meeting; and the fine for unexcused absence from any roll call, if I remember aright, was fifty cents. Half the society's membership of about seventy came on duty to read essays, to declaim, or to debate each Friday night. Thus, if one was not on the program at one meeting, he was sure to be at the next one. These duties were enforced; and order in the meeting was preserved under a rigid system of fines, which were collected in one way or another. Even the most timid member soon found it economical to perform his duty regularly, and before the end of his freshman year practically every student had gained some self-confidence in addressing the society.

Both oratory and debate, as I realize now, were faulty in technique; and neither the graceful speaker nor the polished argument is likely to result from such training. Still I believe that the average Wofford graduate of that time would prove a readier speaker and a more skillful rough-and-tumble debater than the average male graduate of the University of Texas; for our debates were largely spontaneous, and the best part of them always came after the question was opened to discussion by the house. Hence these

The meeting room of the Calhoun Literary Society in Main Building, about 1900. Notice the portrait of Calhoun by Albert Capers Guerry, which is believed to be the model for the official state portrait that hangs behind the rostrum in the chamber of the South Carolina Senate.

organizations furnished a training in the clash of opinion and a preparation for citizenship which, to my mind, are invaluable. That such literary societies seem everywhere to be passing away under the complex machinery of modern college or university administration is a source of profound regret.

In the 19th century, the most important student offices on campus were those of the literary society presidents. A.E. Holler of the Class of 1897 donned his robes to pose for this traditional portrait for the Preston Society register. Beside him is a gavel carved from a lectern in the old courthouse in Hanover, Virginia, that had been used frequently by Patrick Henry. Holler named one of his sons James Carlisle Holler to honor the Wofford president, and numerous descendants attended Wofford, including Margaret E. Holler, Class of 2007.

South Carolina's First Foot-ball Game

On December 14, 1889, Wofford challenged baseball archrival Furman to a football match at Spartanburg's "encampment grounds," which apparently were located west of the campus on Howard Street. It was the first gridiron contest ever staged in South Carolina. According to a college publication, "The Wofford team wished Association rules to govern the game, but Furman protesting, it was decided to play the old rough and tumble game." Wofford easily established its superiority, largely due to the coaching of Yale graduate Edwin Kerrison, Esquire. The pre-game rules discussion may account for the unusual score in the contest, 5-1. The next month, Wofford also won a rematch in Greenville, by a score of 2-1.

The rules likely used by Wofford and Furman were explained in an article by Alexander Johnston in The Century Illustrated Monthly Magazine *for 1887:*

The undergraduates of American colleges, taking the so-called Rugby game of foot-ball, and by working out the scrimmage in a new form, have made it, in addition to its individual opportunities for the exhibition of skill, one of the most scientific of outdoor games in its team-playing, or management of the entire side as one body.

Each side, while defending its own goal, necessarily faces the goal of its opponents, and its object is to advance the ball, by running with it or by kicking it, toward its opponents' goal-line, to plant the ball on the ground on the other side of the opponents' goal-line, which constitutes a touch-down, to kick the ball over the cross-bar of the opponents' goal, or to force the opponents to make a safety touch-down in their own territory.

Passing the ball, or throwing it from one to another, is another feature of the game. Hardly any combination of team-playing and individual skill is more noteworthy. A pass forward is not allowed; the ball must be thrown straight across the field, parallel to the goal-line, or in any direction back of that line.

It is not to be supposed that its opponents are idly watching the ball's progress. The more common way of checking the advance of the ball is by a tackle. Any player may run with the ball. While he is doing so, any opponent may seize him and cry 'Held!' or throw him and hold him until he cries 'Down!' If the tackle is made by seizing the runner above the shoulders or below the hips, it is a foul tackle, and penalties are imposed for it.

The game has, in fact, become a miniature game of strategy, and can best be comprehended by comparing the foot-ball-field to a battle-field, limited by the side-lines, and the respective sides to two armies, managed on military principles by two captains. Four arms of the foot-ball service have been developed. Across the field stretch the foot-ball infantry, the rush line, or rushers. They are the seven heavy men of the team. The two players on the ends of the line, the end-rushes, stand slightly back of the main line. Behind the center-rush plays the quarter-back, answering very much to the quartermaster's department. Behind the quarter-back, and covering the two sides of the field, are the half-backs, the cavalry of the team. The most brilliant playing is done by the half-backs. Farthest to the rear is the eleventh player, the full-back.

The criticisms upon foot-ball have run in two general lines. They are, first, the innate roughness of the game, and the likelihood of severe accident, or even death, from it; and, second, its tendency to degenerate into brutality and personal combat.

The real evil of the game is the betting.

There is satisfaction in knowing that this outdoor game is doing for our college-bred men, in a more peaceful way, what the experience of war did for so many of their predecessors in 1861-65, in its inculcation of the lesson that bad temper is an element quite foreign to open, manly contest.

The *Wofford Influence:*
Exports to Vandy and Duke

Dr. James S. Barrett '55 reflected on Wofford's influence in higher education in the South during remarks delivered at Wofford's opening convocation in 1990. Barrett earned his master's degree at Emory University and then began his career in the United Methodist ministry. He served as president of both Spartanburg Methodist College and Greensboro College before working as head of the United Methodist Church's General Board of Higher Education in Nashville. He was the chief administrative officer of the Spartanburg County Foundation from 1985 until he retired.

"On the city's western border, reared against the sky ..." So sang the Vanderbilt University faithful on a beautiful Saturday afternoon in November 1977. As the alma mater continued, I began to sing with them the words that were so familiar to me: "May she ever be our watchword ... conquer and prevail...Hail to Thee our Alma Mater ... Dear Old Wofford Hail!" And when we finished, I was somewhat shocked to see 50 pairs of eyes focused on me and 50 mouths open in disbelief that Wofford had been the institutional substitute for Vandy. I left for the men's room and failed to return for the second half. I could not abide their snooty stares. But, that was OK: Vandy was down to Tennessee by 30 points and U.T. had already cleared the bench.

Across the campus I trudged to the mess that was on my desk two blocks away, thinking all the while about stories I had heard. Stories that Wofford and Vanderbilt were coupled by a common heritage. Did the similarity of the alma mater signal some truth in those thrice-told tales that came from the likes of Coates and Cauthen? Or had I read it in Dunc's history on assignment from Lewis Jones?

I knew some of the sketchy details about the battles between the old Commodore Vanderbilt and the Methodist bishops over governance, so I decided to go to the archives in the Methodist Board of Education that afternoon to confirm or dispel the connection. Now, lest you conjure up false images, the archives were in my office!

On yellowed pages bearing the date 1910 were words to this effect,

"It is the undeniable fact that Vanderbilt emerged as a truly important center of classical learning with the arrival of Professor Shipp and three of his young colleagues from Wofford College in South Carolina" (Charles Forster Smith, William M. Baskervill, James Kirkland).

Chancellor Kirkland
~Courtesy of Vanderbilt University

I closed the file—my mind was at ease—they had told me the truth at Wofford!

Shipp, the teacher of English literature, became Wofford's second president after a distinguished faculty career at Chapel Hill and immediately following his tenure as president of Greensboro Female College (now Greensboro College). At Vanderbilt, he led the theology faculty, became quite proficient as an ecclesiastical historian, and wrote the early definitive history of Methodism in South Carolina.

His initial importance in the Vanderbilt story is the key role he played in defining the organizational difference between a church and a university. I believe that definition came, much to the dismay of the episcopal corps, as an attitude he brought from William Wightman and Wofford College.

But Shipp's legacy does not end with that episode. The ugly divorce between Vanderbilt and the Methodist Episcopal Church, South, left the Southern church without a center for theological education, a role that had largely been created by Dr. Shipp at Vanderbilt and now perceived to be indispensable for the denomination. The loss of Vanderbilt as a church-related university was the impetus that drove Bishop [W.A.] Candler of the ME Church, South to convince his brother, the Coca-Cola king, that little Emory at Oxford should move to Atlanta, where a great new university, complete with schools of theology, medicine and law, should rise. And this new university be rightly related to the church. In some ways Emory University is Shipp's legacy and Wofford's legacy too. And, I might add, when the dust cleared in Nashville, the wise folks looked to Wofford again; this time to employ a Wofford-educated faculty member named Kirkland to become their chancellor.

And while all this was going on in Nashville and Atlanta, similar events were taking place in Texas and the Southwest. The Southern Methodist University was founded for many of the same reasons that brought Emory to Atlanta. Southern Methodist University is now the modern expression of a dispositional and institutional trail leading back to Spartanburg through Nashville and Atlanta.

Wofford's first president, William Wightman, is usually credited with writing the documents that set this college moving. And without fanfare they guide her direction even to this day. If you want to understand the meaning of liberal learning you need go no further than Wightman's speech on the day the cornerstone was laid for the building we gather in today. And, if you need further validation of Wightman's considerable influence, travel to Alabama and see his signature on what is now Birmingham-Southern, where he also served as president prior to his election as a Methodist bishop. The charter of Wofford College is copied by Birmingham-Southern and by Florida Southern and at least two other colleges.

I've one more connection to draw before leaving this brief history lesson. And that connection is with Trinity College in North Carolina, the small school adopted by James B. Duke that became Duke University.

At the time Mr. Duke made this momentous decision, the president of struggling Trinity was a gentleman named [John] Kilgo. Kilgo was a Wofford graduate and had been on the Wofford staff as a fundraiser. According to the record, he was neither well liked nor much respected among the people in South Carolina. However, his organizational and oratorical powers were considerable and he made his way to Trinity College in time to catch Mr. Duke's fancy. He was able to convince this benefactor that a great university needed to rise in the South that was committed to national educational excellence and have at its institutional center a religious concern and a Christian dimension. It was William Preston Few, from the Wofford faculty and a graduate of Wofford College, who built the educational prestige of Duke University. Like the great Chancellor Kirkland at Vanderbilt, Dr. Few was an educational giant in his generation.

Need I say more to demonstrate the influence and impact of this place called Wofford? I think not.

I must hasten now to share with you the meaning of it all as interpreted by one who has loved the college without shame and almost without criticism for 40 years.

From wherever you have come and for whatever reason you are here, you have joined yourself to a wonderful place. A place where

Dr. John M. Bullard is the organist.

The William Preston Few Organ

From 1969 to 1996, the beautiful Holtkamp organ in Leonard Auditorium, built in memory of Mary Duke Biddle, served the Duke Memorial Chapel. When the university acquired a new instrument, it was decided that this organ would be placed in Wofford's Main Building to honor Dr. William Preston Few (A.B. Wofford, 1889; Ph.D. Harvard, 1896), Duke's first president. Gregory A. Hand of Charlotte was responsible for the painstaking process of enlarging and revoicing so that the music perfectly blends with the acoustics of the auditorium.

you can be yourself, even if it means you play the fool; a place where you can grow; a place where you can learn; a place where you can integrate wisdom and piety—learning and goodness—if you will; a place where people will care for you, struggle with you and even love you when you are unlovable; a place where truth will win; a place where learning makes a difference.

The folks in Nashville may continue to sing about the university on their city's western border. But those of us who know the real story will knowingly smile and harmonize about the Spartanburg northern border college that gave her life.

And I can only hope and pray you will celebrate the greatness of your college as you now achieve and prevail.

Wofford College
Spartanburg, S.C.
26 February 1937

Roy D. Young Studio
Mount Vernon, Iowa

Third Generation
1902-1942

WOFFORD AND THE MIND OF THE SOUTH

by Doyle Boggs

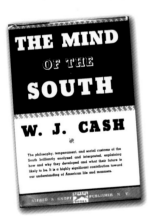

In the summer of 1917, Spartanburg saw a city rise on its borders that had a population larger than its own—the Army's Camp Wadsworth. In addition to the 30,000 doughboys training there, the project brought to the area hundreds of civilians working under government contracts, including a former clerk in a textile mill store, John Cash. With him came a teenage son, Wilbur, known to his friends as "Sleepy" Cash. (He had a nearsighted squint aggravated by frostbite incurred as he drove an open truck through the snow and sleet.) During the 1917-1918 academic year, the young man took classes at the Wofford Fitting School and participated in the Student Army Training Corps. In 1918-1919, the year of the Armistice and the great Spanish influenza epidemic, Sleepy was a student in his first year at Wofford College and a corporal in the training battalion.

He eventually earned his degree at Wake Forest, but it is easy to imagine that W.J. Cash's years at Wofford deeply affected his outlook on life. Indeed, the college's surroundings were a microcosm of Southern culture that he later would describe eloquently in his masterpiece, *The Mind of the South*. There really were four Souths in Cash's time, and Wofford students could see them all from windows in their rooms in the James H. Carlisle Memorial Hall.

Around Morgan Square, south of the campus, was a booming business and courthouse district, offering a hint of a city skyline. The rural South was nearing the bottom of a desperate cycle of expensive credit, sharecropping and boll weevils, but farmers and cotton bales seemed to be everywhere in certain seasons, because Spartanburg was a railroad and trolley hub city. To the east and west along the Southern Railway were two recently developed textile mills, surrounded by their villages. This "Mill Problem" South represented a case study of industrialization without modernization that created economic energy, but only allowed laboring families to exchange one kind of poverty for another. Finally, around the

northern rim of the campus, there were African-American neighborhoods, all seemingly invisible to white elites after segregation was written into law after 1890. One of these, around Cumming Street, was dubbed "Back of the College."

Was there a role for Wofford College in influencing and improving such complex surroundings? A new generation of administrators and faculty responded with a resounding, if paternalistic, yes. Limited to modest tuition income and a small appropriation from the Methodist Church, they did not have the resources to interpret this challenge as "outreach" in the same way as do modern state-supported universities or community colleges. However, they were confident that if they offered a small group of select students a liberal arts education of true quality, their graduates could have a great impact on the church, the state, the nation and, ultimately, the world.

They set to work at the dawn of the 20th century: Henry Nelson Snyder (president and professor of English, 1890-1949); A. Mason "Old Mace" DuPré (dean and professor of mathematics and Latin, 1895-1949); Daniel A. DuPré (treasurer and professor of natural sciences, 1872-1930); J.A. "Uncle Gus" Gamewell (secretary of the faculty and professor of Latin, 1875-1940); A.G. "Knotty" Rembert (professor of Greek and Bible, 1887-1933); John G. Clinkscales (professor of mathematics and astronomy, 1899-1940); David Duncan Wallace, (professor of history and economics, 1899-1947); and Coleman B. "Frog" Waller (professor of chemistry and biology, 1904-1947). Other gifted teachers, most with earned doctorates, came a bit later.

Ironically, the story of Wofford's drive toward academic prominence began not in the classroom but outdoors. In 1854, the campus had been envisioned as a landscaped promenade along a ridgeline overlooking a picturesque courthouse village. However, throughout the 19th century, old pasture fences and furrows of abandoned cornfields were obvious in several places, and the grounds were allowed to grow up in native pines, shrubs and grasses. The nights were so dark in the thick forest between campus and village that students trying to take a shortcut occasionally lost their way.

Snyder and Dan DuPré were determined to change that. "Youth should see its own aspirations symbolized in buildings, in shaded vistas, in green-carpeted lawns, in noble trees, all mellowed by time and agelong associations into a sacredness of unforgettable memories," Snyder wrote. "This too is higher education, and it need not be books *versus* shrubbery, but books *and* shrubbery, and the good angel of higher education, if there be any left, must provide for both." So, oak trees replaced the pines, roads were surveyed for vehicular traffic, and three striking new brick buildings were erected—the John B. Cleveland Science Hall (1904), the Whitefoord Smith Library, still standing and now known as the Daniel Building (1910), and Carlisle Residence Hall (1912).

The faculty gave due consideration to the Rhodes Scholars nomination process, and in 12 years, the college sent three young alumni to Oxford—John Lee Hydrick '08, J. Lyles Glenn '12 and Edwin F. Moseley '16. Glenn was selected for the honor in 1914, but he abandoned his studies when the war began, distinguishing himself in the international relief effort in Belgium and as an ambulance driver in the French Army. After Americans entered the war, he served as a lieutenant and was wounded in the battle of Catigny. While working for the Herbert Hoover Relief Asso-

This rare full-color photograph from the late 1930s perfectly reflects what Dr. Snyder called "the mellow beauty of the Wofford campus." Note that ivy has been allowed to climb up the walls of "Old Main."

Rhodes Scholar
  J. Lyles Glenn '12 *(left)*
Rhodes Scholar
  Edwin L. Moseley '16 *(right)*

The Rev. David E. Camak

U.S. Senator Olin Johnston

ciation, Glenn met the future president, who later appointed him as federal judge. A United States Supreme Court appointment seemed a logical possibility, but Judge Glenn died at the age of 46 in 1939.

At home, the Wofford family also produced some active participants in Wilsonian Progressivism. In 1911, with the quiet support of President Snyder and several Spartanburg mill owners, the Rev. David E. Camak (Class of 1903) organized the Textile Industrial Institute. The pioneering program (much later to be known as Co-Op) allowed adults to earn a diploma by splitting time between mill work and basic schooling. The future Governor and United States Senator Olin D. Johnston '21 was an early TII graduate and completed his Wofford degree after serving in World War I. Eventually, Camak's concept evolved into Spartanburg Methodist College, a process the founder described in a memorable book, *Human Gold from Southern Hills.*

In 1914, Professor Clinkscales displayed exceptional moral courage by entering the South Carolina Democratic primary. Running for governor on the raucous county-by-county stump tour, he advocated compulsory elementary education, an idea far ahead of its time in the Palmetto State. Clinkscales did not have much of an organization, but he had spoken frequently in Methodist churches raising money and recruiting students for the college. Winning in Spartanburg, Cherokee and Union counties, he finished fourth in a field of 12 contenders on the first ballot, trailing three future governors, John G. Richards, Richard I. Manning and Robert A. Cooper. Wofford graduates of that era remembered, "Clink" as a genial mentor, a mathematician of modest theoretical skills, and a tremendously effective public speaker. Quite a few added a

John G. Clinkscales

comment about an impressive mustache, which actually could be tied in a knot behind his neck.

Professor Gamewell was Spartanburg's gentle intellectual guide from 1897 until his death in 1940 as he coordinated a lecture series known as the Wofford Lyceum. Under its auspices, statesmen, politicians, explorers, scientists, authors, famous lawyers, poets and gifted

J. A. Gamewell

men and women of the stage appeared. Some dined and stayed overnight in Professor Gamewell's campus home, later used as an infirmary and now known as the Hugh R. Black House. "Leadership" was Lyman Abbott's subject. Dr. D. J. Stafford presented Shakespeare in readings from "Macbeth" and "Hamlet." William Jennings Bryan, Woodrow Wilson and John Sharp Williams spoke on the political outlook of their time. Branch Rickey's subject was, of course, "Baseball." Nellie Tayloe Ross gave an amusing account of her experiences as governor of Wyoming. Dhan Ghopal Mukerji, East Indian poet and mystic, appeared in native dress with a turban of snowy white. One of the most interesting Lyceum events must have been the appearance of Booker T. Washington, who read from his autobiography, *Up From Slavery.* The book was published in 1901 and Washington died in 1915, so this visit came at the height of "the strange career of Jim Crow" and would have involved dealing with many complications in the rigidly segregated campus and city.

After World War I, Wofford's primary academic goal was to achieve accreditation through the Southern Association of Colleges and Schools. In November 1895, Vanderbilt University's distinguished chancellor James H.

Kirkland (an 1877 Wofford graduate) called a meeting in Atlanta to discuss the formation of such an association, with Wofford represented by Snyder and Rembert. The program adopted at that meeting was farsighted, even courageous. In fact, four of the 16 campuses present were willing to endorse association standards they knew they would not be able to meet for some time. The major obstacles for Wofford were a need to stiffen requirements for freshman admission and the operation of Bamberg and Spartanburg "fitting schools," in which regular college faculty taught. Phasing out these popular residential preparatory schools required a costly and painful process that was not completed until the early 1920s. Wofford then achieved membership in the association, joining Converse College, the College of Charleston, and the University of South Carolina. Accredited status has been continuous since that time.

In spite of all this achievement and the wide respect President Snyder enjoyed in national higher education circles after World War I, little headway had been made in strengthening Wofford's endowment, which was valued at less than $1 million. The college was painfully dependent on its annual support from the Methodist Church, which amounted to about one-fourth of the operating budget. This financial weakness became obvious when Southern farm prices collapsed in the 1920s. Hard times intensified after the stock market crash of 1929. At the height of the Great Depression, some of the faculty worked without pay for seven months. Emergency economizing and a special appeal to South Carolina Methodists were necessary.

Time also had taken its toll on some of the older faculty, none of whom were eligible for retirement pensions or the fledgling Social Security program. Several professors became well known among the students for absent-mindedness. Many years later, Dr. Harold Hutson '33 retold the apocryphal campus story that "Uncle Dan" DuPré once walked into a geology classroom in Cleveland Hall where students were waiting. He opened his class book and took the roll by calling out 35 names. No one answered, since it was Section B that was sitting before him, and he had called the roll for Section A. He then reportedly declared, "Since no one is here, the class is dismissed." President Snyder wrote very movingly in his autobiography about this issue, "What do you do with your old men? Capitalize their service, their character, their personality; hold on to

Peddling his way through college

Dr. Ferman Bishop '42 graduated from Landrum High School and enrolled at Wofford at the age of 16. It was necessary for him to continue working in his father's service station in order to meet tuition expenses, and so he opted to live at home.

Limited passenger rail service was available and there was some access to a car or truck in emergencies, but in good weather, Bishop nearly always rode his old-fashioned, one-speed bicycle all the way to the campus, 26 miles each way. He usually left home at 6:30 a.m., and "with a good tail wind," he could sail down the foothills in time to arrive at Wofford by 8:30. Over the course of his college career, Bishop is said to have cycled more than 2,500 miles. Computing his expenses, he said he wore out one rear tire, broke a front axle, and wore out several sets of pedals, all of which were repaired at a total cost of $12.53.

Bishop was the great-nephew of Edgar L. Archer, the 1871 alumnus and an important early benefactor of the college. He served as an officer in the Navy during World War II and completed his doctorate in American literature at the University of Wisconsin in 1955. After leaving Madison, he was a professor at the University of Colorado, Wichita State and Illinois State, where he retired in 1987. He died in September 1997.

Special thanks to J. Walton Lawrence '34, editor and publisher, emeritus of the News-Leader *in Landrum, South Carolina*

them as long as life lasts; and memorialize them among the enduring records of the institution. … Isn't this one of the elements in what we are trying to say when we talk so much about liberal education? If it isn't, it ought to be, and if a college president is not dumb and blind to what really counts, he will be greatly pleased to have such 'old men' around."

Undaunted, the Wofford community in the 1930s set its sights on one of the most challenging goals conceivable—securing a chapter of Phi Beta Kappa. Formation of the United Chapters of Phi Beta Kappa in 1883 ushered in an era of careful and selective expansion beyond the Northeast, but in 1930, there still were only 17 chapters in the 10 Southeastern states. The formal effort to obtain a charter for Wofford began in that year when Phi Beta Kappa members Snyder, Wallace and Dr. John West Harris '16 signed and sent the initial report to the national senate. (Harris is remembered throughout the

country as the founder of the National Beta Club, which still has its headquarters in Spartanburg.) Finally satisfied that the college's financial health had been restored, national PBK representatives presented the charter of Beta Chapter of South Carolina to five resident faculty members January 14, 1941. Subsequently, ten students were selected as the chapter's first members in course. This stands as perhaps the single most significant date in Wofford College's first century, affirming nationally recognized academic distinction, an unflinching commitment to the liberal arts and sciences, and the achievements and character of a lengthening line of distinguished faculty and graduates.

Later in 1941, there occurred other significant events. Just as the New Deal, progress in public secondary education, and military mobilization were causing the sectional characteristics it described to fade, *The Mind of the South* was released to the

Student instrumental and vocal ensembles (Glee Clubs) were extremely popular on campus and in the Spartanburg community before movies and radio came to town after World War I. This is the 1913 orchestra: Paul Allen, Paul Whitaker and E.P. Pendergrass, violins; H.N. Dukes, J.H. Hood, and G.E. Whitesides, brass; W.M. Turbeville, percussion; and, in the center of the front row, J.C. Harmon, pianist and manager.

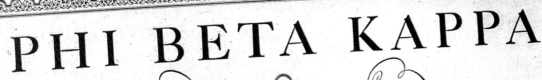

PHI BETA KAPPA

founded ΦΒΚ *Dec.* 5, 1776.
Williamsburg, *Virginia.*

ΦΙΛΟΣΟΦΙΑ ΒΙΟΤ ΚΤΒΕΡΝΗΤΗΣ

CHARTER
To

Olin Blair Ader

Walter Albert Stanbury, Jr.

Herbert Edward Vermillion

David Duncan Wallace

Henry Nelson Snyder

Members of ΦΒΚ *Greeting.*

W...... liberal principles of our Society fhould not...... liberal arts and fciences, are willing and defirous to propagate...... the Society in praifeworthy inftitutions of higher learning; and...... are infpired by an un-

public on February 10. In July, W.J. Cash died in Mexico, an apparent suicide. On December 7, Japanese aviators attacked the United States at Pearl Harbor, and World War II began. For Benjamin Wofford's college, as well as the South, the early 1940s signaled the passing of an era, but successive generations received a special inheritance, a college shining with academic honors.

The Original Terrier

That's Jack, front row center, in this picture of the 1909 Wofford baseball team. Legend has it that he was a neighborhood dog who was adopted by the players after he raced out of the stands and drove off an opposing runner who was trying to tie the score. A cartoon showing a Jack-like dog doing gymnastics appeared in a Wofford *Journal* about 1910. By 1914, when football resumed after an 11-year absence at Wofford, the nickname Terrier was firmly established for the college's athletics teams.

A *Professor's First Impressions*

After 44 years of service on the Wofford faculty, Professor Edward Hampton "Peg" Shuler wrote this article in 1954 for the Spartanburg Herald. He had come to Wofford in 1912 after completing his undergraduate studies at Clemson College. Shuler's background in surveying, mechanical drawing and basic civil engineering provided attractive elective courses for students who would live and work in a rural state and serve as Army officers. Shuler became well known in Spartanburg as a member of civic and fraternal organizations and as a member of the board of trustees of the city's public schools. He was beloved for his "faintly ironic sense of humor that allowed him to take the world and its troubles in stride." Shuler died at the age of 94, on May 3, 1980, in Spartanburg.

When I was asked by the Centennial Committee to write a story about Wofford as I found it in 1912, I agreed with alacrity. When I started to write, however, I found that I could not recall all events with what formerly I called precision—yes, I know now, "Tempus fugit."

When I arrived at Wofford, I was not a total stranger, for while a student at Clemson, I visited Spartanburg many times. The campus impressed me with its potential beauty. While not spacious, it was just in the correct proportion for its buildings. It had two elements of charm that are rarely matched on a campus its size: seclusion and scholarly atmosphere.

For the size of the student body, the buildings were fairly adequate, and with the exception of Carlisle Hall, which was new, all needed repairs. The Main Building had a steam heating system, but the size of the boiler permitted use of the radiators in the chapel only on special occasions. All the classrooms were heated with stoves or open grates.

There were no administrative offices in Main Building. The president's office was his study at his residence. When I had to go to Dr. Snyder's office with its book-lined walls I seemed to be in the presence of the spirits of Shakespeare and other great poets—it was truly a scholar's den.

The treasurer's office was the study of that princely Southern gentleman D.A. DuPré in his campus home. The room eventually became a part of the registrar's office. It was there where I received my first paycheck from Wofford, and many times, I visited, chatted, laughed, and enjoyed exchanges of views about science. When in this room, I often thought of Michael Faraday. Professor DuPré was in charge of the buildings and grounds. He hired all the workers on the grounds and buildings, and all college money was handled by him.

The student body, including the preparatory students, numbered 504. The customs on the campus in those days appeared strange to me. I had just come from a military atmosphere, so imagine how I felt when a student lifted his hat to me. Wofford students did that in those days. The custom vanished with the advent of World War I.

One custom did exist that I liked very much: the students dressed well. From their dress and appearance, they looked as if they came from homes of comfort and plenty. Most of them did, and more: they came from homes of ambition and culture. If a student came to classes or chapel not dressed in the prevailing style (hat, coat, white shirt, collar and tie), he soon felt that he was out of place. Formal occasions were fairly frequent and of course convention prescribed nothing less than "tails."

In those days there were no written rules. When it became necessary to place in order a rule, the president merely announced that so and so is to be the case; and thus it was. Speaking of rules in those days, strange as it may seem, smoking was not allowed in any of the buildings. A professor was permitted to

Science Hall

Whiteford Smith Library

Wofford College, Spartanburg, S. C.

Fitting School

Main Building

smoke in his office if he had one.

All infractions of the rules were handled by the faculty as a whole. I have attended some stormy sessions of the faculty trying to decide on the proper penalty to impose on a boy for over-cuts, Rembert usually leading the defense and D. D. Wallace prosecuting. Usually Clinkscales or Waller would move to adjourn, and President Snyder would rebuke the boy with such frightening words as "preposterous," etc., and scare him so that he would never cut again.

In those days all diplomas were written in Latin. For nearly 100 years that was the custom. Of late we have gone modern, a step we may regret, and now our diplomas are in English. It has been also the custom to give each graduate a Bible along with his diploma. Each member of the faculty is supposed to sign his name in the Bible. I belong to a good many orders and societies where rituals and ceremonies are the custom, and over the years I have seen religious ceremonies, but to me this custom of presenting a Bible with the diploma stands out. May it ever be Wofford's proud tradition.

We had a good library for our time and size, presided over by Miss Mamie DuPré and while our offerings, intellectually, were not as extensive as they are now, they were of such high quality as to create the envious esteem in which Wofford is held in educational circles the country over.

One of Wofford's bids for fame was its outstanding faculty—small in numbers, but

SPARTANBURG, S.C. Science Hall. - Wofford College.

giants in their chosen fields of teaching. When measured by scholarly teaching and attainment Wofford was out in the front rank of colleges of our size. The entire faculty was the administration. All the records were kept in a long box in the faculty room or in the president's office, and were accessible to all members of the faculty. The affairs of the college were in the charge of committees, and as usual, the chairman had to do the work.

The year 1912 saw the opening of Carlisle Hall for its first year of usefulness. Many strides have been made since that time, modernizations have taken place galore, but nothing has taken place to eclipse the glamour of those days nor dim the luster of that galaxy of pedagogues who put Wofford out front and who by sacrifices have left to the world a legacy of ideals to challenge each generation.

Carlisle Memorial Hall,
Wofford College, Spartanburg, S. C.

The golden age of U.S. postcards occurred between 1900 and 1920. These views of the Wofford campus are from the collection of Steve Garris.

Henry Nelson Snyder

enry Nelson Snyder faced a dilemma. On the evening of June 7, 1902, Wofford trustees offered him the presidency of the college, hoping he could fill the very large shoes of James H. Carlisle.

At the time, the 37-year-old Georgia native, Vanderbilt University alumnus and Wofford professor was nearing completion of the requirements for a doctorate at the Universität Göttingen in Germany. Snyder was an exceptional mentor of bright students, who often became disciples. (They sometimes called him "Heine," referring to the imprint of his graduate studies.) The conventional wisdom was that he soon would follow former faculty members William Baskervill, James H. Kirkland and Charles Forster Smith to one of the nationally focused research universities that were starting to emerge outside the circle of the elite campuses of the Northeast.

Though trustees made the job sound simple—"maintain Wofford's tradition of fine education and leave a little room for potential new direction"—Snyder endured a long night of self reflection. He wondered whether and how he could take Wofford, given the meager available resources, to the next level. In the final analysis, it was a challenge he did not refuse. He passed up other intriguing offers and the final portion of his degree studies to begin a 40-year presidential tenure that would do much to ensure a successful future for the college.

Snyder knew from the start of his presidency that, by necessity, the Methodist Church would continue to play an enormous role in shaping Wofford College. Snyder's presidential career was spent, in many ways, creating a delicate balance between the needs of a growing educational institution and those of its religious benefactor. He kept a healthy respect for the Methodist Church at all times, creating a mutual trust that allowed him to become the president of the church's board of education, a position of considerable power. All across the United States, Methodists came to see Snyder as a sort of missionary for education. He played an instrumental role in the reunification movement of the various branches of Methodism, which had been divided since well before the Civil War, and he spent considerable time on the road as a national speaker and committeeman.

There were, of course, struggles along the way with regard to how Christian doctrine and practice would fit into the curriculum and campus life, but Snyder met each challenge with an appropriate response, never upsetting the balance that hung between the church and the academy. Even when he went so far as to allow non-Methodist faculty to teach at Wofford, an unusual practice in a denominational college at the time, he did so delicately and with high regard for the church's desire to have only leaders with impeccable morality at the front of Wofford's students.

In President Snyder's later years came new challenges and opportunities. Highly successful in fundraising for two decades, he successfully faced a test of vision and character in the lean years of the Great Depression, which started in the South early in the 1920s and continued until the economic mobilization for World War II. President Snyder's commitment to the Spartanburg community continued after his retirement in 1942 through his role as the first president of the Spartanburg County Foundation, adding yet another chapter of service to the life chronicled in his rich autobiography, *An Educational Odyssey*.

Henry Nelson Snyder's legacy stands firm today, an intangible something that encourages tomorrow's young leaders to embrace even the opportunities they do not feel prepared to undertake.

—*Kristi Keenan '96*
editor, South Carolina Magazine

This fine portrait of a young Henry Nelson Snyder by Josephine Sibley Couper hangs in the living room of the president's home.

How to Choose a College

This article by Wofford's President Henry Nelson Snyder appeared in The North Carolina Christian Advocate August 15, 1940.

As I consider the kind of college where I am to spend four of the most important years of my life, years that will give direction and quality to all I might be and do, I am matriculating for life. I am choosing my alma mater, my spiritual and intellectual mother, who will be always with me. She is mine and I am hers to the end. Therefore I should choose carefully.

I should begin by studying the kinds of publicity sent out by the colleges I know. If it seems to claim too much, it probably has not much to claim. If it stresses sidelines, it is probably neglecting the main business of education.

I should not pay too much attention to the differences in costs at various colleges. As is the case with so many other things of value, cheapness in price often means cheapness in quality. It is well to look into this as we count the dollars and cents to be invested in a college education. It may be wiser sometimes to decide to attend the more expensive institution.

Then I should want to know something of the campus and buildings and other physical equipment of each college I considered. Do all these possess distinction, beauty, and charm? I do not ask palaces for dormitories, nor do I want mere size or garish display in buildings, but I do desire to live in surroundings that have something of grace and dignity. Suitable buildings, a pleasing landscape, a congenial atmosphere will add to my appreciation of things beautiful and give me memories that will abide throughout life.

After this, I should go very closely into its strictly educational standing and purpose of each school, being sure that, above everything else, the college is an educational institution. After investigating its "rating" by the approved standardizing agencies, after satisfying myself about the adequacy of its library and laboratory equipment and other physical facilities, I should remember that back of all these lie certain intangibles that are even more important.

I might ask myself such questions as these: Is the intellectual and moral atmosphere of the institution sound? Are its scholarly standards high and genuine? What about its faculty, their training, their productiveness in their special fields? Are there among them a few really great teachers, men and women with commanding and inspiring personalities? What sort of boys and girls attend this or that institution? I would try to find out if they are the serious kind who were seeking the best, and enough of them seeking it to give a stimulating tone to the whole institution and to create an atmosphere congenial to right development of personality.

Qualities like these intangibles are hard to discover in an institution, but I should make a further effort to find them trying to get acquainted with some graduates of each college. After all, its real measure is to be seen in the kind of men and women upon whom it has placed its stamp. These are its dividends, and the final test of whether it has done its work poorly or ably. Of course I am thinking not merely of the "big" names on its rolls, the alumni to whom it points with so much pride, but also to men and women who on the common highways of life illustrate what their college taught them. By always standing up to be counted on the side of the best things of life, do these people of the "rank and file" reflect honor upon the school that nurtured them?

Finally I think I should choose a college of my own church. There are certain religious values that are too essential to be left out of the processes of education. In college I should acquire not only knowledge in the ways of making a living, but also understanding of the real meaning of life and the kind of character that stands up to all the test of experience.

Members of an intercollegiate debate team in the 1920s.

Student Life

There were many important changes that took place at Wofford in the early years of the 20th century, most of which occurred very quickly just before and after World War I. While debate and public speaking remained very important for a group of students competing at the intercollegiate level, the literary societies were in a pronounced decline, and they disappeared entirely after World War II. In 1911-12, a modern student government organization was created, and John Lyles Glenn was elected first president. Student publications such as *The Journal*, the yearbook (first called the *Aurora*, then the *Bohemian*), and a new weekly newspaper (the *Old Gold and Black*) began to attract large staffs, enjoyed wide readership on campus, and could be financed primarily by selling advertisements to Spartanburg businesses.

"Ma" Helms, housemother for Snyder Hall.

Gifts from local businessmen led to the construction of Andrews Field House and Snyder Field, thereby strengthening Terrier athletics teams. At the same time, however, there were no scholarships to speak of, and the intercollegiate program of that era is best described as competitive rather than highly successful.

According to Dr. Lewis Jones '38, "Students roosted in two dormitories: Carlisle, considered the more modern of the two; and Snyder, considered the more prestigious by the particular fraternity groups who had gathered themselves therein. Each residence hall had a hostess (one, "Ma" Helms was a truly revered saint), and each dorm had its own dining room where meals were served family style (no cafeterias), with all eating simultaneously and noisily after a blessing. Students were summoned to meals by loud handbells rung raucously by joyful janitors going up and down corridors—amid loud threats of bodily harm in exchange for such thoughtful service. Meals were a very early breakfast, heavy "dinner" (at an ungodly 2:30 p.m., classes having ended at 2:15), and "supper" at 6:30. At two meals, grits was standard fare, and daily at supper, there was rice (this, after all, was South Carolina). At Sunday dinner, the students (always with Sabbath coat and tie, plus even a bit of decorum) received also a repulsive bag meal for Sunday supper. After all, the cooks had to get time off from one of the week's twenty-one meals."

After World War I, the opportunity to host a unit in the Reserve Officers' Training Corps was extended to Wofford and other independent colleges. The battalion achieved federal recognition on October 18, 1919. That first year, more than 100 students enrolled in the course. Although ROTC was voluntary at Wofford during the 1920s and 1930s, nearly all the students took military science. The small stipends paid to junior and senior cadets often made the difference between staying in and dropping out of college, and, at a time when dress shirts and ties were expected classroom attire, wearing uniforms to class stretched clothing budgets. Many graduates received commissions in the Regular Army or Army Reserve, and a large number of them served with distinction as officers in World War II.

—Doyle Boggs '70

With dancing and drinking prohibited on campus, formal "stag dinners" at downtown hotels were popular activities for the social fraternities. Both President Snyder and Dean DuPré may be identified in this photograph of a Sigma Alpha Epsilon gathering in the late 1930s. The young man in the left seat on the first row is the future Professor Lewis P. Jones '38.

Amazing DuPré

One Saturday afternoon, several members of the Class of 1932 followed the Wofford football team to a game at Furman's Sirrine Stadium. Any student in the residence halls who planned to travel more than 15 miles from the campus was required to sign out, in the same manner as a soldier leaving his barracks with a weekend pass. Violating the well-known rule, the group impulsively decided to stay overnight in downtown Greenville. What the young men found to occupy their time that evening is not recorded, but they rose the next morning in time to attend Sunday School at the Buncombe Street Methodist Church. After they had been seated near the front of their classroom, they realized that the visiting teacher that morning was none other than A. Mason DuPré, the dean of Wofford College.

It was too late to flee. The students stayed for the lesson and afterward congratulated Dean DuPré on the high quality of his presentation. Back in the residence hall at Wofford they awaited their fate. On Tuesday morning, they were summoned to the dean's office. He first reminded them of their sins; they had left Spartanburg without permission. But then, he said, they had demonstrated good judgment by coming to Buncombe Street to hear him speak. In that balanced situation, he would only issue them a warning. According to classmate Harold Hutson, it is noteworthy that one of the students said to have been a part of this escapade eventually became the senior minister at the downtown Greenville church.

That story tells much about Wofford student life in the 1920s and 1930s. By that time, many of the distinctive characteristics of the 19th century classical college had faded. The faculty once had handled business management and student affairs in a collegial fashion under the leadership of its president and secretary; these duties were turned over to two new administrative officers, a dean and a treasurer. There was an honor system all right, but it was not written down, and nobody signed a pledge to observe it. It was a systematic, authoritarian application of moral principles laid down by "Amazing" DuPré, or more often, "Old Mace."

Dean DuPré, Wofford class of 1895, was a native of Abbeville, South Carolina. Only distantly related to the DuPré family so prominent in the early history of the college,

Dean Arthur Mason DuPré

his father served as the county sheriff at a time when the job was intensely political and sometimes downright dangerous. Young Mace studied and taught Latin and mathematics, two disciplines seemingly appropriate for someone rigidly committed to a life of logic and self-discipline. For a number of years, he was headmaster of the Wofford Fitting School until, in 1920, he was appointed the first dean of the college. When there was a problem or infraction, the dean settled it, and it is said that no one was ever known to have successfully argued Old Mace into changing decisions about a principle or college rule.

David Duncan Wallace wrote in his history of the college, "It is well that Dean DuPré was a good man, for he would have been a terror as a bad one."

—Doyle Boggs '70

Peg, Fish *and* Graveyard *and the* Study *of* Foreign Languages

Generations of Wofford students have sung the lyrics to the college's alma mater: "On the city's northern border," by K.C. Frazer '20. Fewer are familiar with "A Wofford Hymn," an ode to the college penned by Professor John L. "Jack" Salmon. Here's a verse:

> *Wofford! Bright star of an age that is gone,*
> *With honors unsullied shine on*
> *Wofford! Thy sons, in the light of thy fame,*
> *Tread paths of thy sons that are gone*
> *Undaunted we dare, the banner on high,*
> *To battle for God, state and thee*
> *Thy old gold and black unstained we pledge,*
> *To yield to thy songs that shall be*

Salmon wrote the song while at Harvard, on leave from the Wofford faculty from 1925-1928. It wasn't his only stab at poetry—a collection of love poems to his wife is found in *To Lynne*—but it stands as a testimony to Salmon's love for the college.

Salmon was among a trio of professors in the modern foreign languages who came to Wofford in the first three decades of the 20th century and earned distinction for defining the college's approach to their field. But they are best remembered for their relationships with their students and their love of the college.

Students gave each man a nickname: Jack "Fish" Salmon, William "Peg" Bourne and James "Graveyard" Chiles.

Salmon's students picked a predictable play on the professor's last name. Bourne's name was obvious, too—he had a wooden leg. The story of Chiles' nickname is less certain. One account has it that his class was considered exceedingly difficult, a challenge to make it out of (academically) alive. Another story is that the moniker refers to Chiles' quiet, dignified demeanor.

Foreign language instruction in those days —until the 1970s, arguably—hardly resembled the field as it developed late in the 20th century. Latter-day students are expected to travel as part of their study and appreciate other cultures. Students are immersed in the language in class and in supplemental work in high-tech language labs. French professor Dennis Wiseman credits his colleague Susan Griswold with bringing all that to Wofford. Before World War II, few students anticipated international travel, and learning a foreign language was considered a step toward becoming more exact and expressive with the English language.

Chiles came to Wofford in 1914, distinguished in his field. During a one-year stint at the University of Wisconsin, he wrote a

Dr. James A. Chiles *(left)*
Professor W.R. Bourne *(right)*

Professor Jack Salmon and his wife, Lynne, celebrated their wedding anniversary at a campus dinner in 1981.

textbook for German students, *German Prose Composition*. A revision of the book was later used by the United States military in World War II. At Wofford, Chiles founded the Delta Phi Alpha, a national fraternity for German students.

He earned a reputation as a tough teacher, but one who was committed to his students and his field. "In the classroom he was a strict disciplinarian, and he demanded and received careful preparation," wrote his colleague Salmon in an obituary column about Chiles. In the same essay, Salmon quoted John Olin Eidson '29, a dean at the University of Georgia and student co-founder of Delta Phi Alpha: "Anyone who ever knew Dr. Chiles felt a strength of character which imparted strength to all around it. His calm but firm demand for the fulfilling of one's responsibilities was one of the finest teachings which he gave to his students." Salmon added, "His was a character without pretense or sham."

Peg Bourne '23 was similarly known for his demanding courses. Dr. Richard Robinson '61, professor emeritus of mathematics, tells of taking Bourne's classes—he and four or five others managed to finish with a passing grade. Robinson believes the rigor taught him valuable lessons about perseverance. "Somehow, I think, folks realized what it did— for at least the survivors—was to instill a sense of excellence," Robinson remarked. Another former student, Jim Mahaffey '68, wrote: "If, in our work at the boards, he caught a student unprepared, he proceeded to lay him low

(very low) before the class. On the other hand, he never hesitated to award laurels to the deserving individual."

Bourne took the mission of the college as seriously as he took his own classes. In an essay published in the Spartanburg *Herald-Journal* during the college's centennial, he articulated a view of that mission: Wofford, he argued, isn't looking to teach young men to become "mechanics," trained for a particular trade but unable to grapple with life's mysteries; Wofford shouldn't produce mere "playboys," likable young men who never stand out for their contributions to the larger society; but neither is Wofford's mission to turn out the "intellectual neurotic who is forever chasing rainbows." Bourne's hope was for Wofford to produce the "truly educated," who "must develop, over and beyond knowledge, a conscience and an abiding integrity."

Salmon's love for Wofford was demonstrated in more ways than verse. He taught modern languages at Wofford between 1921 and 1964. Popular with students, the *Old Gold and Black* picked up on his trademark "well-worn briefcase," calling it "something of a Wofford tradition." And, upon his retirement, the *Old Gold and Black* described the Salmons as "possibly the most popular chaperones on campus."

Another tribute at Salmon's retirement read: "He has shared in making the finest traditions of the college. Always he has been a gentleman and a scholar. ... He is a diligent worker, a loyal friend, and a wholesome influence whose life has enriched a great host of Wofford students."

—Baker Maultsby '92

TO LYNNE

Beauty is just skin deep, 'tis said,
But that is false, spoken or read.
Beauty lies deep within the heart,
Of soul and mind, it is a part.

Love's not blind, it never was,
But beauty is as beauty does.
Love sees beauty of every kind,
Whether of form, whether of mind.

Lovely spirit, beauty of face,
Beauty of voice, infinite grace.
Each one is yours, and love's bright goals,
For all to see, beauty of soul.

—Jack Salmon

Creative Participation: Wofford's Journal of the 1930s

An important era for Wofford writing came in the 1930s. Students published four or five editions of *The Journal* each year under the leadership and encouragement of Professor Kenneth Coates. These literary magazines still stand as remarkable illustrations of the breadth of student interest and initiative. Each issue included original stories, poems and short plays along with book reviews, political and social commentary, academic and personal essays, reviews of other college literary magazines and humor.

In these editions of *The Journal*, explorations of topics such as "The Futile Search for Ultimate Reality" and "A Liberal Education" appeared beside analyses of current political and social events. In May 1934, J.R. Cross '35 challenged the leadership of the state over the ratification of the 18th Amendment, charging that those voting for Prohibition "will not stand up for their convictions," and adding that "the sad thing is that many of those who voted dry, drink wet." In April of the same year, Kempson DeLoache '38 asked, "Will the other nations of Europe permit Hitler to satisfy his unbounded ambition?" In 1936, L.H. Hall '37 published an interview with a retired German Naval officer who was aboard the U-boat that sank the *Lusitania*.

Other writers for *The Journal* in the 1930s took on controversial social issues. In April 1936, Peter Moody wrote one of the most talked-about pieces ever to appear in any Wofford publication, "To a Cotton Mill Worker." [The full story may be found in another Hub City publication, *Textile Town*.] In "Notes of a Census Taker," a writer identified as WHO asserted, "We should know the Negro better." The statement may strike a reader in 2005 as racist in its phrasing and in some of its assumptions, but nonetheless, it took a firm stand for cross-racial understanding.

Several contributors during the period obviously were concerned that students were limiting their exploration of the world outside popular culture. WHO suggested, "Clearly students read very little other than the stories in the magazines." If this were in fact the case, then *The Journal*'s writers attempted to express serious concerns and to broaden the interests of the campus community. The late Professor Harris Chewning recalled Coates' insistence upon and staunch support of freedom of expression, "He was known as a friend of the students. ... He was especially concerned about freedom of the press and from censorship for student publications. Every few years an editor would get in hot water for publishing something indiscreet or too radical or rebellious. Kenneth was always loud and vigorous in the student's defense."

Not all was serious in *The Journal* of the 1930s. In April 1934, WHO published the tongue-in-cheek "How to Make a Success of College," revealing the extracurricular distractions that keep students from their studies. At the end of 1934, students published a spoof of their own publication, "The Churnle: The Litturury Pooblikashun of Woffort Kollitch."

Accounts of the 1930s note that Kenneth Coates' encouragement of the students who published poetry, fiction and drama in *The Journal* was vital to the publication's success. Pickett Lumpkin '37 wrote that in class, Coates "always loved discussion and argument. It didn't matter much to him if we wandered off the subject if the going was good. I had a course with him in modern playwriting and in creative writing. Always, his method was to get us to participate, both in class and out of class. Our exercises seemed always to point toward doing something creative and new."

Such "creative" participation, both in the classroom and out, marked *The Journal* of the 1930s and left a legacy for those who followed.

—*Carol Brasington Wilson '81*
Associate Professor of English

Professor Kenneth Coates taught creative writing to several generations of Wofford students and crafted editorials for the local television and radio stations.

Editorials

I Want to Revolt, But . . .

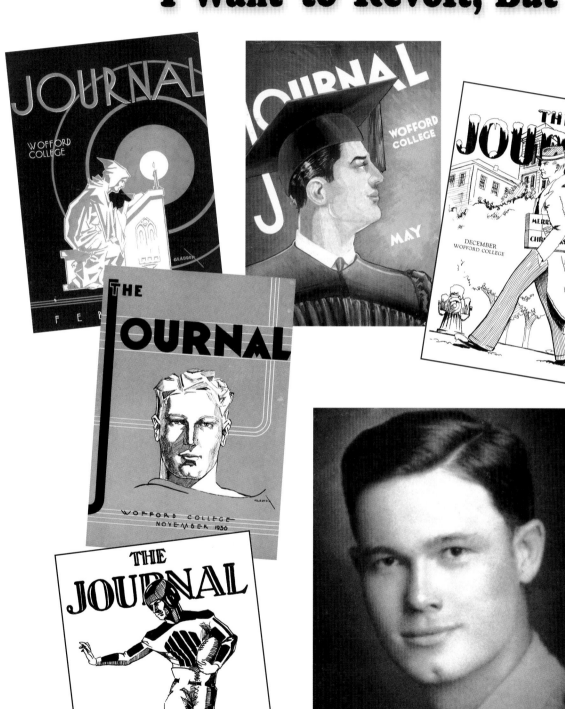

The art of Bill Gladden '39, which appeared on numerous covers of The Journal, set a very high tone for the publication. Serving as an infantry company commander in World War II, Gladden was killed in action in Europe on October 9, 1944.

Notable Alumni *from the* Third Generation

Marvin L. Holloway '33 started his business career at the height of the Great Depression by door-to-door peddling of bottles of perfume, powder and vanishing cream at 98 cents each. In 1938, he answered a want ad and became associated with the Tampa Motor Club, the American Automobile Association's smallest affiliate. It had only 97 members and its offices occupied 400 square feet in the basement of a chamber of commerce building.

Within a year, Holloway had become the club's manager. He began recruiting new members, improving services, lobbying against small-town speed traps, and consolidating small clubs into more regional organizations. By the time he retired in 1990, he was chairman of the board and chief executive officer of one of the association's largest affiliates, the AAA Auto Club South. Shortly before he died in 2002, Holloway's generous donation to Wofford for the Roger Milliken Science Center was a key to ensuring its completion.

Dr. Albert C. Outler '28 edited a definitive collection of the writings of John Wesley and was a noted theologian, author and ecumenical leader who taught most of his career at Southern Methodist University. He was the official Methodist delegate to the Second Vatican Council and was the first Christian in the Wesleyan tradition to receive the Pax Christi Award of the Benedictine Order. He also won an award from the American Jewish Community for his contributions to advanced understanding between Christians and Jews. Outler was the inaugural speaker in the Wofford Lecture Series in Religion and Ethics, and he was one of the first winners of the Council for Advancement and Support of Education's Alumni of the Year Award. An endowed chair in religion at Wofford bears Outler's name.

Dr. Eugene Pendergrass '16, who has been called "the father of American radiology," earned his medical degree at the University of North Carolina. For many years, he was a pioneering physician, teacher and researcher in cancer treatment at the University of Pennsylvania School of Medicine. He was also one of the first to treat Japanese victims of atomic warfare. Pendergrass received the Distinguished Service Award of the Pennsylvania Medical Society and the Medal of the American Cancer Society award, joining Dr. Jonas Salk and Dr. John Gibbon, the inventor of the heart-lung machine. The South Carolina Science Council posthumously inducted Pendergrass into its Hall of Science and Technology in 1997.

Dr. Louis B. Wright '20, author of more than 50 books, served as the director of the renowned Folger Shakespeare Library from 1947 to 1957. He received 28 honorary degrees from institutions such as Princeton, Amherst, Yale and St. Andrews in Scotland, and was a member of the Order of the British Empire. At the time of his death in 1984, he was serving as a historical consultant to the National Geographic Society. His autobiography, *Barefoot in Arcadia*, speaks warmly of his days at Wofford, and he returned to the college to speak at the inauguration of President Charles F. Marsh on April 29, 1959.

Austin T. Moore '20 attended the Medical College of South Carolina after graduation from Wofford. He did his residency as an assistant to the distinguished Dr. A. Bruce Gill at the University of Pennsylvania. He then returned to Columbia, South Carolina, opened a clinic, and began a practice of orthopedic surgery in 1927. In less than a decade, he earned a national reputation and was elected to membership in the American Academy of Orthopedic Surgery. In 1942, Dr. Moore reported and performed the first metallic hip replacement surgery in the United States. The original prosthesis he designed was made of the metal vitallium. It was about a foot in length and bolted to the cut end of the femoral shaft. Dr. Moore died in 1963, but improved versions of his prosthesis, still known as the "Austin Moore," remained in use into the 21st century.

Paul Hardin Jr. '24 was a gifted scholar during his college days and an undefeated intercollegiate debater. After graduating from the Candler School of Theology in 1927, he served churches in North Carolina, and then he became pastor of the First Methodist Church of Birmingham, Alabama, in 1949. In 1960, Hardin was elected as a Methodist bishop and appointed to return to South Carolina. A year later, he was also asked to fill an episcopal vacancy in the Alabama-West Florida Conference. In that capacity, he was one of the clergy to whom the Rev. Dr. Martin Luther King Jr. addressed his famous "Letter from the Birmingham Jail." "Bishop Hardin's sense of fairness to persons of different viewpoints, yet his own powerful commitment to the goal of an inclusive church," are said by historians to have been essential in the merger of South Carolina's African-American and white United Methodist conferences in 1972. Hardin also served in 1972 as president of the United Methodist Council of Bishops, and then he retired. He died in 1996. Paul Hardin III, the eighth president of Wofford College, is one of his three children.

The Honorable C. Bruce Littlejohn '35 was admitted to law school after his junior year and was awarded a Wofford degree after completing prescribed additional requirements at the University of South Carolina. He likes to claim he remembers his Wofford commencement speech word-for-word—he dropped by the president's office one afternoon to pick up his diploma, and after a quick handshake of congratulations, he was instructed to reimburse the treasurer for the printing costs on his way out! With time out for military service during World War II, Justice Littlejohn practiced law and served in the South Carolina House of Representatives until 1949, where he was speaker for a two-year term. The General Assembly elected him to a South Carolina circuit judgeship in 1949, and then to the state Supreme Court in 1967. He served as chief justice from March 1984 until he retired. Active and productive into his 90s, Justice Littlejohn willingly has done "chores" for a variety of organizations and civic projects and is also the author of three books.

Hugo S. Sims Jr. '41 was a combat hero in World War II, serving with the 501st Infantry Regiment, 101st Airborne Division (the Screaming Eagles). He was awarded the Bronze Star in the Normandy campaign and the Silver Star for action during Operation Market Garden, "a bridge too far." While serving as a battalion intelligence officer, Sims earned the Distinguished Service Cross for leading the "Incredible Patrol," the story of which was featured in *Life* magazine. Firing only two shots and taking no casualties, he and five other soldiers captured 32 German soldiers. After the war, in addition to working as a practicing attorney, Sims founded a real estate development company and was a banking executive. He was elected to the South Carolina House of Representatives (1946-1947) and then to the United States House of Representatives (1949-1950). Serving on the Wofford Board of Trustees from 1976 through 1988, he placed particular emphasis on achieving competitive salaries and benefits for the faculty and staff.

One Man's Wellspring *of* Generosity

Edward King Hardin '32, retired Chester County probate judge and former Wofford trustee, died Jan. 13, 1992, at the age of 79. Vice President Larry T. McGehee wrote this article upon Judge Hardin's retirement in 1990.

About 45 miles away, there's an old man from Wofford's class of 1932. At the end of November, he retired as probate judge for his county. They had changed the salary structures for public officials just before he retired. His had been raised to $25,000 a year, probably the most he had ever earned in a year in his lifetime.

For years, we at the college have been accustomed to getting at least one letter a week from him. Sometimes it is a note of encouragement, some word of excitement about something good going on at his alma mater, or some expression of appreciation for some college milestone passed. Sometimes they are copies of letters he sent to all his classmates asking for support for the college. More often, the letters contain checks, sometimes for $25, sometimes for $50 and occasionally for $100.

We've given up trying to acknowledge all his letters, because that means getting some more thanking us for thanking him. There's no way to get ahead of him at letter writing.

Daily he scours several newspapers from the two Carolinas, and often his checks are memorials to Wofford alumni who have died. In between obituaries, there are checks for the Annual Fund, for the general endowment fund, or for his Class of '32's endowed scholarship, for his family's endowed scholarship, or for any special college drive of the moment that requires matching gifts.

Judge Edward K. Hardin '32

Last year, despite his income, his gifts totaled more than $5,000. I am told that what he has been doing for years for his college he also has been doing for his local church.

I am convinced that he does without lunch to make such generosity possible. With his life mostly behind him, it is amazing to find someone his age believing as much as does he in progress and improvement.

His wife seems to share joyfully in the pleasure he takes in giving, although he teases about having to wait until she is out of town each spring to file his tax return so she won't see how much he gives away.

He entered the college about the time Hoover entered the White House and graduated about the time Hoover left. It was hard times for both of them.

He served in combat in World War II and can recall minute details about those of his classmates who were killed in battle.

Although he never makes the connections explicit, I think there is some tie between his giving and his gratitude for having survived both Depression and the war and some sadness for those who didn't.

He has served on the college's board and chaired it, has received the college's outstanding alumnus award, the Algernon Sydney Sullivan Award, and an honorary degree. But those honors and service don't seem to be the wellsprings of generosity that the reputation of his family's name and his experience in hard times have been.

Since there is no one else running him even a close second for the number of gifts he makes each year, his annual competition has come to be himself. Each year, he has tried to outdo what he did the year before. Usually he has succeeded.

The folks in the courthouse gave him a nice party in the grand jury room. Lots of people dropped in to see him off. Strangers to the courthouse had no trouble finding the party. He had left a note in the same scrawled handwriting as all those letters on his office door, telling where he was and how to get there.

Wofford gave him a tie for the occasion. It is gold with black stripes, with an embossed emblem on it of "Old Main." He reports he is wearing it with pride in his retirement. It seemed the appropriate gift. He is himself the best old school tie we know.

Wofford Takes on Ty Cobb, 1913

The *Spartanburg Journal* of Saturday, April 4, 1913, carried a headline, "Ty Cobb's Bunch Play Here Today," and predicted a victory for the barnstorming professionals over the Wofford College team, but a lively contest nonetheless. Reporting the next Tuesday, the same paper noted that Cobb's bunch had won a close one, 9-8, but that the ninth inning proved especially amusing.

"Osborne, a Wofford player, was coaching on the third base line, and Ty was pitching. What passed between the man and the child could not be heard in the stands, but the Wofford boy bristled up like a Bantam rooster and wanted to fight. He was just so small and Cobb was just so big that the whole incident was really amusing. After the words, Cobb stated that he would see the player after the game. About 613 [sic] boys gathered about Cobb intent upon killing him, or doing something else equally as harmful [sic], and the prompt arrival of officers saved Cobb's life."

But the story didn't end on the field. Two days later, on Thursday, April 9, the *Spartanburg Herald* headlined: "Tyrus Cobb and Wofford Player Fight in Hotel." Both the Terrier team and Cobb's All-Stars were in Greenville to play Furman University on Monday, April 6. Traveling salesmen brought to Spartanburg the suppressed news of a fist fight between Rutledge Osborne, Wofford student from Anderson, South Carolina, and Tyrus Cobb. "One report was that Osborne publicly cursed Cobb in the dining room of the hotel; another was that Osborne drew a pistol, which was wrested from him."

The *Spartanburg Journal* of the same day reported that "Dr. Snyder, president of Wofford College, lectured the boys [the student body], and deplores the affair," but would not bring charges against the student or team.

The full story came out in the *Spartanburg Herald* of April 11, 1913:

"Mr. Osborne yesterday admitted that he drew a pistol when attacked by Cobb, but justified it on the ground that Cobb was much larger than he and had made threats against him.

"After his trouble with Osborne in Spartanburg Saturday, Cobb, it is said, declared he would 'beat Osborne's face into jelly' when they met on Monday in Greenville. Osborne said that he borrowed the pistol to protect himself, but tried to avoid the difficulty."

The newspaper carried Osborne's account: "'Cobb went to [Wofford] Coach McCarthy's room and asked my name. When I was told this, just before dinner, I slipped up to my room and put the pistol in my pocket.

"'When dinner was over, one of my teammates and I took the elevator for the room to dress. As the elevator started, Cobb and one of his men stepped in. When we arrived at the stop, he grasped me by the collar and pulled me out into his room, my companion going to the first floor for the rest of the team. I was thus alone with Cobb, Coles, McMillan and another member of Cobb's team. He struck at me and I naturally drew the gun. This made him release me, but Cad Coles slipped up behind me and wrenched the gun from my hand. Cobb then jumped on me and it was an easy matter for a man of his size to beat me up considerably. I did not hunt a scrap and I hated to be mixed up in one. Cobb acted cowardly and overbearing, and I, being only a boy, acted on the impulse of the moment.'"

Osborne later transferred to the University of South Carolina and graduated in 1916. Years later, his service as chairman of its board of trustees led to naming the USC central administration building for him. Cobb, who played in more than 3,000 games, holds the record for runs scored and is among the top five all-time players in RBIs, stolen bases and hits.

No record exists of his ever returning to the Wofford campus.

—*Larry T. McGehee*

Several members of this baseball team from the mid-1910s played against Ty Cobb's barnstormers at "Wofford Park." The grandstand was located on the northeast corner of the present Snyder Field.

"Frog"

On offense, most football teams in the 1920s lined up in a double wing or "spread" formation. Just prior to the snap of the ball, the backs went through a series of choreographed movements designed to confuse the defense. The tactics eventually led to a rules change imposing a penalty for "backfield in motion." [To see how it worked at Notre Dame, watch the movie, "Knute Rockne, All-American."]

Carroll F. Reames '26 played quarterback for Wofford in that era, and it was his responsibility to call the shifts: "one, two, three, hike." As he moved, he gave an odd little jump that gave him his life-long nickname, "Frog." Contemporaries remembered Reames as the "best defensive back known in all the galaxy of Wofford stars, past and present." Reames went on to become a legendary principal during a 41-year career in the public schools in Anderson, South Carolina. He died on February 10, 1995. ~Courtesy of Pi Kappa Phi fraternity archives.

Claude Finney *and the* 1928 Terriers

There was much excitement as the Wofford football team reported for fall practice in 1928. Hopes were high that for the first time since 1919, a winning record might be possible.

An All-America tackle at Annapolis and former Navy officer, Tommy Schaffe returned as head coach, after making a promising beginning in 1927. Schaffe's most memorable quality was his toughness. He put his team through all sorts of conditioning exercises and, in addition, went in for much heavy scrimmaging. "He used to think nothing of grabbing you by the hair and really chewing you out for making a mistake," said one of his players. "He didn't cuss, but that really didn't seem to hamper him any. He could really make you feel stupid."

In addition to being a no-nonsense taskmaster, Schaffe was also a shrewd judge of talent. In those days, college coaches were as likely to be seen scouting campus intramural games as they were visiting high schools, and it was on one such occasion that Schaffe saw a junior baseball standout named Claude Finney running with the football. Finney became the Terriers' first backfield substitute. Said the Spartanburg *Herald*, "Though not a big man (5-8, 175 pounds), he is hard to put down once he gets underway. He seems destined to be one of the most valuable backs Wofford has."

"Basically, we ran the single wing with the guards pulling and blocking on the end sweeps," Finney recalled years later. "Leather helmets, shoulder pads and cleats were still optional in those days, and face masks were illegal. It was rough." In one game, Wofford ran 53 plays into the line, eight end runs, and threw nine passes. "We had to do almost all our scoring on straight power football. We didn't have a good passing game, or we would have been world-beaters."

The Terriers won their first two games rather routinely, but the Carolinas took notice when Wofford shut out Davidson, 7-0. It was front-page news in the *Herald*, and inspired this paragraph from sports editor Wilton Garrison, "The drive gained power every time and reached its peak in the final period, when the ball, covered with gold and black blood splotches, was rushed across the goal line."

Wofford reached the climactic game of the season, against The Citadel at the Spartanburg Fairgrounds, with a record of 6-1-1. The Bulldogs scored first, but Wofford responded with a 65-yard drive for a touchdown. "I got knocked goofy during the drive," Finney recalled, "but I still managed to get up and later scored from the three yard line." Late in the game, the Bulldogs decided to pass from behind their own goal line, and Dargan and Lever broke through to score a safety for Wofford, giving the Terriers a 9-7 victory. The student body and the crowd of 4,000 carried the coaches and players off the field.

Nothing on paper exists to compare Finney with those who went before or after. However, it is documented that he scored 56 points in 1928, leading the state. He was also named to the All Southern team and was Wofford's MVP, the first recorded winner of that distinction in football. In 1961, a veteran's committee of the South Carolina Sports Hall of Fame elected Finney to membership—truly amazing considering that he played only one full season as a starter.

An excellent student, Finney coached for a year, and then enrolled at the Medical College of Virginia. He returned to Spartanburg to practice medicine for many years. He died November 15, 1984.

—*Doyle Boggs '70*

The 1928 Terriers—Loren King and George Brown were the ends; Clyde Lever and Harry Oates played tackle; Perrin Dargan and Allen Turbeville were the guards; and Russell King was the center. Joe Kennedy, Doug Jones and Leland Jackson joined Finney, number 65, in the starting backfield. The kicking game was outstanding, with Oates punting and Dargan handling extra points. ~Courtesy of John Dargan

Baseball Major Leaguers: Ellerbe *and* Wood

After serving in the Navy for a year during World War I, Frank Ellerbe '18 signed a professional contract with the Washington Senators in 1919, where he played third base. Traded in 1921 to St. Louis, he promptly went four-for-four in his first game. In 105 games that year for the Browns, he recorded a .288 batting average. He followed that with a .246 mark at the plate in 91 games the following season.

After eventually seeing action with Cleveland and Kansas City, the recurrence of an old knee injury forced him to retire in 1925. He knew Ty Cobb well and con-sidered him the best baseball player of his era.

At Wofford, Ellerbe was a 1917 All-State selection in football, and it is said that he played in every minute of every game that season. Highlights included quarterbacking Wofford to a stunning 20-0 victory over South Carolina. In baseball, he was the Terriers' starting shortstop and captain during the 1917 season.

Later in life, Ellerbe was a par golfer and, with his brother, built and operated one of the first golf courses in the Pee Dee area of South Carolina. The son of a South Carolina governor, he went on to serve in the South Carolina House of Representatives in the late 1920s and was a community and church leader in Latta, South Carolina. He died July 7, 1988.

*   *   *

One Sunday evening in 1928, Charles Asher Wood '30 lost his chance to earn a Wofford diploma, but he earned a lifelong nickname and went on to enjoy a brief day in the sun as a professional baseball pitcher.

The Spartanburg native and three other students were playing bridge on campus, an activity prohibited on Sundays by the unwritten honor code. Wood had the misfortune to be dealt 13 spades for a "laydown grand slam." When the local newspaper published an article about this very rare event, he was immediately expelled, even though others in the same room were playing poker.

"Spades" (the nickname was even included in his obituary in 1986) became a very good minor league pitcher. He went on to pitch 122 innings in two seasons with the Pittsburgh Pirates. In 1930, he put together a 4-3 record, but finished with a 5.12 earned run average. The next season, he finished 2-6 with a 6.05 earned run average.

Wood later was an executive with Yukon Mill and Elevator Co. in Severy, Kansas.

Frank Ellerbe posed for this publicity picture during his pitching career with the Washington Senators.

The ball and glove were used in the early 1920s by the future US Senator Olin D. Johnston.

Wofford at War

On December 7, 1941, Spartanburg was enjoying a pleasant, seasonable Sunday. In nearly all the churches, the sermon reflected the text, "Thou Shalt Not Kill." The ministerial association had agreed to preach about highway safety.

As the temperature rose past 50 degrees, Professor and Mrs. Jack Salmon left their home on the Wofford campus to go for a drive. In midafternoon, they heard the news on the radio—the Japanese had attacked Pearl Harbor.

Years later, Mrs. Salmon remembered "Fish" taking her hand and saying, "That's war,

served in Europe through the war and retired in 1971 as an Air Force lieutenant general. In the later stages of the war, Montgomery was the deputy plans officer for the 20th Air Force during the B-29 campaign against the Japanese. He too became a general officer in the 1950s, commanding the 8th Air Force.

Christmas 1941 found the campus in a somber mood. In the December 1941 issue of the Wofford alumni bulletin, President Henry Nelson Snyder wrote, "Four times in its history, Wofford has been called to war, and its officials, faculty and students have, in each period of strain and crisis, met all the obligations

darling." The couple had no children of their own, and their thoughts immediately turned to Wofford alumni, some of whom were even then in harm's way.

For example, former Spartanburg Eagle Scouts Joseph H. Moore '36 and J. Beverly "Monty" Montgomery '38 were on active duty with the Army Air Corps. Flying the obsolete P-40 Warhawk fighter during the campaign in the Philippines, Moore recorded two of the Air Corps' first wartime kills before he and the other pilots were evacuated to Australia. He

required of them with fortitude, fidelity, and in the spirit of high and generous sacrifice. We offer to each of our far-flung alumni, best wishes for either the experience or the memory of an American Christmas under a flag which as never before is the free heart's only hope and protection in this hour."

Just a few days after the message was written came bad news concerning a Wofford graduate. Married on Christmas Day 1941, Lt. Roy Robertson '35 of Spartanburg, was killed just three days later when his plane crashed

Army Air Corps Preflight Cadets drill on Snyder Field during World War II. From this view atop the north grandstands, Andrews Field House and Carlisle Hall can be seen in the background.

while on anti-submarine patrol off the North Carolina coast.

Another Air Corps lieutenant and former Wofford football star from Spartanburg, Henry Elias, had left college before graduation to fly with the 23rd Fighter Group (the old "Flying Tigers") in the China Theater. Col. Robert L. Scott wrote the story of this unit in his 1943 bestseller, *God is My Co-pilot*, and described Elias as "my most unforgettable character, a man who brought a little sunshine into the grim reality of war. He had a reply for every person, and a comeback to every joke." On September 2, 1942, Chinese witnesses reported a dogfight over Nanking during which Elias took on four Zeroes and was killed. A Chinese officer made a dangerous 160-mile trip by buffalo cart to retrieve the body for burial in the American pilots' cemetery.

It was no wonder that the 1943 *Bohemian* yearbook opened, "The student body realized the seriousness of the crisis in human affairs and returned to school only because they believed that by doing so they were better preparing themselves for a part in the nation's war effort. Many of us have brothers and friends fighting in various parts of the world. This year, we came to school with a new purpose and a new determination that those who have died and those who will die in this war shall not die in vain. ...The heart of Wofford is unchanged and changeless."

Aubrey Faust '43, Wofford's first All-American in football, was killed in action in Normandy during World War II.

On February 11, 1943, came the historic news that the Wofford campus would be turned over to the Air Corps. After the final chapel, the students filed out, singing the alma mater. The first-year students and sophomores attended classes at Spartanburg Junior College, and the juniors and seniors took classes at Converse. [The full story is told in an essay by Dr. Phillip Stone '94 in the Hub City Writers Project book, *When the Soldiers Came To Town*.]

Most of the remaining upperclassmen were physically unqualified for the military and were pursuing majors that involved critical scientific research. "By going to summer school, I was able to graduate a year early," remembered the late Dr. William P. Cavin '45, who later served as chair of the chemistry department. "I had fewer than 30 classmates, and I did not have a chance to get to know them very well. I was the only man in most of my classes."

Professor and Mrs. Salmon also were displaced. Their 1854 campus home was remodeled into an infirmary. Salmon taught Spanish and served as an informal dean of men at Converse. Other than Kenneth Coates, who wrote newspaper and radio editorials, Wofford faculty taught the Air Corps students. The opportunity was a godsend for these older men, because the alternative would have been unemployment.

The honor roll of war dead at Wofford reached 73 names, quite remarkable for a small college where fall enrollment had never exceeded 500. Several of those who died were among the best and the brightest of the graduates of the 1930s, men like Aubrey Faust '43 and Bill Gladden '39, both of whom were killed while leading infantry units in the Normandy campaign. They, and all the others, are remembered on a bronze plaque in Main Building.

"Only this is changeless," said the 1944 *Bohemian*, "the courage and strength of Wofford men who picked up a grenade or bayonet because the nation had a dirty job to do, and it was their nation. They were guided by tomorrow's vision—Wofford students back in Wofford classrooms hearing Wofford professors. Dr. Snyder giving new chapel speeches. Rebuilding Dr. Wallace's distorted globe. Back to normalcy and loud sport jackets. Hot bull sessions and dining hall grub. And there will always be a Wofford, on the city's northern border."

—Doyle Boggs '70

During World War II, Wofford honored its alumni in the armed forces with a banner with blue stars for living alumni and gold stars representing those who had been killed. This view also shows Leonard Auditorium as it was configured between renovations in 1902 and 1961.

Fourth
Generation
1942-1968

THE COLD WAR GENERATION

by Phillip Stone

As his 40-year administration drew to a close, President Henry Nelson Snyder and the trustees had made tentative plans for building the Wofford endowment and modernizing the college's facilities. The endowment remained small and the college dependent on annual support from the Methodist Church and contributions from individual alumni and friends. American entry into World War II postponed the campaign, which proposed to raise about $500,000 for endowment and facilities improvements, and Snyder retired after Commencement 1942. College leaders understood that the war would profoundly affect most aspects of the college's life, and they continued Snyder's efforts to prepare the campus for postwar life.

Snyder's successor was Dr. Walter Kirkland Greene. A member of the Class of 1903, he is the only graduate to hold Wofford's presidency during its first 150 years. Greene earned a doctorate at Harvard and came to Wofford from Duke University, where he had been dean of undergraduate studies and professor of English. He spent the early years of his administration guiding the college through the war, but with victory in sight, his administration was looking to the future. Barely a week after the Japanese surrender, the college announced a major postwar plan, "The Wofford of To-Morrow" [sic], that called for significant improvements to the college's facilities.

Under the plan, the college would add a new academic building, a new science building, a student activities building, an honor society and fraternity hall, a chapel and two new residence halls. The document also called for an expanded library, a swimming pool in Andrews Field House, renovation of Main Building and improvements to the grounds. The Wofford of To-Morrow proposed to increase the endowment by $300,000 and to replace the $85,000 endowment that had been lost at the end of the Civil War. The total campaign goal was $1.5 million, and as of

September 1945, the college had received more than a $250,000 dollars in pledges. However, a series of controversial events involving Methodist higher education in South Carolina diverted the college's focus from the planning document.

Throughout 1947, South Carolina Methodists debated a series of proposals to merge single-gender Wofford, Columbia and Lander Colleges into a denominational university that would serve men and women. An initial plan, proposed in the spring of that year, located the institution on a new campus in Spartanburg County. That concept was rejected in favor of another study, but at a later special session of the Methodist Annual Conference, and after a full day of legislative wrangling, church leaders voted to place Wofford and Columbia under a single administration and board of trustees. Control of Lander was offered to Greenwood County. The plan took effect in November 1948. Greene became president of both Wofford and Columbia, with a dean of administration on each campus to direct internal affairs. Although supporters of full merger may have considered this a step toward that goal, the plan proved unworkable. At its 1950 session, the Annual Conference returned each campus to its own president and board of trustees. The state's Methodists promised to take a more active role in fundraising for both colleges. Fatigued by the campaign and controversy within the church and by the strain of presiding over two colleges separated by 100 miles, President Greene announced his retirement in 1951. Thus, at a critical time in its history, an opportunity to move Wofford ahead was missed.

While their leaders were trying to secure funds for campus improvements and debating the future, Wofford students, many of whom were veterans, worked hard at being average college students. With a rapid increase in the number of students, the faculty underwent major changes in the late 1940s. The college had never had a retirement plan for its faculty, and many professors taught beyond their 75th birthdays. Greene implemented a retirement plan that required professors to retire at age 70. Six of the longest-serving faculty members, with a combined 238 years of service, retired in 1947. The faculty, which had numbered 24 in 1940, grew to 43 members by 1950. At that time, only nine professors had served before 1940, and more than 30 had joined the faculty since the end of World War II. As the president's report to the trustees noted, "It is a young faculty of men whose scholarship is thorough, whose teaching ability is superior, and whose character offers excellent leadership to the college student."

After a yearlong search following Greene's retirement, the trustees announced that Dr. Francis Pendleton Gaines Jr. would become Wofford's sixth president in August 1952. Taking office at age 33, he established the record as the youngest president in the college's 150-year history. The son of the distinguished president of Washington and Lee, Gaines had lived on college campuses for nearly his entire life. After earning his doctorate in history at the University of Virginia, Gaines came to Wofford from

Wofford Military Dead of the Cold War Era

~Korea~
Norman E. Bowen '49,
December 27, 1952
Robert F. Haynes '37,
November 28, 1950
Avery W. Williamson '34,
February 14, 1952

~Vietnam~
Leyburn W. Brockwell Jr. '51,
May 1, 1967
Audley M. Federline Sr. '59,
November 19, 1966
Furman W. Massingale '70,
May 29, 1972
John S. Reaves Jr. '68,
July 8, 1969
Harold S. Sale Jr. '64,
June 7, 1967
Ted J. Taylor '68,
July 15, 1971

Between 1950 and 1970, most Wofford students volunteered for ROTC training for at least two years. Curtis Bell '55, who later served Wofford as a professor of mathematics, instructs fellow cadets on the operation of an anti-tank recoilless rifle during a leadership laboratory.

In the mid-1950s, seven non-residential fraternity lodges were constructed and, after an absence of some 50 years, "the row" again became part of the Wofford campus scene.

Southern Methodist University, where he had been dean of students.

Almost immediately, the president, trustees and faculty began planning for the college's centennial and for its future needs. The college remained short of funds both in the operating budget and in the endowment. As of 1952, the college's endowment was approximately $950,000, and gifts never exceeded $40,000 per year. Gaines also hoped to address some of the college's lingering facilities problems. While the college had built one new residence hall and expanded Andrews Field House and the library since World War II, no new academic buildings had been erected for decades. The aging residence halls and academic buildings were in constant need of repair. Even with GI Bill tuition payments, budgets were often very tight, and the college ran operating deficits in more years than not. In 1954, the trustees approved a $1.3 million centennial campaign to try to address some of these problems.

In 1955, Gaines and the trustees asked the Annual Conference to expand the membership of the Board of

Trustees from 13 to 21, with a quota of 11 laypersons and 10 clergy. One of the new trustees was Roger Milliken, the president of Spartanburg's Deering-Milliken Company. Noting that, at the time, only 12 percent of alumni contributed to the college's Annual Fund, Milliken pledged to give the college $1,000 for each percent increase in alumni giving. This pledge generated national publicity as well as gifts to the 1956 Annual Fund from more than 74 percent of the alumni. Pursuading Milliken to join the board proved to be among Gaines' most significant accomplishments.

Throughout the generation after World War II, Wofford reflected the culture of the 1950s and early 1960s. Members of the all-male student body came largely from small towns in South Carolina, attended mandatory chapel and dressed in coat and tie for Sunday dinner. A large percentage of their adult role models had served in World War II, and these young men expected to serve for at least two years as officers in the armed forces, which were partially mobilized throughout the Cold War years. First-year students had to endure a period called "rat season," which was designed to teach them about Wofford traditions and to increase school spirit. They wore beanies, made signs for pep rallies and performed silly tasks at the behest of upperclassmen. Stories about fraternity events, football and basketball games, Homecoming and ROTC filled the pages of the *Old Gold and Black*. While the

Dean Philip Covington and his wife Liliane (left) greet first-year student Bob Dobbins '70 in the fall of 1966. Covington recruited an interesting and able faculty and defined "the Wofford Way" for several generations of students.

Wightman Hall was a new addition to the campus in the late 1950s. The building in the foreground was a student center and canteen, sometimes known as the "Dog House."

arts were not well represented on campus during these years, a number of students participated in Professor Sam Moyer's Glee Club. The group performed regularly all year, but the highlight of the year was the two-week long spring bus tour, usually in the South Carolina Lowcountry.

After five years as president, Pendleton Gaines surprised the campus by resigning in August 1957. Though he had succeeded in attracting new supporters and increasing the college's endowment, Gaines never seemed comfortable around Methodist ministers or lay leaders, or with some of the older faculty. Having previously worked at several larger colleges and universities, Gaines perhaps believed Wofford to be provincial, and he found the faculty resistant to change.

Dean of the College Philip Covington became acting president for the 1957-58 academic year while the trustees searched for a new president. Covington possessed a strong sense of what made a good faculty member for a liberal arts college, and he was largely responsible for recruiting a generation of excellent professors. One often repeated story is that Covington hired John Harrington to teach geology after talking with him on an airplane. When Covington died, Lewis Jones spoke at the funeral, recalling a 1980 letter sent from a house named Toad Hall in Frogmore, South Carolina. Covington had written, "Personally I dislike any change (good or bad) in Wofford and its unusual folk. I'd like the whole thing preserved forever, as it was when all of us were young." Jones continued that it was Covington who invented the college apologia that he called "the Wofford Way," which sometimes he also exemplified. For those not familiar with it, Jones said, "the phrase is akin to the majestic implications in that phrase associated with England—its way of muddling through."

In 1960-61 Main Building was gutted for a major stabilization and revitalization. While the exterior work was faithful to Edward C. Jones' classical design, the classrooms were radically altered, the auditorium was expanded to hold a larger student body, and a new north-side portico was added.

An annual presidential duty in the era of Charles F. Marsh was the crowning of the Homecoming Queen. She was usually a student at Converse, Columbia, Winthrop or Limestone who was sponsored by one of the social fraternities.

In 1958, Dr. Charles Franklin Marsh, a Wisconsin native who was dean of the faculty at William and Mary, became Wofford's seventh president. With leadership from Marsh and the trustees, many of the long-delayed improvements to the campus finally took place. While aging Carlisle and Snyder Halls remained in service, Greene Hall and Wightman Hall were added in the 1950s. The innovative Wightman Hall (since demolished) housed students in suites rather than on long halls and abandoned barracks-style showers in favor of slightly more private facilities. There was also a new campus-wide cafeteria on the first floor. House-mothers, who were an important part of campus life, supervised these residence halls, and students often were subject to room inspections by the dean of students. Fraternity lodges were completed in 1956, returning to the idea that Greek-letter organizations might benefit from permanent meeting spaces on campus.

President Marsh's first years on campus marked a building boom unseen since the early 1900s. During the 1960-61 academic year, "Old Main" underwent a thorough renovation that essentially reconstructed the building inside the original walls. After the demolition of the obsolete Cleveland Science Hall, the Milliken Science Building was erected and opened in 1961. Two additional residence halls, named for President A.M. Shipp and Dean A. Mason DuPré, rounded out the construction projects of the early 1960s. With this new housing, the college's enrollment was allowed to grow to 1,000 students by 1963.

In his address at President Marsh's 1959 inauguration, Dr. Louis B. Wright '20, the director of the Folger Shakespeare Library, spoke of "the essential business of a college." Historically, Wright argued, the American college was designed to produce "the intelligent leadership that a democratic society required." In Cold War America, colleges were "serious institutions where a picked body of intelligent men and women work at a maximum efficiency to develop their minds, bodies and personalities." In addition to predicting a greater emphasis on writing, history, languages, science and mathematics, Wright expected the better colleges to offer a greater emphasis on the fine arts. While America needed more scientists and engineers, Wright also believed that in an increasingly interconnected world, Americans needed a greater understanding of other cultures. As Wright's address noted, many aspects of college life in the early 1960s reflected a Cold War mentality. Continued research into atomic energy and the launch of the Soviet satellite Sputnik in October 1957 brought a new emphasis to the physical sciences throughout America. The college continued to define its principal missions as providing a superior liberal arts education and the development of character, but added an emphasis on producing leaders who could be "bulwarks of freedom," as one college publication called them, in cities and towns throughout the nation.

Crossroads of the New South

"More than any single action by the government, the Interstate and Defense Highway System changed the face of America. ... Its impact on the economy—the jobs it would produce in manufacturing and construction, the rural areas it would open up—was beyond calculation." So wrote Dwight D. Eisenhower in his 1963 Presidential memoir, *Mandate for Change*.

After World War II, the emerging interstate system indeed changed the landscape of Spartanburg County. A few miles north and west of the central city, one of the major north-south highways in the interstate grid, Interstate 85, crossed Interstate 26. The latter highway facilitated travel to Columbia and Charleston, and as its mountain sections were completed, it became a much faster and easier connection to the Midwest via Interstate 40 and Interstate 75.

The Spartanburg Chamber of Commerce dubbed this intersection, "The Crossroads of the New South." Neville Holcombe '26, mayor from 1953-61, Richard E. Tukey, who headed the chamber, and other civic leaders achieved significant success in marketing that concept abroad. Spartanburg became the American headquarters for more than 100 foreign-owned companies. Many of them were textile-related, but the effort was successful in bringing a new economic diversity to the area.

Spartanburg's busy
East Main Street, circa 1960,
east and west views

Wofford and the *G.I. Bill*

In 1944, as the most destructive war in human history moved toward its final act, the United States Congress passed a piece of legislation that would have a tremendous impact on postwar American society: the Servicemen's Readjustment Act, popularly known as the GI Bill of Rights.

In his State of the Union address that year, President Franklin D. Roosevelt called for an "economic bill of rights," which would create "an American standard of living higher than ever before known," including the right to a job, a decent standard of living, a home, health care and an education. An increasingly conservative Congress was not willing to pass such an ambitious agenda for all Americans, but there was a bipartisan consensus that such rights should be granted to those who had served the country during the war.

The Wofford Dames (wives of the veteran students) were an active and important campus social organization in the late 1940s. This picture was made at one of their "first Wednesday" meetings in Carlisle Hall.

Thus was born the GI Bill, which granted veterans of the war assistance in buying their own homes, starting their own businesses, and going to college. The result was a tremendous growth in the American middle class and an unprecedented boom in the nation's colleges. The GI Bill of Rights granted veterans as much as $500 a year for college. Students who had interrupted their Wofford educations returned to finish, and others who had never had the chance to start college belatedly began. The composition of the student body became, almost overnight, dominated by veterans of the war. All branches of the services and all theaters of operations during the war were represented in the Wofford student body. For several years, veterans outnumbered non-veterans.

During the 1946-47 academic year, over two-thirds of the students were veterans. For the entire year, the *Old Gold and Black* had a weekly column, "Kilroy Wrote This" (a play on the ubiquitous "Kilroy was here" graffiti scribbled everywhere American soldiers went during the war years), that was devoted to items of interest to veteran students. The paper regularly published short biographies

of selected veterans such as Howard Moody, a member of the Army Air Corps, who was shot down in 1943 and held by Germany as a prisoner of war for more than a year. The Veterans Club organized social events, including a dance, which was held at the USO facility on North Church Street to avoid violating rules that banned dancing on campus.

Along with the sudden influx of so many students came inevitable growing pains. A major issue was housing. The college scrambled to accommodate the unusual number of married students, some with children. (In 1949, even as the number of veterans declined, the *Old Gold and Black* reported that 21 percent of the students were married, and all but a handful were veterans). The college, with government money, built 32 apartments on the site of some old tennis courts for married student housing, which became available in January 1947. (Later, this became the site of the Sandor Teszler Library.)

Despite the assistance of the GI Bill, life was not easy for these veteran undergraduates. Many found that the $90 per month in government aid did not go far enough in inflationary times. Some wives took jobs in Spartanburg, adding not only income but also some tension to family life. To ease their isolation, the spouses formed a Veterans' Wives Club. Forty women attended the first meeting. The college set up a "course on contemporary facts for veteran students' wives," some of whom took the class for college credit.

The veteran student body was, however, a short-lived phenomenon. The class of '49 saw 150 veterans graduate out of a class of 200, and in the following fall, non-veterans became the majority again for the first time since 1946. In some ways, the veterans had been a distinct group in Wofford's long history; in others, they were quite the same. As one returning veteran observed in 1946: "All during the war years, no matter where we might have been, a wave of longing and homesickness swept over us when we thought of those twin towers 'on the city's northern border,' and all that Wofford had meant to us."

—*Mark S. Byrnes*
Assistant Professor of History

The *George Cooksey Story*

I n June 1944, Janet Cooksey received this telegram from the adjutant general:

The Secretary of War desires me to express his deep regret that your husband, Second Lieutenant George D. Cooksey Jr. has been reported missing in action since 12 June over France. If further details or other information are received you will be promptly notified.

For most men serving in Europe during the Second World War, the chilling message would have been the end of the story, but that was not the case for George Cooksey '48. He became "Georges Derrieux," wine merchant from Dinard and member of the French Underground.

It all started the day Cooksey bailed out of his flak-riddled B-24 at about 4,000 feet and landed in a wheat field in Rennes, France. To the man on the side of the road watching him land, he said, *"Bonjour, Monsieur. Je suis American. J'ai faim."* Cooksey wrote later, "I had two years of high school French and one year in college—with a Southern accent. Why I said I was hungry, I don't know, unless I thought he might take me to his home and out of sight." Luckily, that's just what the farmer (Monsieur Roger) did.

Using photographs Cooksey kept in his escape kit, Monsieur Lambert, a grocer from Combourg, produced a French identity card with all the proper stamps for a certain Georges Derrieux, wine merchant from Dinard. "Georges," dressed in shirt, pants, sweater, beret (and, finally, shoes—it took a little while to find any big enough), had a series of uncomfortable encounters with German soldiers. Even in his disguise, he said, "I don't think I ever was at ease when they were around."

He also recalled uncomfortable encounters with impetigo and appendicitis, but despite the apprehension and discomfort, there was the joy of forming lasting friendships. Cooksey even attended a French baptism, which flowed with champagne and included course after course of food. Liberated by the advancing Allied armies before Christmas in 1944, Cooksey was soon back with Janet and her parents at the Polo Lounge of the Beverly Hills Hotel. He was only 21 years old.

George Cooksey came to Wofford in 1940 when he was 16; he left it a veteran of World War II. "I felt the veterans that were coming

George Cooksey *(second from left)* was chosen to chair the Senior Order of Gnomes in 1948. He is shown with fellow Gnomes Eben Taylor, Dewey Bell and Paul Wood, "the most prominent and influential members of the Senior Class."

back gave a lot of maturity to college programs," said Cooksey. "It started upgrading education overall."

Upon graduating from Wofford in 1948, Cooksey joined the newly created United States Air Force. He spent many years in research and development involving ballistic missile and space activities, and he was involved in the space program prior to the Russians' launching of Sputnik in 1957. His last assignment was in the office of the Secretary of the Air Force Special Projects. He retired from the Air Force in 1969.

Cooksey then spent 20 years with the McDonnell Douglas Corporation, retiring as manager of the corporate office in San Diego.

Cooksey began going back to Brittany in 1953 and continued to stay in close touch with the friends he made during the war. In 1994, he participated in a number of 50th anniversary celebrations of the liberation of France during World War II. He was honored individually at two of those ceremonies, and he spoke at several schools, educating young French students about the war. "Almost every city had some kind of celebration on the day it had been liberated," said Cooksey.

—Mary Beth Knight '96

This article originally appeared in *Wofford Today*, a few months before Cooksey's death on December 16, 1996.

A *Science Retrospective*

For his 2001 January Interim project, Geoff Thomas '04 helped the college prepare for the opening of the Roger Milliken Science Center by interviewing retired faculty members Dr. B.G. Stephens '57 (chemistry), Dr. W. Ray Leonard (biology), Dr. Dan Olds (physics and computer science) and Dr. James Seegars (psychology). The original audiotapes are permanently housed in the college archives along with complete transcripts. Karla Parris '04 chose and edited these excerpts.

In the early 1960s, Cleveland Science Hall *(right)* was demolished and replaced with the new Milliken Science Hall *(above)*. "The Pit" *(opposite page top)* was an impressive feature in the new building.

Geoff Thomas:
When you were a student here, your classes were in Cleveland Science Hall, correct?

Dr. B.G. Stephens:
Cleveland had a lot of character. It was an old wooden building with brick veneer; the fire marshal would have had apoplexy if we had that building here now. But it was well maintained. We had the equipment to do what needed to be done, all the reasonably modern day-to-day laboratory equipment. On the ground floor was the chemistry department. It had a chemistry stockroom and all the laboratories except organic chemistry. In the basement you had the organic chemistry lab. If you looked out, you could see the dirt under the floor of the building. I took two semesters of organic chemistry down there and then an advanced organic chemistry course. The upper floor was devoted to physics, and Professor E. H. Shuler, who taught mechanical drawing and surveying, had his drawing tables up there. In the dome was the planetarium.

The Milliken Building that replaced it in the early 1960s was modern and efficient, but it had very little character. Because it was designed by a firm (so I have always been told)

from Massachusetts, believe it or not, it had redundant heating systems but no air conditioning. It was hot in July, trust me. The amphitheater was called "the pit." It could seat about 130 to 140 people. It was tight in there, and I mean damp, with no air conditioning. I always felt that I was getting ready to do an autopsy on that table in the pit. Now, we have made it a much more friendly room. The building had a full basement, which by the way, was designed for use as a college bomb shelter in those days of "massive retaliation."

Before I left the chemistry department in 1971, Joe Lesesne was the academic dean, and he appointed a committee of scientists chaired by Ray Leonard with me as the grant writer to develop a program for funding by the National Science Foundation. We received a commit-

ment of $300,000 if we matched it—a lot of money in those days. Only Lyndon Johnson's alma mater received a larger grant under that NSF program! President Paul Hardin convinced the Daniel Foundation to make the match that would be used to air-condition the Milliken Science Building.

Geoff Thomas:

In the early 1960s you were asked to come back to Wofford as a member of the chemistry department. Perhaps you would like to share with us why you decided to come back, why you decided to be a part of the Wofford community once again.

Dr. B.G. Stephens:

I was in graduate school at Clemson finishing my PhD. It was early in the summer of 1963. I was helping my mother paint a room in her house. I had on old Bermuda shorts, a T-shirt and tennis shoes, and I was covered up in paint (more on me than the house, you know how that goes). I got a call from Dr. James Loftin that Wofford was looking for someone to be the fourth member of the chemistry department and would I be at all interested? I said, "May I come by next week?" He said, "No, you need to come right now." There was some desperation about getting recently educated scientists into the academic world at that time, and probably rightly so. Anyway, without changing clothes, I had a meeting with President Marsh, Dean Covington, and Dr. Loftin. We sat around in Dr. Marsh's living room, and by the end of the day, I was hired.

Dr. B.G. Stephens '57 joined the Wofford faculty as a professor of chemistry. He later served as dean of the college, and then as vice president for technology.

Dr. Ray Leonard headed the department of biology for many years and was the second faculty member to be named to the Kenan Professorship.

What attracted me was the opportunity to come back to a place that I thought was on the move. Mr. Milliken had gotten involved with the college by then. They had built a new science building, and were planning to grow from something like 700 students to about 1,000. I think we had a class of 16 to 18 new faculty members that fall. Also, I was assured I would have the opportunity to do research here and it turned out that I was able to do that, even involving several undergraduates in published research.

Geoff Thomas:
What was your biggest challenge in teaching pre-meds and biology majors?

Dr. Ray Leonard:
When I left Vanderbilt, there was a big argument going on as to whether DNA or protein was the genetic material. They didn't know. The lag back then between publishing and getting a textbook out was about a ten-year period. So even though Watson and Crick had made the fundamental discovery in 1953, it hadn't even gotten into a book that was published in 1956. So I had to go to the original sources and get the materials just to keep up with [advancements]. Things were going so fast that they weren't getting into the books. But you see, my chemistry background put me in good stead to do that. And I have to tell you, that's the thing that kept me going

Dr. Dan Olds chaired the physics department, and then went on to develop the academic and administrative computer center.

all my years at Wofford—keeping up with the new studies that were coming out in cell and molecular biology.

Geoff Thomas:
I understand that you received a grant from the National Science Foundation that brought the first computer to Wofford College.

Dr. Dan Olds:
Dr. Charles Marsh was our president in the 1960s, and I was interested in bringing computing resources to the campus. I went to national meetings about computing and the liberal arts, and I would talk to President Marsh about the ways I found to get funding for a computing resource for the college. Finally, in the spring of 1968, we agreed that he would budget some special college funds, and I would contribute some physics department funds, and we would get started with academic computing. (At the moment, I am just talking about academic computing. On the administrative data processing side, they had a punch card system called unit record equipment, and they had had it for a couple of years by this time.) The academic computer center was housed in the physics department area of the science building, but we did what we could to make people understand that it was not a physics department resource, but a college resource. We got started with a really clunky yellow-paper Teletype typewriter and a dial-up line to a computer service in Raleigh.

Shortly after this, the Southern Regional Education Board in Atlanta coordinated an effort by several colleges to sell the National Science Foundation on an experiment in computing for colleges. So each of the colleges got some funding, and we were able to continue. One of the wonderful things the NSF money did for us was make it so that we no longer paid by the hour for our use of the computer; we paid a monthly flat rate. I wasn't

in there sweating as the poor students typed one key at a time at $10 an hour on our single terminal.

In the subsequent months, we were able to add a second Teletype, which wasn't on line, but you could sit there and punch paper tape. When your chance came to get on line, you could run through your paper tape rather than type slowly and get your program in.

In January 1969, more resources were in place, and I ran an Interim project on computing. Those students worked day and night to get their time to schedule this one computer line and get their programs running. That was our initial experience with academic computing. At that point, I became, in addition to chairman of the physics department, director of the academic computer center.

One Friday the president called me and said, "We can probably get some money from Hoechst Fibers to buy a computer." We sent them a proposal on Monday morning, and they gave us $50,000. Thus, we spent $49,999.98 on our first on-campus academic computer, a Digital Equipment Corporation PDP-11. When we got our own system, we were able to add video terminals and some printing terminals.

Geoff Thomas:

Dr. Seegars, when you were first introduced to the psychology program at Wofford, what state was it in?

Dr. James Seegars:

Embryonic. Psychology had been taught in the education department. When I came, Dean Covington's assignment to me was to build an academically strong department. I first hired Dr. James Patrick, who had recently retired as chairman of the department of psychology at Ohio University. He said he would love to come for a year and be a mentor to me.

Our emphasis right from the beginning was to make our major a laboratory-based Bachelor of Science degree. All of our students were required to take eight hours of physiological psychology and eight hours of experimental psychology, so they spent a long time in the lab. In those days, only your best colleges did that, the Davidsons and the Dukes. Fortunately, the chair of the biology department, Dr. Ray Leonard, was my golf partner. He helped me with the neuroscience side, and he supported our approach. At one point, we had over 100 psychology majors. We really grew fast, faster than three people could

handle. It is more manageable now, but that is how we got started.

Eventually the dean gave us some money to bring in a consultant, a scholar named Nathan Azrin, who was nationally known in psychology. I told him, "What we want to do is teach students how to understand behavior, what causes behavior, how to predict behavior, and how to change behavior." So he sketched on paper what he called a three-track curriculum. We had a clinical track in which we talked about how an organism develops under normal circumstances (child development, adolescent psychology and behavior pathology), and sometimes deviates from the normal. We had an experimental track, which was a cluster of courses designed to address the question of how the environment influences behaviors and changes personality. And we had a physiological track, focusing on how the internal organism causes behavior. We talked about things like neuroanatomy, vitamins, diet and the neurological makeup of the organism, including genetics.

This was our core curriculum during my whole tenure at Wofford. Many colleges and universities require students to take three classes in this cluster and two of this cluster and four of this cluster—they have a large potpourri of classes. We only had three faculty [members], so potpourri was out of the question. Our students had to move through the curriculum together. But this actually was a huge benefit, as the students became strongly bonded. Seniors would be very helpful to the sophomores, because they had been through the same courses. Almost all of our majors did quite well in graduate school. We felt very good about the curriculum.

Dr. Jim Seegars was ahead of his time in developing an experiential curriculum in the psychology department. A hall in the Roger Milliken Science Center has been named in his honor.

Emigrés on the Faculty

Communist revolutions across the world during the first half of the 20th century gave many colleges in the United States their first real opportunity to attract faculty with international backgrounds. Marie Gagarine of St. Petersburg, Russia; Dr. Joaquín Fernández DeVelasco and Dr. Ricardo J. Remírez de Estónez, both from Havana, Cuba; and Dr. Ta-Tseng Ling of Changsin, China, taught at Wofford in the 1960s and beyond. All were instructors in their native languages except for Ling, who taught government.

Marie Gagarine

In 1887, Count Mussin Pushkin and Princess Dolgoroukoff celebrated the birth of a daughter, Marie, in St. Petersburg. Growing up as a Russian aristocrat, she had many childhood memories of the Tsarist court. She married Prince Michael Gagarine, who served in the Russian military. As the clouds of World War I gathered, she was determined to learn nursing skills as an emergency means of survival.

Several years later, while working as a military nurse in a small town north of Warsaw, she learned of her husband's death. Gagarine realized that the Russian government was nearing collapse, and she decided to take her three children to safety in another country as soon as possible.

After many adventures, they were able to escape to Istanbul, Turkey, crossing the Black Sea on a small, leaky French minesweeper. Gagarine found work as a governess for a French family. Eventually, she and two

Gagarine

of her sons settled in the United States and became American citizens.

Gagarine taught French and Russian at several academic institutions before moving to Spartanburg in 1959 to be near her son, Dmitri, who worked for Milliken & Company. Her subsequent appointment to the Wofford faculty marked two firsts at the college: she was the first woman instructor, as well as the first faculty member to speak and teach Russian.

Marie Gagarine was active well into her 90s. She appeared in plays with Wofford's Theatre Workshop and Spartanburg Little Theater. She continued her hobbies of walking and mountain climbing. Once, when classes were cancelled because of one of Spartanburg's occasional snowstorms, she walked to the campus and dismissed the bad weather as "a heavy frost." She told her life story in a fascinating autobiography, *From Stolnoy to Spartanburg: The Two Lives of a Former Russian Princess*.

She died in March 1982 at the age of 95. The determined demeanor of this tiny Russian princess impacted many of her students. "Our perspectives have been broadened, our sights have been set higher, and our belief in our nation and its values is much more intense," one of her former students remarked after her death.

Joaquín DeVelasco and Ricardo Remírez

Joaquín F. DeVelasco and Ricardo J. Remírez were practicing attorneys in Havana before Fidel Castro came to power in 1959. DeVelasco joined the Wofford faculty in 1963, and Remírez came in 1964, both teaching Spanish in the department of foreign languages.

DeVelasco

DeVelasco was a government official under the ousted Batista regime. Having studied civil law, economics, political science and English, he was a director of the legal department of information in the General Accounting Office. He barely escaped with his life after the

Remírez

revolution, and in fact, was reputed to be on a target list for Castro's agents during the 1960s. He lived quietly with his sister in Spartanburg, participating in church and civic club activities. After retirement and a long illness, DeVelasco died in March 2002.

A younger man involved in the private practice of law, Remírez, like many others, supported Castro at first. However, after receiving information from an inside source, Remírez became involved in an anti-Castro underground movement that printed anti-Communist propaganda and stored weapons and equipment. One of Remírez's neighbors who worked for the government became suspicious, and the underground group encouraged the Remírez family to leave the country. Years later, they understood that they were fortunate to have left when they did. According to an article Remírez wrote, "once a family applies to leave, the father and mother immediately lose all rights as Cuban citizens. They no longer have jobs and must depend upon family to support them during their years of attempting to leave the country."

Remírez became widely known in South Carolina's Hispanic community and was a leader in such organizations as the Spanish South Atlantic Modern Language Association, but he eventually took a leave of absence to care for his mother in Miami. Seeing her having difficulty communicating with her physicians, he put his translation skills to use in developing an innovative and successful methodology that allowed patients who did not speak English to describe their symptoms. He also became interested in the real estate business and eventually resigned from his Wofford post. As of 2004, he continued to live in Florida.

Ta-Tseng Ling

Born in Changsin, China, Dr. Ta-Tseng Ling led the first part of his life in a country torn by disorder, war and revolution. Well-educated and with the stately bearing of the traditional Chinese gentleman, Ling served in a series of impressive positions for the government of the Republic of China, which after October 1949, was located on the island of Taiwan. He was a research assistant for the Ministry of Foreign Affairs, Consul General in Chicago and Los Angeles, and deputy director of the Foreign Ministry's personnel department. He then moved to Honduras to be Chargé d'Affaires at the Taiwanese legation.

After globetrotting for 20 years, Ling and his wife, Christina, finally settled in Spartanburg in 1966, where he became an assistant professor of government at Wofford. He was promoted to professor of government in 1975 and retired in 1986. He was an effective teacher, well liked by both his college students and young participants in the college's Summer Program for Academically Talented Students.

Not long after his retirement, in April 1989, Ling and his wife died together in a traffic accident near their home in Spartanburg. At the funeral, Dean Dan Maultsby praised Ling's dedication to Wofford: "His sense of worth was in doing his best to meet responsibility and to serve the college. He cared more only about his family."

—*Kristin Sams '05, with Doyle Boggs '70*

Ling

The *Gus Papadopoulos Story*

Constantinos Neofytos Papadopoulos did not speak English when he enrolled at Wofford in 1951. He had graduated from high school that spring in his native Kavala, Greece, a country still in turmoil following Nazi occupation and a five-year civil war. He had come to the United States to pursue a family member's recommendation to attend Wofford, a college in a town where the Greek community was very strong. "I was a 19-year-old baby," said Papadopoulos. "I knew nothing about America. I didn't really start to understand the country until eight or ten years later."

Quickly becoming known to his classmates as "Gus," Papadopoulos registered for his first semester. The late Dean Philip Covington recommended he defer taking first-year composition until he learned the English language. The optimistic student resisted and enrolled in that course and four others anyway. The composition class was the only one he did not pass. He repeated it in the spring term and earned a C. From then on, his grade point average was a solid B-plus.

Gus Papadopoulos '54 enjoys the dedication of the building named in honor of his father.

Papadopoulos said the key to his quick success was simple: "Hard work and persistence." He added that Greek high schools were very comprehensive because students went directly from there to advanced university programs or professional schools. Typically, students only finished high school before starting their careers, so he felt very prepared for all subjects other than the English language or composition. When he enrolled at Wofford, he not only knew Greek, but also French.

By 1954, Papadopoulos completed the requirements for graduation in only three years. He so mastered the English language that he won a public speaking contest his senior year. The administration asked him to make the award-winning speech at a centennial celebration function. Papadopoulos followed President Pendleton Gaines to the podium. His speech about the German occupation of Greece and his country's civil war in 1944-49 so inspired the audience that they immediately raised the funds to furnish the common areas of Walter K. Greene Hall. A plaque in the lobby of the residence hall commemorates the occasion.

Following graduation, Papadopoulos and his brother embarked on a whirlwind week-long cross-country trip in search of a promising location for him to start a medical practice and therefore, to enroll in medical school. They traveled as far as Los Angeles and were halfway back across the country when they stopped in Houston, Texas.

Papadopoulos had found his new home. He enrolled at the Baylor College of Medicine and earned his medical degree in 1958. Five years later, he earned his United States citizenship. He settled in the Houston area, working as an anesthesiologist. His medical career included working with Dr. Michael DeBakey on resections of aortic aneurysms. DeBakey went on to become a legend in cardiovascular surgery. While still practicing medicine, Papadopoulos became a successful businessman, forming the real estate venture Delta Troy. His developments became so successful and time-consuming that, in 1974, he left medicine altogether.

Devoted to Wofford since the day he graduated, Papadopoulos has served for many years on the Board of Trustees. Board meetings have given Gus and his wife, Maria, a ready opportunity to reconnect with family and the local Greek community. (Maria, who graduated from Converse College, grew up in Spartanburg.) As of 2004, Papadopoulos remained active in the real estate development business, serving as the president of Papadopoulos & Associates. He and Maria have four children and four grandchildren.

"Whatever I have, I owe to Wofford," he said. His contributions led him to become the first graduate to give more than $1 million to the college. His gifts included funds for a new office building with a beautiful reception room. The Neofytos D. Papadopoulos Building, named for his father, opened in October 1986.

—*Sarah Ross Cohen '88*

C.C. Norton's Christmas Carol

This Wofford Christmas memory from an anonymous graduate of the mid-1960s was first read several years ago at an alumni meeting in North Carolina.

"Chapel" was a requirement in our time—twice a week and it could be painful. Time dulls the memory of the bad ones, but there were plenty. There were some very good ones also—John Carradine and Marcel Marceau come to mind. However, none could compare to the last chapel before Christmas.

Chapel began at 11 a.m., and normally the first-year students filed into the balcony of Leonard Auditorium as late as possible, but not on this occasion. It soon was evident that many seats were filled by members of the Spartanburg community. The administration and faculty were all present. The students filled every seat, and often chairs had to be put in the lobby. Students with nicknames like Tuba, Zeus, Igor, Lurch and Stinky, whom we all thought had discovered a way to avoid *all* chapel programs were actually neatly dressed and sitting tall in those wooden seats.

On the stage was a small desk upon which were a book and an inkwell from which protruded a feathered quill and a single candle. A straight-back chair behind the desk was the only other item on the stage, and the heavy curtain was drawn. The lights dimmed, the audience broke into applause, and from behind the curtain came Dr. C.C. Norton, a senior faculty member. He walked to the desk, acknowledged the applause and took his seat. Immediately a hush came over the auditorium, a stillness we had not heard in that place since being threatened by Dean Logan during "rat week."

"Marley was dead" came the words from Dr. Norton … and the familiar tale of Scrooge, Bob Cratchit, Tiny Tim and the true meaning of Christmas had begun. The book was a prop, for Dr. Norton had long since committed every proper English word and every inflection to his memory. The abridged version went on for 45 minutes, in which he held that audience of 1960s cynics and skeptics totally spellbound. We could hear the chains when Marley's ghost appeared, and on more than one occasion there were lumps in the throats and tears in the eyes of each of us fortunate enough to have been compelled to attend. Finally, "God Bless Us Everyone" was read, and Charles Dickens' wonderful story had ended. Dr. Norton had once again brought down the house, and the standing ovation was as genuine and heartfelt as any could ever be.

For those of us who attended Wofford College during the C.C. Norton era, that performance will forever be part of those wonderful memories we have of Christmas. We left the Wofford campus for the holidays, but Dr. Norton gave us a present that we carry for life.

Dean C.C. Norton (known in his early days on the faculty as "Cutie" because of his dapper wardrobe and carefully groomed mustache) was equally at home in the classroom or playing Ebenezer Scrooge.

Life Off-Campus

Between 1945 and the mid-'60s, Spartanburg was prosperous and conservative, though class and racial tensions simmered below the surface. Coming largely from Southern families with above-average educational and economic backgrounds, both Wofford men and Converse women found the city to be a comfortable environment. "Uptown" clothing stores like Greenewald's and Prices' would establish credit accounts for student customers, and Belk-Hudson and the Aug. W. Smith Co. were convenient first-class department stores.

For 18-year-olds, it was also a time when the town was "wet" with respect to beer and wine, and the campuses were "dry," at least in theory. In retrospect, the bonds between town and gown seem to have been very close.

Students frequently enjoyed pizza at Mama Morrelli's, dinner out at the Piedmont Steakhouse, house parties at the Lake Lanier Tea Room or Lake Lure's Fowler Brothers' cabin, though George Martin '59 recalled that college students rarely spent lavishly on entertainment. "Nobody had much money," he said. "Not nearly like what kids have now." But, he added, "Two dollars would usually get you through the night."

ROTC was theoretically voluntary, but most students participated for at least two years. It was a way to earn a little spending money, not to mention a guaranteed job after graduation. The monthly check would go toward downtown movies, beer at Smitty's (where curb services allowed students to drink in their cars!), a shirt from Prices' or hamburgers at Simple Simon's or the Beacon. An upscale date could be enjoyed at the Village Supper Club. "They served mixed drinks," Martin recalled, "and you ate dinner with grown-ups."

Wofford students occasionally veered "to the other side of the tracks." In his mystery novel *The Star of Sutherland*, Gene Breaznell '71 based his mythical Sutherland College upon his experiences at Wofford. The first scene is set at the Tradewinds Lounge.

Breaznell can't quite recall the bar that inspired the Tradewinds, but he said, "It was a real dive." Breaznell came to Wofford from Connecticut, and, he said, "being from the North, it was intriguing to me to go to redneck pool halls."

The Tradewinds *could* have been Porky Pig's (though it stands to reason that Breaznell wouldn't have forgotten that name.) Situated on the eastern outskirts of town, Porky Pig's could get pretty rough. Martin recalled that Wofford students were forbidden from going there after one particularly nasty barroom fight.

Musical offerings in town sometimes drew Wofford students off campus. The Spartanburg Memorial Auditorium, next door to the college, brought gospel acts, jazz, big bands and country music. Martin remembers seeing Louie Armstrong and Ella Fitzgerald in concert. Breaznell saw Loretta Lynn at the height of her popularity. "The greatest thing was that after the show, she went out into the parking lot, sat on the hood of a car, and played requests for the college kids," he said.

By the late 1960s and early 1970s, down-town Spartanburg was developing a particularly vibrant music scene. The Upstairs Club was known for live Beach Music. The Sitar was a popular spot for music, drawing big-name Southern Rock acts like the Allman Brothers and local heroes, the Marshall Tucker Band.

—*Baker Maultsby '92*

Students of the Cold War generation enjoyed bowling *(left)*, fraternity road trips to the South Carolina beaches and chili-cheeseburgers at the Beacon, a local institution owned by John B. White Sr.

Frost and Sandburg: An Historic Encounter

On March 14, 1950, a determined-to-survive, complex and energetic Robert Frost visited Wofford College to speak to students and faculty at the then-traditional Lyceum, the college's public lecture series. Wofford's Lyceum had a proud tradition of inviting important guests to speak on the campus. Frost, with his visit, took his place among such speakers as Woodrow Wilson, Booker T. Washington and William Jennings Bryan.

And students? That spring, as they have done in all years at Wofford, the students were leaning slightly toward spring break, and the professors were hitting the mid-semester slump of paper and test grading. It's hard to imagine much hoopla on campus, even for Robert Frost.

What makes Wofford's Frost visit even more unusual was that poet Carl Sandburg drove down from his home in Flat Rock, North Carolina, that night, and the two literary legends engaged in banter about poetry in front of the audience gathered there. A stack of reel-to-reel tapes in the Wofford archives preserves the entire encounter. The late Herbert Hucks '34, then the college's associate librarian, was present when Frost arrived that evening to read. He acquired the poet's permission to tape the reading and set up his machine down front. More recently, a digital copy was made of the tapes, assuring their survival.

The friendship between Frost and Sandburg extended back 40 years by the time they argued at Wofford College. Sandburg first met Frost in 1917. He liked him immediately, calling him "the strongest, loneliest, friendliest personality among poets today." It seems Frost and Sandburg saw each other often as they each developed their careers. Sandburg moved from newspaper reporter to, by the 1930s, a true "man of letters," with published poetry, novels, essays and a huge, soon-to-be-famous biography of Abraham Lincoln. By the time Sandburg moved from near Chicago south to

Flat Rock in the mid-'40s, his papers alone filled two boxcars.

Frost stuck close to poetry, only poetry, and Sandburg, in the early years, often made comments about Frost "barding around" the country while he held down a regular newspaper job. Sure, Frost was a farmer, but he was always teaching and lecturing, too. So their differences, which still had glint on them in 1950, were both personal and political: Frost, the son of a frustrated politician, believed a poet should be a poet and a poet only; while Sandburg, a deeply political man, was active in the public affairs of the country through four presidents and two world wars.

Several biographers report that during the Second World War, Frost refused to do what he called "propaganda" work for the Roosevelt war effort. Sandburg jumped right in, but he never really forgave Frost for the reluctance to write for the government. "The state's one function is to give," Frost said the night he read at Wofford. "I must remember that as a Vermont Democrat."

So Frost and Sandburg brought differences deeper than meter versus "freedom from meter" into the chapel of Old Main on the night of March 14, 1950. It's obvious from letters that Sandburg considered Frost a friend, in spite of their differences. But Frost? As always, Frost is harder to pin down. In the early 1920s Robert Frost began criticizing Sandburg adversely. "His affections have almost buried him out of sight. He is probably the most artificial and studied ruffian the world has had." Frost even said that he did not like to be put in the same category as Sandburg when it came to poetry—"We're entirely different in our work. He has a good heart. He says in his poetry that the people say yes. I saw the people say yes and no."

Upon arriving in Spartanburg, Frost stayed at a downtown hotel and invited Wofford students and faculty to come down and interview him the afternoon he arrived. There is a photograph in an issue of the *Old Gold & Black* that shows those in attendance as then students Ed Berckman, Clyde Ariail, Ralph Cannon and Professors Hunter, Covington, and Whitaker. The Wofford English professors and literary students asked Frost questions about art and literature. Frost insisted on bringing literature into the everyday, calling poetry "an athletic event" and explaining, "Athletics are the nearest kin to poetry that they require skill and mastery of performance."

Dr. Ralph Cannon '50 retired after a long career as a United Methodist minister. What did he remember, 44 years later, about the visit of the famous poet? "I remember Carl Sandburg in the audience and Frost up at the podium arguing all through the evening. They carried on like Bantam roosters. But what I really remember—my friends and I talked about it afterward—was the effect it had on us as students: two men who were friends could carry on like they were terrible enemies."

That evening, excited applause interrupted Dr. William B. Hunter's introduction to Frost when he announced that Carl Sandburg was in attendance. Hucks remembered that Frost was "a little mad" Sandburg's arrival had upstaged him. But when Frost came forward to the microphone, silence follows on the tape. Finally Frost responded, beginning with the old argument: "I'm a metricist myself and Mr. Sandburg is not a metricist. That's all we differ with, I believe."

Sandburg's voice, barely audible, can be heard from the audience: "I live on a high mountain 40 miles from here."

But Frost, with his quick wit, and his clear sense of where he stood in 1950 among the poets such as Pound and Williams, reclaims the stage: "Oh, Mr. Sandburg, you live on a high mountain. Is it a higher mountain than mine?"

The laughter that follows on the tape shows the audience got it.

Dr. Hunter later wrote about the encounter in *Forum*. In one of the most interesting passages the professor described what happened after the reading: "So we hurriedly decamped and drove into town to a café that was open late ... Over coffee, Frost quickly settled down and the stimulating part of the evening took place. He was one of the great conversationalists of all time."

As a student in the English department during the 1970s, I always heard rumors of the "Frost-Sandburg tape" in the Wofford library, but I never listened to it. I had heard that Wofford was the location of the famous "free verse is like playing tennis without a net" encounter, but I had never talked to anyone who had actually listened to the tapes. When I finally heard them I was amazed at what unfolds as the evening progresses. The recording is part of Wofford's literary heritage, something that makes the college unique among liberal arts colleges. We have the magnetic transcript of a historic encounter. We own a public portrait of a complex friendship between two forces of 20th century literature.

The nature of poetry is metaphor. Frost's mountain still stands, and is even growing like the Himalayas. Sandburg's reputation as a poet lives rounded and inviting like the mountains to our west, where he lived his final years. The Robert Frost/Carl Sandburg encounter, and the valuable tape which preserves every moment of it, is a docudrama of a 40-year poetic struggle between two giant men, a mock-fight to learn from between "terrible enemies."

—*John Lane '77*
Associate Professor of English

C.C. NORTON

Frank Logan, *the* Great Food Riot *and* Other Adventures

Bishop William H. Willimon '68 originally published his memories of Frank Logan, dean of students, in this essay from his book, Family, Friends and other Funny People: Memories of Growing Up Southern (*Durham, NC, 1980*).

S. Frank Logan '41 was named Dean of Students Emeritus after serving the college well in a series of administrative capacities for 34 years. He died in 1995.

I have previously lamented the disappearance from the Southern scene of our eccentrics and "characters." The world seems smaller now; its confines more restrictive. This tendency toward conformity of personality is nowhere more evident than on many of our state's college and university campuses. Modern faculties fancy themselves as professional thinkers. The college teachers of a bygone day were in the job of expanding their students' minds and introducing them to the world in all of its delightful differences. Today's doctoral programs mold people into tame scholarly irrelevance, as humorless as the hundredth footnote on a typical dissertation.

Such was not the case when I came as an open-eyed freshman to Wofford College. One came to college then not so much for an "education" as for an experience. And in those "bright college years" a big part of that experience at Wofford College was Frank Logan, dean of students.

On that first day of orientation, "Logan," as he was affectionately known, took it upon himself to orient us to the rigors of college

life. First we gathered with our parents in Leonard Auditorium for a word from Logan before bidding our parents goodbye. He greeted our parents with: "You're probably looking at the woebegone-looking character who is seated with his parents next to your darling angel and wondering how in the hell he ever got into Wofford College. Well, let me tell you, his parents are looking at your son and wondering the same thing!" By the end of the afternoon our parents left us, aware that their innocent offspring would never be so innocent again.

I know that the *in loco parentis* approach to higher education is definitely passé. But in those days, Logan unashamedly attempted to be the parent-in-residence for every man on campus. He even tried to correct our parents' errors in their child-rearing practices. He knew every boy's name, whether his father had attended Wofford and whether he had ever run afoul with the administration. Logan was the benevolent autocrat of the campus. He knew who you were dating regularly, who you were dating on the side unbeknownst to the person you were dating, what your last semester's grades were, how many times you had cut chapel, and whether your room looked like that of a "Wofford gentleman" or "someone from Clemson."

Logan had an almost religious affection for Wofford, a predictable disdain for every other institution of higher learning in our state, and a deep animosity to all military schools in general. During one of those despised freshmen Saturday chapel programs that he required us to attend, he once had a boy stand who had just transferred to Wofford from The Citadel. The boy's shaved head and gray pants betrayed his brief encounter with that military institution.

"Gentlemen, you see before you a man who made a grievous error in judgment in his selection of a college," Logan said as he gestured toward the forlorn freshman, "but he has repented, his wisdom has won out, and he is now here among us. He deserves a standing ovation for his change of heart." The entire class rose to its feet and applauded.

Logan's idea of a perfect college year was to beat both Furman and The Citadel in football. A win over Davidson in the same season was a cause for almost unbearably ecstatic rejoicing.

Thinking back on it, I sometimes marvel at the influence Dean Logan exerted upon us. He had a rare understanding of the minds of college males and an obvious love for the college and its students.

I remember one of those dreaded Tuesday and Thursday chapel programs (which I fought to do away with when I was in student government but which, looking back, form some of my most vivid college memories). The Spartanburg Symphony, I think it was, was performing for our cultural edification. The

Wofford student body greeted this performance with the usual newspapers, yawns, and serious attempts to look as bored and uninterested as possible. There was also an unusual amount of chatter and noise coming from the captive audience, so much so that the musicians were obviously annoyed.

"Just a minute," Dean Logan shouted from his seat in the faculty gallery as the symphony began another selection, "give me that microphone."

"Now look here," he growled, "You people sit up and shut up and show these folks the respect they deserve. Anybody who would dare to play this kind of stuff before an audience like you deserves our greatest admiration. I don't understand a lot of this either, but by the time you graduate, you should be able to act like you understand it."

The concert resumed, musicians and students not sure just who had been praised and who had been reprimanded.

The most exciting event of my college career (besides the A-minus I got from Dr. Patton in freshman biology) was what came to be known as The Great Food Riot of '65. Actually, food at the Wofford cafeteria wasn't all that bad. But everyone else was having riots in those days so it was inevitable that we would have one too. We didn't like to be behind the times.

The stated cause of our riot was the serving of hot dogs (for the third time in a week) one Sunday evening in the cafeteria. Looking back on it, I suppose the real cause was an excuse to let off some steam before spring exams and to visit Converse on a nice spring evening.

It started spontaneously in the college cafeteria. Food was thrown, then plates, then furniture. Then the students moved from the cafeteria into the yard, setting fire to two large

Dean Logan and his wife, Madeline, enjoy a reunion concert of "Moyer's Men," Glee Club members of the 1950s. Mrs. Logan was a delightful hostess and close friend to many Wofford students through the years.

The setting of the Great Food Riot of 1965: On a spring afternoon, students are seen leaning over the balcony of the since-demolished Wightman Hall. Dean Logan leaped from his car as he pulled up next to the tombstone-like marker for Archer Circle. This campus drive is no longer configured as a circle, but the marker and the name remain.

trash bins, taking over Wightman Hall dorm, chanting, shouting and throwing things down from the upper floors of the dorm. (Wightman Hall, since demolished, was a perfect place for a riot. All of its rooms opened out on exterior walkways, which were perfectly designed for throwing things over the side. Whoever designed it obviously had no understanding of the perverted mind of a college male.)

Someone called the Spartanburg police and fire departments who arrived on the scene to find an apocalyptic vision of chaos and disorder. By this time the entire student body was hanging off the upper reaches of Wightman Hall, chanting and throwing.

The police and firemen must have been inwardly excited about the opportunity to engage themselves in quelling a real live student riot. They were very serious about the whole matter. Why should the police in Berkeley and New York have all the fun? The chief pulled out his new bullhorn (which he had obviously never had the occasion to use) and, after a few minutes of reading the instructions for its use, ordered the rampaging students to stop and disband. His order was greeted with a large balloon filled with water, which hit the chief's car, exploding everywhere.

Then the chief directed two of his men to assault Wightman Hall and arrest the culprits. These two brave souls were turned back by a barrage of wet toilet paper rolls and fire extinguisher foam. Already a group of students was making its way over to nearby Converse College for an old-fashioned panty raid. Would the students then turn and threaten the tranquility of the entire city? Reinforcements

from the highway patrol arrived and sealed off the campus. The lawmen crouched behind their cars, pinned down by a never-ending barrage of water balloons. The chief turned up the volume of his bullhorn and shouted even greater threats. What was going to happen?

It was about this time that a gray, 1957 Chevrolet rounded Archer Circle in front of Wightman Hall. "It's Logan," shouted one of the student revolutionaries. But his warning was not heard above the din of battle. Logan was arriving back at campus after speaking somewhere in the state that afternoon on the topic of "The Making of Christian Gentlemen at Wofford College."

The car made its way through the patrol cars and fire trucks. Logan stepped from his car, demanded the bullhorn from the chief and uttered those immortal words, "Cut the crap out."

Silence descended. One by one, the students timidly filed down from the heights of Wightman Hall and scurried to their respective quarters. The riot ended as quickly as it had begun. Logan handed the bullhorn back to an astonished police chief, got back in his '57

Chevrolet, and drove over to his home next to Snyder Hall. As I said before, Logan was in charge at Wofford.

I could tell you more about the late Frank Logan, about his annual four-page Christmas letter that every alumnus and every friend of Wofford received every year (about two weeks after Christmas); how he always cared enough to know how deeply you were hurt when you were turned down at law school and how he called you into his office to tell you he cared; how he always had time to drop everything else and talk with you about a problem. He slapped you on the back and told you, "Don't worry, you have a lot on the ball and I can tell you're going a long way," (and he could make you believe it). I could tell you how he kept a case of silver tart servers so he could send one to all the Wofford men who always invited him to their weddings, or how he finally let a boy in my class graduate after the boy had spent seven years trying to get a diploma and whispered to the boy as he was leaving the commencement ceremonies, "If I ever visit your office in the future and see that diploma stuck on your wall, I will personally sue you for libel against Wofford College." But that is enough to fill a book.

A man from Columbia told me about the time Logan recruited his son for the freshman class at Wofford. On a visit through Spartanburg, the man had told Logan that he hoped his son Doug would attend Wofford someday. He told Logan the boy was only 10 years old. Well, Doug was surprised to receive a personal letter from Logan the next week, inviting the boy up for a weekend at Wofford. Doug's parents were surprised, but they had been surprised by Logan before. So, Doug left for Spartanburg on a Saturday afternoon bus.

Late Sunday night, Doug returned from Wofford, having had a wonderful time and having thoroughly enjoyed his initiation to college life. When his parents asked him what the weekend was like, the lad replied: "It was great. Two football players met me at the bus station. I stayed with one of them in his dormitory room. I even went to their fraternity party."

Doug's parents commented that this was all certainly good of the two students.

"Well," said Doug, "when I was getting ready to leave on Sunday afternoon, one of the guys told me that he had a confession to make. He said that Logan had told them to look for a redheaded guy who was about six feet tall in the tenth grade. When they saw me at the bus station, they realized that Logan was

mistaken. I was a redheaded boy who was 10 years old and in the sixth grade. They said they wanted to kill Logan. They had a date for me and everything. But they said, after a weekend with me, 'You know, for a kid, you're really a cool little guy.' They said they wanted me to come to Wofford—only that I should wait a few years first."

I think that the present Wofford men are getting shortchanged. But I suppose college campuses are too conservative these days and students are too serious to really appreciate a Frank Logan. They have to turn him over to the old alumni who can still remember the fun they had in college more vividly than the lectures they heard or the books they read, and who know that characters like Frank Logan don't give an education, they *are* an education.

Student craziness in the 1950s and early 1960s was not restricted to rites of spring. One Halloween, pranksters "borrowed" a country outhouse and put it on the steps of "Old Main."

King Teens

Thanks to a chance brainstorm of three student leaders and a responsive administration, Wofford College became and remains a forerunner in academic scholarship assistance. The King Teen Program, ancestor of the present-day Wofford Scholars competition, was instituted in 1949 after a recommendation from Rab Braddy '49, Francis Nicholson '50 and Dick Steadman '51.

"We liked King Teens as a splendid way to honor academic merit, leadership and character as well as a method to introduce the best young men in the state to the merits of Wofford College," recalled the late Dean S. Frank Logan '41. "Off we charged into the academic marketplace of South Carolina, long before the National Merit Scholarship Program began."

The King Teen Scholars Program saw a humble beginning. In its inaugural year in 1949-50, fewer than 30 South Carolina high schools submitted nominations. Lester Johnson of Woodruff earned a $250 tuition scholarship as King Teen. Runner-up Sidney Kelley of Conway received a $100 scholarship.

For more than two decades, being named the King Teen was one of the most significant honors for male seniors in South Carolina high schools. In the early 1960s, the college began to award scholarships to four King Teens per year rather than one, and the number of schools participating increased to more than 200. In 1969, James Cheek of Spartanburg's Carver High School became the first African American to win a King Teen scholarship. In the early 1970s, the King Teen name was dropped, and the more appropriate Benjamin Wofford Scholar was adopted.

The Anna Todd Wofford Scholars program for women was instituted in 1972, and 41 high school seniors participated in the first competition. Dorothy Lynn Smith of Spartanburg Day School and Carol Ann Cudd of Paul M. Dorman High School in Spartanburg each received a $4,000 scholarship, payable over four years, as the first Anna Todd Wofford Scholarship recipients.

—Adapted from the silver anniversary reunion program for King Teens (1974), written by Frank Logan '41

Spartanburg attorney, James Cheek '73 shown here working as an admissions counselor shortly after his graduation from Wofford, was the first African American to win a King Teen Scholarship. This competitive academic merit scholarship program that Wofford pioneered continued into the 21st century, though winners were later called Benjamin Wofford or Anna Todd Wofford Scholars.

Paying My Dues on Snyder Field

Jim "Dasher" Ditty '54, played for Coach Phil Dickens as "the weak side guard" on the Wofford football team. A recent trip to the campus from his home in California triggered these memories. "On visits back to Wofford, I sometimes walk from Old Main along the familiar path to Andrews Field House. Tucked away at the northeast corner of that venerable building is the objective of my lone pilgrimage. A half century ago, in a pair of nondescript, connected rooms that once housed a coach's office and more recently were used as a laundry, a young boy's life was forever changed. Standing in those tiny rooms, my mind drifts back to the way we were ..."

Creaking wood and rattles contrasted with the squeals of metal on metal as the tired, old day-coach swayed along uneven ribbons of steel. On curves, the black steam locomotive was seen far ahead, belching smoke, drivers spinning, powering the long train through Appalachian highlands. Glued to the stained window was one wide-eyed teen-aged boy. He watched in utter fascination at the rolling panorama of green mountains, rushing streams and rocky crags. Never before had he seen such a confusion of land and trees, water and sky; it was grand! A big city boy from Chicago, he had often wondered how mountains looked. Now he saw them, and was captivated.

I was that boy, embarked upon the grand adventure of my life. Trying for a football scholarship, my first stop was the University of South Carolina. In Columbia, there was disappointment. Carolina turned me down. But then, friendly students extolled the virtues of a small college in the Piedmont region of the state. So, on to Spartanburg!

At first, the city seemed less than impressive as my cab transited an impoverished section of town known as Gas Bottom, along present-day Daniel Morgan Avenue and North Pine Street. But then, we passed under a railroad track, rounded a curve, and before my eyes rose one of the most beautiful campuses that I have ever seen, then or now: graceful brick buildings, tree-shaded lawns, gently curving streets, an ambiance of quiet learning amid robust camaraderie. Even today I get a thrill and a sense of belonging, just walking that campus and meeting other alumni, acknowledging that I, too, am a Wofford man.

On the field I was given a welcome chance to show my stuff. The tryout went well, but trepidation reigned as other boys filed out of the coach's office, heads hanging. Then, it happened. Coach Phil Dickens stood framed in his doorway, grinned, and in his grand charismatic way, announced that my quest was

Phil Dickens and Snyder Field, from the 1952 *Bohemian*.

over. "We'll give you a scholarship right here." But it was tough! First, I had to pay my dues on Snyder Field. Those memories are perhaps most vivid. That hot Carolina sun! I lost 10 pounds at the first two-a-day practice. Sweaty pads, hitting, getting hit, hurting, bouncing back, "shaking it off" and going again. Roaring crowds, trying to catch my breath. Mostly winning, sometimes losing, but always "Full Speed."

My favorite photo of Coach Dickens leads off the athletics section of the 1952 *Bohemian*. Bundled in overcoat and wide brimmed hat, his visage looms over Snyder Field. Ever present—overseeing his boys, teaching,

Coach Phil Dickens

From the time that he scored 96 points in a single high school football game at Hartsville, Tennessee, everyone knew that "Phantom Phil" Dickens was a special kind of athlete. During his six-year tenure as head football coach at Wofford (1947-1952), he proved he also was a special kind of college football coach. He had a career winning record of .691 and was the first to take a Terrier team to a post-season game.

Dickens and his principal assistant, Jim Myers, both played under the famous General Bob Neyland at the University of Tennessee. They installed the Volunteers' advanced balanced line, single-wing offense and exploited many recruiting contacts made during their college years.

Highlights of the Dickens era included five straight ties to open the 1948 season (a national record that seems safe with the adoption of overtime in the NCAA); an undefeated 11-0 regular season in 1949, followed by a trip to the Cigar Bowl in Tampa, Florida; a 19-14 upset of Auburn in the 1950 season's opener and the Terriers' first victory over Furman in 35 years in 1951. After the 1952 season, Dickens moved to the University of Wyoming, where he was successful from 1953 through 1957, and later, he was a respected head football coach and athletics administrator at the University of Indiana.

Coach Phil Dickens' teams of the early 1950s often dressed out in solid uniforms of coppery "Wofford Gold." The result of a manufacturer's error, the color was almost exactly the same as the footballs used at the time. The color became popular across the country, but defenses were confused to the point where the rules were changed to outlaw it.

encouraging, cajoling, at times correcting with sharpness. But not any sort of cruel despot some coaches are colored in later years. We always knew that Coach Dickens cared about more than winning football games. As another Terrier once said, "A lot of men could have taught us about football, but Coach Dickens taught us about life." "Winners do what losers won't do. They pay the price of victory." "If at first the breaks go against you, don't give up; put on more steam." These were not just words; they were our way of life.

In my first year at Wofford, one incident indelibly taught the meaning of discipline and honor. Some players began testing training rules that forbade eating between meals, or even frequenting hamburger stands. In midseason, seven players were suspended before the game with traditional rival Presbyterian College. Those seven included four starters and all three tailbacks on the team. (In our single wing, this group represented the entire corps of passers and primary running backs, including one whom Coach Dickens years later described as the best natural athlete he ever coached.) PC had been favored anyway, and the Terriers were given little chance. But the coaches cobbled together an offense. Other players stepped up, and you know what? Wofford won that game! The next week, seven well-chastened players rejoined the team.

In Wofford's classrooms, similar values were absorbed by budding student-athletes. Here were great challenges of the intellect. But while I was struggling to survive academically, a funny thing happened. I found that not only could I learn, but that it was really great fun! Thus, from the twin venues of athletics and academics was born a lifelong respect for excellence and a mighty thirst for knowledge.

More value came from residence hall living, new friends, twice-weekly chapel sessions, visiting various Spartanburg churches, social events and dates. Of course, not all of it was golden for this Yankee from the industrial North. New cultural and religious currents presented formidable social barriers and very difficult personal adjustments, not always well handled. Still, on balance, I made good friends and experienced much personal growth.

This was the heyday of the segregationist Jim Crow laws. One time, my Southern teammates were visibly upset because two black athletes of the Fort Jackson team were not allowed to participate in a scrimmage against us. One teammate from North Carolina gave it voice, stating, "If they are good enough to play for Fort Jackson, they are good enough to play against me." Incidentally, Fort Jackson was loaded with college and NFL stars drafted into the Army during the Korean War. They pretty well turned us every way but loose.

Half a century has now passed since last we ran onto Snyder Field, the cool night air on our faces and the roar of the crowd in our ears. Yet, these values endure: Dedication to excellence, a love of learning, and a determination to live our lives honorably, to always be counted among those who will get the job done.

So, Go Terriers

And when the going gets tough, and we need a few yards

Run the old "Ten on Two".

Fisher DeBerry

Fisher DeBerry '60 believes in setting goals. He has been known for giving his players decals for their watches at the beginning of the season. The decals state simply: Commander-in-Chief's Trophy, conference championship, bowl trip.

During his first 21 years as head football coach at the Air Force Academy (1983-2004), the Falcons achieved those goals more often than not. DeBerry's 161-94-1 record stood high on the list of college coaching achievements, and he led the Falcons to 12 post-season bowl games and 14 of the academy's 16 Commander-in-Chief trophy titles.

In 1996, he served as president of the powerful and prestigious American Football Coaches Association. He received the State Farm Coach of Distinction award in 2001, joining coaches like Phillip Fulmer of Tennessee and Tyrone Willingham of Washington as recipients. He also has been inducted into the South Carolina Sports Hall of Fame and the Fellowship of Christian Athletes (FCA) Hall of Champions.

When Fisher DeBerry visited the White House to accept the Commander in Chief's trophy from President George H.W. Bush, he posed for this picture with two other former Wofford football players, John Miller '67 (then with the Secret Service) and the late Bruce Johnson '70 (then on the Falcon coaching staff).

A *View* from the *Press Box*

Wilson Davis '61 has always had a special interest in Terrier athletics as a result of his four years as student Sports Information Director, beginning in 1957. After his stint at Wofford, he stayed in the communications field and retired in 1999 as director of the University News Service after 31 years at The University of North Carolina at Greensboro. Here, he shares his memories of "a special, bright and shining era" in Wofford athletics.

In the larger world, the Korean War's end and the civil rights revolution served as bookends for 1952-64. The period was a paradox, defined by both peaceful years and momentous events. In 1954 came the United States Supreme Court's landmark decision prompting school integration. Then came Sputnik I in 1957, the end of President Eisenhower's second term, John F. Kennedy's election and assassination, and the Cuban missile crisis. In short, it was an exciting time.

That was also true with sports in South Carolina. At Clemson, Coach Frank Howard was still winning big on the gridiron, and the University of South Carolina Gamecocks were developing their own pigskin magic under Coach Rex Enright and then under Coach Warren Giese.

At Wofford, head football Coach Phil Dickens left in 1952 for the University of Wyoming after compiling an enviable 40-16-7 record and accumulating a troubling financial deficit in the athletics operating budget. Conley T. Snidow, a soft-spoken Virginian who

had won big at Emory and Henry College, replaced Dickens as head football coach. He brought with him Jim Brakefield as an assistant coach. A more realistic football schedule, continuing to include the University of South Carolina, was put in place, and even with budget adjustments, the athletics program enjoyed a large measure of success. This was in the Jim Crow era, quite a few years before the arrival of talented African-American players. Nevertheless, the Terriers attracted top-notch athletes, including talented transfers from larger programs. As is still true today, Terrier football or basketball players often served as student body presidents—as exemplified by Jeter Hammond Jr. '56, Donald Fowler '57, Charlie Bradshaw '59 and Jim Dunn '60.

Snidow was head football coach for 14 years, compiling a 77-59-4 record. After the 1957 season, he doubled as director of athletics. In January 1967, Brakefield succeeded him as head coach and won 28 of 44 games during his tenure. As student SID, I

Football teams during the era of Conley Snidow and Jim Brakefield drew large and enthusiastic crowds to Snyder Field.

followed two real pros in Henry T. "Sonny" Smith Jr. '57 and Melvin E. Derrick Jr. '54, who left big shoes to fill. In those days, the student SID took a full load of 18 academic hours and also found time to work about 25-30 hours per week publicizing the Terrier teams. Majoring in English, I sought to be equally conversant about literary works such as the *Iliad*, the *Aeneid* and William Wordsworth's sonnets as I was about Terrier football. Overall, it was an enjoyable time in my life.

I was brought to Wofford as student SID by Joel Robertson '41, the genial head basketball coach and business manager of athletics. A few years earlier, in 1952, Ellerbe "Daddy" Neal '53 was setting records for Robertson's cagers. In his final season, Neal averaged 32.6 points and 26.5 rebounds per game. Robertson told me once that he thought Neal, almost seven feet tall, was the best big man ever to play collegiate basketball in South Carolina. In 12 years as Terrier coach, Robertson had a 157-124 won-loss record.

Robertson left after the 1957-58 season and was replaced by coach Gene Alexander from Erskine College. Alexander was a competitive man who hated to lose, but also one who cared profoundly about his players— "his boys." His Erskine and Wofford teams compiled a 487-385 record, and his 1959-60 Terriers, led by Trap Hart '60, and Bill Barbee '60, had a 25-6 mark, and advanced to the quarterfinals of the NAIA national tournament in Kansas City.

I remember with special fondness the 1957 Terrier football team, which finished 8-2 and was ranked No.1 nationally by the NAIA at one point that year. That was the season that quarterback Charlie Bradshaw '59 and end Jerry Richardson '59 both were named to the Associated Press Little All America squad: Bradshaw to the first team and Richardson to the third team. Three others—tackle Roger Hagy '58, guard Jim Rampey '58 and running back Frank "the Bull" DePrete '58—made honorable mention Little All-America. Bradshaw could have graduated that year, but returned to play with Richardson again. The Terriers fell to 3-7 in a rebuilding year. Richardson still made second team Little All America and went on to play in the NFL.

During the 1952-64 era there were other football Little All-Americans: end Jack Abell '54, halfback Joe Hazle '55, tackle George Rice '57, offensive guard Dan Lewis '62 and defensive back Archie Black '65.

I also spent many pleasant spring afternoons in the Wofford dugout as Jim

The Andrews Field House arena, built in 1929, was obsolete by the 1960s, but there was still plenty of excitement there on cold winter nights when Gene Alexander's Terriers played "Little Four" teams.

Brakefield's Terriers played good baseball on Law Field. Trains from the old Clinchfield Railroad chugged by in the background, giving it all a wonderful pastoral setting. I remember the competitiveness of Fisher DeBerry '60 on Brakefield's baseball teams. That same trait helped make DeBerry a successful head football coach at the Air Force Academy.

Despite the passage of more than 40 years, I still remember many happy times from my student days—good professors, special friends on campus and in the news media—and lots of Wofford wins. There were talented Terrier athletes, too numerous to mention, and good coaches, which taken all together, helped make 1952-64 a special, bright and shining era in the history of Wofford athletics.

After graduation, I returned to North Carolina, but I have always been grateful for those years at Wofford. I am reminded also that it was through a story I wrote on Terrier football player John Tate '58 for *The Burlington Times-News* that I met Jean, my wife. At the time, John's mother wrote to thank me for the story, and since I had recently moved to their hometown, she asked me to stop by so she could thank me in person. When I did, I also met John's sister, Jean. That was in 1961. We were married three years later.

Moyer's Men: *The* Glee Clubs *of the* 1950s

Every spring break during the 1950s and early 1960s, the members of the Wofford College Glee Club packed their tuxedos (provided at a low cost through Belk-Hudson on Main Street in Spartanburg) and headed out on a tour through Lowcountry South Carolina.

The Glee Club created a sense of responsibility in its members, recalled Clyde Aiken '55, and the tour was where they were able to showcase this responsibility. When the students arrived in a town they would be guests of the local townsfolk and would reward each town with a stirring performance at a local church—usually Methodist, of course. Among the "many wonderful experiences and beautiful memories," Aiken remembered "meeting the warm, wonderful folks in the towns … meeting the girls."

The architect of these epic tours was Professor Sam Moyer, and the group he showcased across South Carolina was affectionately dubbed, "Moyer's Men." Two buses were required to accommodate more than 60 singers and staff.

Moyer directed the Glee Club for 21 years. Like many Northerners who discovered Spartanburg during World War II, he married locally and settled in the area. When he accepted the chair of the music department at Wofford, the big, red-haired, loud and loving Moyer was an immediate success both with students and audiences.

Dr. Talmage Skinner '56 described Moyer as "a showman of the first rank," and said his concerts were always packed. The club consisted of "a few good singers … but everyone sang with great heart," he said. The 10-day tour was the highlight of the club, but the icing on the cake was the return to Wofford. The closing concert was held at Memorial Auditorium, usually filled to its capacity of 3,100.

Moyer's Glee Club recruited dozens of young men to Wofford and encouraged them to stay and earn degrees. Freshmen and seniors "just merged like cars on an interstate," Skinner said. Recruitment was undoubtedly influenced by Moyer's closing comments at each concert; "Go to the church of your choice, but send your sons to Wofford."

Moyer died suddenly in 1963 at the age of 46. More than four decades have passed since then, but through recordings, current members of the Glee Club still can get a taste of what Moyer's Men sounded like. No program would have been complete without the singing of the Wofford Alma Mater, which they performed magnificently. Another memorable selection was "Do Not Forsake Me, Oh My Darling" from the popular movie *High Noon*, which began with the beating of drums and flowed in and out as Moyer divided the men up for different verses and pitches. The club also devoted about half their concerts to timeless sacred songs: "I Believe," "Beautiful Savior" (this selection featured a great solo) and "The Creation."

Moyer's Men always will be a part of Wofford because they brought the college into the communities of South Carolina, and their era has helped define a century-long legacy of great choral music at Wofford.

— *Emmett Sheridan '06*

During Wofford's Centennial year, 1953-54, the Glee Club posed for this formal portrait. Clyde Aiken '55 recalled that on its spring tour, the lead bus in their two-bus convoy lost its brakes as it approached an intersection. "To avoid hitting other cars, the driver tried to make a right turn but overturned and the bus landed on its side," Aiken said. "Bill Kinney crawled out of a window and called out to me on the ground, 'Catch me!' just as he jumped. I do not remember which of us hit the ground hardest. That night, the sacred part of our concert took on a new meaning for all of us, and the Lord's prayer had never been done with such personal and collective meaning."

"After graduation, I was married, out of money, and uncertain of my future when one day I had a call from Sam Moyer. He said a man in Spartanburg wanted to pay for a Methodist Wofford graduate to attend theology school, and he had recommended me to T.P. Hartness, who owned the local Pepsi-Cola bottling company. Mr. Hartness said, 'Sam Moyer says you are OK. How much do you need?' He paid for the next two years at Emory and changed my life." —Talmage Skinner '56

Moyer's men held two highly successful Homecoming reunions during the mid-1980s. Among the groups performing were the Tennessee Dew Drops, as they appeared in the mid-50s *(above)*, and as they appeared at one of their reunion concerts *(right)*.

A *Generation* of *Leaders* for the *Church*

Generational theorists tell us that people born between the years of 1925 and 1942 are part of what is known as the *Silent Generation*. For Wofford College, these were the students of the 1950s. Their parents and their friends fought in *the* war, they typically married during or soon after their college experience, and their children would boom onto the scene as idealists ready to take on society. All this was especially true of those students seeking a vocation in religious spheres.

Wofford produced a generation of church leaders during the 1950s who populated diverse areas of ministry, proclaiming a message of faith, hope and love during often uncertain and unstable times. Not all of them came to Wofford expecting to spend their lives serving in the church, but the atmosphere was compatible with creating and cultivating their vocation as future ministers.

In the 1950s, the college had a well-rounded and inspirational faculty and offered an array of activities and events that inspired and confirmed calls to ministry. Perhaps above all else, Wofford nurtured strong bonds of friendship between these soon-to-be church leaders that motivated them to explore, discern and ultimately serve together.

The encouragement received through the classroom experience in the 1950s broadened and shaped their young minds. In particular in the religion department, it was the one-person show of Dr. Charles Nesbitt leading them solidly into the future. Because of his courageous historical-critical approach to biblical studies, Wofford students were later bored to tears by introductory seminary courses. Adding to Nesbitt's offerings were William B. Hunter's courses on Shakespeare, Milton and classical literature. Others, from President Marsh to Professor Charles Cauthen '17 and Lewis P. Jones '38 in the history department, offered direction in areas other than biblical studies.

The teachers made the subjects come alive and helped students to begin to be comfortable with the vast array and ambiguity

of knowledge. The pursuit of knowledge was an important attribute these young visionaries would take with them as they moved from Wofford to seminary and into the life of the church.

The Wofford of the 1950s saw students busy in the classroom and also in extra-curricular events. Though not pressured to involve themselves in local churches, many students attended, and churches in the community expressed their desire to be a part of the lives of the students. The college also had two weekday chapel services where guest ministers often presided. Occasionally during the course of the semester, students would lead worship and speak on religious themes.

The Student Christian Association (SCA) at times had more than 100 members. There, Wofford's future church leaders had opportunities to reach beyond the walls of the college to the surrounding community in such activities as the Gas Bottom Project, a Saturday playground program for African-American children in a nearby neighborhood just east of the campus. In the SCA they also began to form the bonds of friendship with other

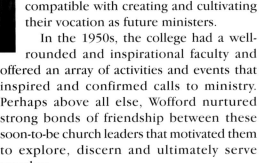

Dr. Charles Nesbitt

Dr. Charles Cauthen

A fund-raising brochure called "the Wofford of To-morrow" (1945) featured this map touting the impact of Wofford alumni across South Carolina.

KEY TO SYMBOLS

+ Wofford Ministers
● Wofford School Administrators
★ Wofford Men In Congress
  or Legislature

students. It was also where they began to define who they were and give shape to their futures.

The Wofford community and its culture provided a place for students to fully experience one another, their professors and the staff, and also the family, friends and significant others not a constant part of their on-campus experience. Wofford was a place that was patient with its students, especially with those who may have entered its hallowed hallways some years beyond the traditional college age. Together these future church leaders worked on assignments, played in intramural sports, worshipped, joked and laughed, and consoled each other in times of disappointment and failure.

It was this environment of freedom, respect and civility that allowed students to embrace Charles Wesley's vision that "knowledge and vital piety" can and should be joined.

—The Rev. Lyn Pace '99, with special thanks to Bishop Marshall Meadors '55, the Rev. C. Allen Senn '59 and Dr. Charles Barrett '55

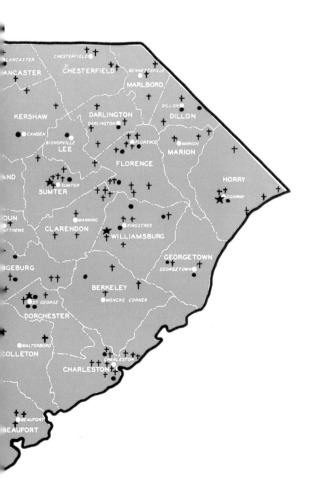

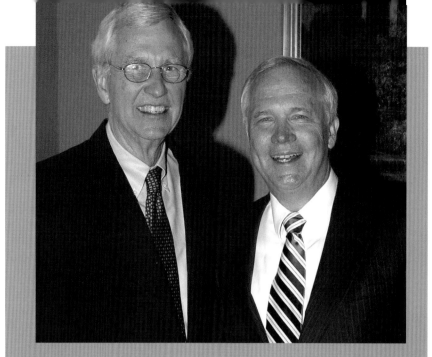

A native of Florence, **Bishop Marshall L. Meadors, Jr. '55** *(left)* earned his Wofford degree with Phi Beta Kappa honors. After seminary studies at Emory, he joined the South Carolina Conference, serving churches in Greenville, Anderson, Marion, and North Myrtle Beach. He served as a trustee of Spartanburg Methodist College and as a member and chairman of the South Carolina Commission on Aging.

Elected bishop in 1992, Meadors presided over the Mississippi Conference for eight years. Observing his work with the Council of Bishops' Initiative on Children and Poverty, the United Methodist Interpreter called him "the Children's Bishop." He also served as president of the Mississippi Religious Tolerance Conference. In 1999, he was a member of an interdenominational peace mission to Serbia that helped bring resolution to the Kosovo conflict.

Meadors received an honorary degree from Wofford in 1979, and in 2000, received the Alumni Distinguished Service award. Following his retirement in 2000, he returned to South Carolina and in 2001, joined the Wofford Board of Trustees.

Born in Greenville, **Bishop William H. Willimon '68** was elected to Phi Beta Kappa at Wofford. He earned degrees at Yale and Emory and served churches in the South Carolina Conference until 1976, when he was appointed the Duke Divinity School faculty. In 1984, he was named minister to the university and professor at Duke, and in 1989, became Dean of the Chapel at Duke.

In 1976, he was named the Young Alumnus of the Year by the National Alumni Association, and in 1994, he received an honorary degree from Wofford. Willimon is a prolific writer and commentator about issues facing the contemporary church as well as an editor-at-large of an influential journal, *The Christian Century*. In 1996, a Baylor University group named him one of the 12 most effective preachers in the English-speaking world.

Elected bishop in 2004, Willimon was appointed to serve the North Alabama Conference. He served as a member of Wofford's board of trustees from 1980 to 1992 and again from 1997 to 2005.

— Phillip Stone '94

Jim Kilgo's Gift of Storytelling

James Kilgo '63 was blessed with the genius of storytelling and the discipline of friendship. Anyone who sat across a campfire from him, or shared a cup of coffee in a café knew both. Jim spun stories out of love—for landscape, for language, for the listener, and often as not, for God. We who loved Jim will remember him as a writer of beautiful sentences, a teller of tales.

Jim Kilgo joined the department of English at the University of Georgia in 1967 and taught there until his retirement in 1999. He headed the university's creative writing program in the 1990s, winning five outstanding honor professor awards as well as a creative research medal and Sandy Beaver Award for Excellence in Teaching.

He maintained friendships out of deep loyalty, keeping up with a network of long affections stretching far afield from his home in Athens. With his death in December 2002, after a long battle with cancer, Wofford lost one of its most loyal graduates, and quite possibly the finest alumni writer of his generation.

Jim's final book, *Colors of Africa*, brought the essayist and novelist back into familiar territory of his first book, *Deep Enough for Ivorybills*: hunting, its pleasures and deep contradictions.

Colors of Africa was Jim's account of a three-week safari in the Luangwa River Valley of Zambia in 2000. When he accepted the invitation to travel to Africa, Jim did not plan to hunt, choosing instead to merely accompany his big-game hunting host on the trip of a lifetime—to observe, reflect and prepare to present his account of "the colors of Africa." Near the end of the hunt, Jim was offered a chance to hunt a kudu, an antelope of legend. "Will I be worthy?" the writer wondered as he brought his story to a close.

As would be expected by anyone familiar with Jim's other essays, *Inheritance of Horses*, *The Handcarved Crèche*, *The Blue Wall*, and his novel, *Daughter of My People*, he did not ignore the complexities inherent in hunting—especially big game hunting. He had a deep need to justify his participation in the hunt, and he realized that such justification could only come from within.

Already many are claiming that Jim Kilgo's travel narrative *Colors of Africa* will take its place alongside those other bold explorers of Africa in prose: David Livingstone, Ernest Hemingway and Isak Dinesen.

—*John Lane '77*
Associate Professor of English

John C. Kilgo *(left)*, whose diploma from Wofford was a master's rather than a bachelor's degree, was recruited by the college to serve as a financial agent (development officer) in 1890. The trustees built a beautiful campus home for him, which still stands and is known as the Kilgo-Clinkscales House. Brilliant intellectually, eloquent and energetic (but with an abrasive personality), Kilgo moved on to become the president of Trinity College and a Methodist bishop in North Carolina, where he assembled a powerful coalition to promote the denominational colleges and restrain the development of the state university system. James W. Kilgo,class of 1881 *(right)*, was John C. Kilgo's brother, and the great-grandfather of Jim Kilgo, the writer. His son, a 1905 graduate, was James Patrick Kilgo.

This picture of the fourth and fifth generations was made when Jim received an honorary degree from Wofford in 1998 *(left to right)*: John Simpson Kilgo III '04, James L. Kilgo '02, John S. Kilgo Jr. '69, Jim Kilgo '63, John Carlisle Kilgo '89.

What's Going On Up There?

When President Charles F. Marsh made these remarks at the Alumni-Senior Banquet in June 1962, he reminded the audience that he had come to Wofford as a first-year president when the members of the graduating class were first-year students. These remarks [edited for publication in this book] constituted a prophetic warning about the challenges that his administration would have to face as the pace of change intensified across the South and the Baby Boom generation began to arrive at Wofford. The title of this speech "What's Going On Up There?" does not, of course, refer to Heaven or to the newly explored world of John Glenn, Scott Carpenter and their fellow astronauts. The phrase "up there" refers to the "hill," the traditional site of any college campus.

Charles F. Marsh served as Wofford's president from 1958 through 1968, a time of great social change throughout the South.

The question "What's Going On Up There?" is sometimes made a bit more pointed by expanding it to "What's Going On Up There Anyway?" and by following it with the second question "What's wrong at the college?" Usually, this means, "Unless the college does what I think it ought to do about a specific matter that irritates me, I'll withdraw my support, financial and otherwise." Actually, this thinking is typical of many colleges and, unfortunately, particularly so of those colleges like Wofford which have extremely close and affectionate ties with a church and with alumni and other interested people who live relatively close, geographically, to the campus. ...Many of you right here in this room can think of particular things that have caused you to tee off against Wofford in your innermost thoughts, conversations with other off-campus friends, or directly to the officials of the college.

Have any of you ever become irritated over the honorary degrees that Wofford has awarded, or the fact that such degrees have not been awarded to someone you esteem highly?

Have any of you begun to downgrade the college because it has not admitted one of your young friends or relatives, after careful consideration of his academic potential?

Have any of you queried hotly, "Why don't they fire that student or faculty member right now?" because of something that you have seen in the press but about which you have no further information?

Have any of you shaken your heads about the possibility of Wofford's slightly increased tuition and fees "pricing the college out of the market for students" when at the same time you have done little to influence your local Methodist church to contribute the Conference goal of $2 per member to the College

Familiar to Spartanburg residences for decades, this sign marked the North Church Street "front door" to the campus well into the 1980s.

Maintenance Fund, or to increase your annual contributions, and those of fellow alumni, to the Living Endowment Fund?

One of the most disturbing things to all of us at the college is the protests made by some constituents because one or more students or faculty members or visiting speakers express publicly a point of view concerning public affairs contrary to their opinions. This protest sometimes takes the form of a demand that such individuals be summarily dismissed from the college or otherwise disciplined or, in the case of visiting speakers, is stopped from appearing, under the guise of protecting our basic American freedoms and upholding Wofford's traditional ideals. ...

It is pertinent at this point to remind this audience of President Snyder's views on the role visiting speakers play in fulfilling this purpose. In his autobiography, *An Educational Odyssey*, he says: "Now as I recall the procession of American greats who came to Wofford for the commencement occasion...I must feel a sense of satisfaction over the quality and standing of those who delivered what were called 'messages' on these occasions. ... They were selected because they had done or said important things...and they spoke without any visible restraint in an atmosphere of liberty and tolerance, though their audience might be far from agreement with their utterance."

So the next time when you feel your blood pressure boiling because of some isolated incident at the college and, hot on the trail of a suspected conspiracy against the welfare of

Wofford, you ask "What's Going On Up There Anyway?" think of the frightened householder who reported to the police that he'd been struck down in the dark outside his back door by an unknown assailant. A young police officer sent to investigate returned very soon to headquarters with a lump on his forehead and a glum look on his face.

"I solved the case," he muttered.

"Amazingly fast work," his superior complimented him.

"How did you do it?" The young officer explained: "I stepped on the same rake."

We at Wofford admit readily that we make mistakes and pick up headaches through stepping on our own rakes. I can assure you, however, that there is nothing basically wrong, and hope that you will be less inclined to evaluate it in terms of isolated instances which have nothing to do with the basic educational strength of the college. ...

Frankly, the great disappointment I feel at this moment concerning my four years at Wofford is the slow progress made in improving what really counts—the quality of the educational experience offered to our students. Even more discouraging, if possible, is the lack of vital interest on the part of many members of our family, including faculty members, in the almost life and death necessity of making much greater educational improvement at Wofford if we are to survive as a significant educational institution. Higher education is an increasingly dynamic area in which many innovations and experiments are being made with apparent great success in

providing better educational opportunities to students.

Yet very few of the many communications you and other friends have sent me have been concerned with the basic quality of education at Wofford. Few of you are alarmed about the increasingly poor competitive position of the college in the market for able teachers and students. Our tardiness in developing significant opportunities for independent study, for study in foreign countries, and for associations at Wofford with foreign students, for greater interdepartmental course offerings, for learning something about non-Western history and culture, for electronic language study and for programmed learning in various fields is apparently of almost no concern to most Wofford supporters.

But enough of this caviling about petty complaints, possible overemphasis on physical improvements, and painfully slow improvement in educational quality at Wofford. The effect of several years of rising admission standards is beginning to be felt. Both faculty members and older students have commented on the greater seriousness of purpose and

intellectual interests of this year's freshmen. Letters to the editor of the *Old Gold and Black* have actually taken the administration to task for appearing to place more emphasis on our proposed student union than upon improving such an important educational facility as the library. While the writers did not realize that we are already at work on making significant improvements in the library which will be completed long before our new and, I may say, greatly-needed student center is started, I have been delighted at this manifestation of student insistence upon educational excellence.

I should be grossly negligent if I did not refer also to the splendid recognition three of our 1962 graduates have won for their college and themselves in winning Woodrow Wilson awards for graduate study. I am particularly pleased, also, that three of our new initiates into Phi Beta Kappa are entering Methodist theological seminaries next fall, thereby carrying on the great Wofford tradition of intertwining academic excellence with moral

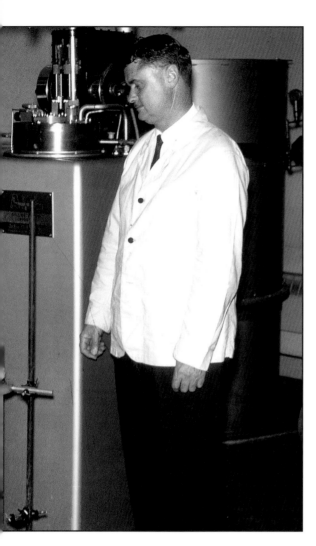

students and from outside sources. They will be helpful in developing a new 10-year plan for the college. All members of the teaching and administrative staff will soon become involved in a comprehensive self-study of the college which must be well underway by September 1963 to conform to the requirements of the Southern Association of Colleges and Schools.

In other words, when you and other friends of the college ask the question in the next few years, "WHAT'S GOING ON UP THERE?" I am confident that we can answer "Plenty!"

And it is all directed at making Wofford a better place to send the best young people you know for a quality education with a Christian emphasis. ... "

As the Baby Boomers approached college age, the federal government established loan programs so that colleges could expand their housing to accommodate larger enrollments. Shipp and DuPré Halls were built at Wofford during this period, and they featured a pioneering suite arrangement that has accommodated numerous changes in residence life.

and religious emphasis.

Though we have a long way to go, faculty salaries have been increased and definite plans been made to make certain that the key factor in educational strength at Wofford—a competent, stimulating and dedicated faculty—is given first priority in the allocation of our financial resources. The faculty has taken favorable action on the first recommendations of two new committees on the superior student and on foreign study and foreign students and has made various changes designed to strengthen the curriculum and to tighten academic standards.

During the past year, the committee structure of the Board of Trustees has been reorganized to provide that each trustee will become the board's expert in [one aspect] of the work of the college and report, through one of four basic committees on education, student affairs, development and finance, at meetings of the Board of Trustees. These reports will be based on information derived from faculty and administration members and

Fifth
Generation
1968-1987

THE *BABY BOOMERS RECREATE* THE *"WOFFORD WAY"*

by JoAnn Mitchell Brasington

Wofford used this college logo in the late 1960s and early 1970s.

(preceding pages)
Tommy Thompson made this aerial photograph in 1989 when he was working on the book, *Wofford College: A Time to Remember.*

Before January 1968, few Wofford students were eager to leave the warmth of their homes at the end of Christmas break for exams on Wofford's rainy and cold January campus. That changed with the college's first Interim. For many students, Interim 1968 provided an opportunity for their first flight in an airplane, their first trip outside the United States, their first experience with another culture and way of life. During this first Interim, Wofford students left their chalkboards and desks to live among the ruins of the ancient Roman Empire, with Spanish-speaking families in Mexico, or with hippies in San Francisco. They studied jazz in New Orleans, art in Florence, Italy, and international politics at the United Nations in New York City. They explored possible careers in the ministry, teaching and medical research. They developed and produced the campus's first play and created the foundation of the Wofford Theatre Workshop. Thanks to Interim, the walls of Wofford were expanding along with student consciousness.

Dr. Charles Marsh considered Interim one of the great accomplishments of his 10-year tenure as president of the college. He, Dean Philip Covington, and other older members of the faculty and administration had been observing the student climate slowly change during the mid-1960s. By the time the first Baby Boomers enrolled at Wofford in 1964, they had watched the assassination of a president, witnessed the invasion of the Beatles, and heard Martin Luther King Jr.'s "I Have a Dream" speech. Rock 'n Roll, television, and the threat of nuclear holocaust were now rooted in American life. Marsh's so-called Oasis of Tranquility was gone, and college administrators could no longer work with parents to shelter students under the relative safety of the campus oak and dogwood canopy.

Interim, as well as other efforts at curriculum change, faculty recruitment and racial desegregation was the Marsh administration's way of expanding the college experience for this new group of students. They were rejecting everything 1950s and would soon make changing their corner of the world a high priority, right up there with enjoying an extended period of adolescence.

Dr. Joab M. Lesesne Jr. was a graduate student in history at the University of South Carolina when Wofford began debating the issue of desegregation. According to Lesesne, the state was badly divided. While opposing forced desegregation in principle, many whites thought that change was inevitable and that the state could never thrive economically unless it moved past the issue. While at USC, Lesesne, who at the time had no Wofford ties, became friends with a member of the Wofford Board of Trustees who hoped to forestall integration, and Ross Bayard, a doctoral candidate from the Wofford faculty who favored voluntary desegregation on an accelerated timetable. From the carrels in the McKissick Library, the three often discussed the issue of higher education desegregation at Wofford and throughout the state. There Lesesne learned that Marsh was taking a strong but diplomatic position, saying that it was

Librarian Frank Anderson, Dean Philip Covington, Dean Joe Lesesne and Professor Bill Scheerer plan the "Remember the Cowpens" Interim of 1968.

Douglas Jones Sr. '69 was the first African American to receive a degree from Wofford. He is shown here at commencement 2004 with two of his children, Moneefa Jones-Taylor '95 and Jarvis Jones '04. Albert W. Gray '71 was the first black student to enroll at Wofford, but he served a tour in Vietnam prior to his graduation.

important for church-related agencies and colleges to integrate voluntarily and take the lead on this issue.

On Nov. 20, 1963, President Marsh made a presentation to a divided Board of Trustees at the Poinsett Hotel in Greenville, asking them to seriously consider "whether or not Negroes should be admitted to Wofford." At the meeting Marsh said that he had "no personal objection" and could "see strong moral and ethical reasons" to admit African-American students. He asked trustees to put their personal feelings aside and think critically about the issue.

Marsh and trustees in favor of admitting African-American students feared that Wofford would become isolated from the budding economic and educational progress in the state and nation if it did not soon desegregate. Trustees and alumni against voluntary desegregation were afraid of conflict and loss of financial support from their hometown churches and communities. Still, the Southern code of civility and good manners that kept most South Carolinians—both black and white—on the high road during this emotionally charged time, kept the Wofford Board of Trustees unified and focused on the most important issues: the advancement of the college and the opportunity to serve a broader constituency.

While Wofford was quietly discussing and studying the issue, the federal government began to offer financial incentives to integrated colleges. Trustee Roger Milliken also pledged

to help Wofford overcome any loss of funds withheld by alumni and churches as punishment for the board's decision to desegregate. Following the May 1964 board meeting, Wofford became one of the first historically white independent colleges in the Cotton Belt South to admit African-American male students voluntarily. In the fall of 1964, Wofford's first black student, Albert W. Gray '71 of Spartanburg, arrived on campus joining other Weejun-wearing men as they watched the Cold War extend into Vietnam and the nation increase its military involvement there. Over the next several years, the *Old Gold & Black* covered war protests and draft card burning with the same earnest indignation that it reported football losses, rat season injustices and student pranks.

Whether stealing the clapper from the college bell in the misguided hope that no bell would mean no classes (at least until the culprit could finish a paper or cram in a little more study time), dismantling the milk machine in DuPré, swiping all of the copies of the barely dry *Old Gold & Black* or skipping chapel, these first Baby Boomers found strength in their token rebellions against authority and tradition. They shared a seriousness of purpose—probably not the purpose their parents or professors would have chosen for them—but a commitment nevertheless to join, even if relatively quietly, the moral crusade spreading across college campuses around the country.

When Marsh retired in 1968, he described

Dr. Susan Griswold, recruited to upgrade foreign language studies, was the first woman to chair an academic department at Wofford.

the Wofford students of the day as "more able intellectually, more serious in their search for the meaning of life, more independent in thought and action, less amenable to the influence of parents, teachers, administration, and old people generally … more affluent and less provincial." These were the students that Paul Hardin III inherited. President Hardin's administration, supported by younger members of the faculty, is most remembered for aligning the college alcohol policy with state law, ending compulsory chapel assemblies, instituting a modern student government and the Code of Student Rights and Responsibilities, ending the era of house mothers, and admitting women as full-time day students.

Members of the Wofford community posed for this picture during the "Graz Summer" of 1969. They included Dr. J.R. Gross, Dr. '47 and Mrs. John Q. Hill, Marshall Walsh '71 (enrolled in a summer studies program in Europe), Dean and Mrs. Philip Covington, Daniel Iseman '70, Dr. John Bullard, Dr. Ross Bayard and Tom Lentz '70. Dr. '57 and Mrs. B.G. Stephens were members of the team that prepared the Graz Report, but they were not present when the picture was made.

In addition, Hardin and his administration worked toward lessening the racial divide on campus. In an editorial in the *Old Gold & Black* early in Hardin's administration, one African-American student wrote that Hardin and his staff—one of whom was Bobby Leach, an African American hired specifically to serve as a mentor for black students—were "the only ones who welcomed us." The opinion was shared by some and softened by others. The editors of the *OG&B*, however, agreed. On Dec. 5, 1969, a student editor wrote that integration at Wofford "has been a miserable failure in assimilating" the college's seven African-American students. "Something must be done to bring the Negro into the Southern

community. College students must take the lead."

And they did. Tom Leclair '71, a member of what he calls Wofford's "small but lively group of counterculture members" says that the Hardin administration's focus on actively recruiting and assimilating African-American students "contributed immeasurably to the Wofford experience by opening, broadening and diversifying the experience."

A similar theme of openness and broadened perspectives appeared in 1969 when Wofford received recommendations from the Graz Report, commissioned earlier by the administration to review the college and its impact on the surrounding community. According to the report, Wofford and the other three colleges in Spartanburg needed to collectively mobilize their students to play a more prominent role in the community. The report said that, in addition to benefiting the community, students who participate in life outside the isolated bubble of college campuses are less disillusioned following graduation. Following the report, the college widened its doors to community outreach programs and encouraged students to participate.

Although women had occasionally attended Wofford since the 1890s, the arrival of full-time female day students in 1971 caused a reaction. Among the first women on campus during the time were Robin and Shelley Henry, daughters of English Professor Ed Henry; Donna Green, daughter of Economics Professor Hal Green; and Leslie Smith from Spartanburg. An article in the local newspaper on March 7, 1971 reported in the style of the times, "Wofford males are lucky, all four girls are pretty, intelligent and sensible about this period of adjustment." The article continues that Green "wears her grungies [bellbottom jeans and loose sweaters] to class. …Donna, tall, slender and very attractive, tries to avoid the commotion she causes by wearing a dress."

Some male students opened doors for their female peers; some closed doors in their faces; others ignored the women, treating them as they once treated girls who went to their high schools. Shelley Henry Sperka '75 recalled several faculty members who were "not ready" for the addition of women in the classroom. Professor John Harrington, however, was extremely supportive, she said. These first women during the 1970s shared a single restroom on campus in Main Building, and they had no access to locker facilities before or after physical education classes. Still, they proved their competency, tenacity and resilience and helped make easier the college's decision to admit women as resident students a few years later.

With Vietnam détente in 1972, student restlessness at Wofford and around the country began to wane. When Lesesne accepted the job as president of the college that same year, he knew that he would need to deal with two issues relatively early in his administration—one was finding creative means of funding Wofford's distinctive educational program and the other was full, residential coeducation.

As the Baby Boom generation began to graduate from high school, it soon became obvious that the higher education structures in most states were inadequate. As had been the case with the World War II veterans, it was clear that energetic young people represented a national resource, well worth a public investment. State leaders began funding technical education programs and increasing the size of public university systems in an attempt to serve the new volume of students. They also increased operating subsidies at public universities to minimize tuition and fees for in-state residents. In 1962-63, for example, the resident student comprehensive fee for a year at Wofford amounted to $1,500,

compared to $988 for state-supported Clemson. By the late 1960s and early 1970s, independent colleges felt the impact of a widening tuition gap, particularly if the prospective student was willing to consider the option of a commuter community college or university branch campus. A number of

once-vibrant independent colleges folded or were permanently weakened during this period. Others, such as Lander and the College of Charleston in South Carolina, successfully lobbied to become state-supported at a substantial cost to taxpayers.

In 1973, the South Carolina General Assembly implemented the state's Tuition Grant program. It was available to students on independent campuses who were state residents and who could demonstrate financial need. In the first year about 100 students received $150,000 in education aid; the number of students benefiting from the program doubled by the next year. In addition to state grants, federal Basic Educational Opportunity Grants (later known as Pell

Dr. Donald Dobbs was a legendary biology professor at Wofford for decades, and his students performed exceptionally well in medical schools.

By the end of the 1970s, there were more than 200 women studying at Wofford, and they were beginning to have an influence on campus life.

In 1984 Anne Springs Close became the first woman to chair the Wofford Board of Trustees. By that time the board included several minorities and women.

Quick action by Spartanburg firefighters saved Main Building from destruction in 1971, and adequate insurance coverage ensured that the damage could be repaired quickly.

Grants) became available to middle class families, further making private education affordable.

Still, Lesesne knew he needed to continue what Hardin started by courting the support of national foundations. The tide seemed to turn when Wofford received a $400,000 grant from the National Endowment of the Humanities in 1973 to implement a revised and expanded humanities curriculum. The approved proposal, which incorporated some of the best suggestions of the Graz Report, provided for graduation requirement changes, two new majors, seminar-type humanities courses, and reading and writing laboratories on campus.

In a 1974 convocation address, Lesesne used the example of Watergate to illustrate the college's need for community. Also preaching human decency and personal responsibility, Lesesne said that Wofford and other institutions should end the era of "administrative isolation syndrome." The speech set the tone for an open-door administration—an administration that realized it would need all the help it could get raising funds, expanding Wofford's admissions reach beyond the state and immediate region, and improving the academic and physical infrastructure.

With an energy crisis slowing the country down to 55 miles per hour, Wofford seemed to be speeding up, in more ways than one. Naked college students were streaking across campus, and the South Carolina

Conference of the United Methodist Church had approved a plan to expand the Board of Trustees from 21 to 27 members, also abandoning a traditional quota of 11 lay members and 10 clergy trustees. The King Teen program was changed to accommodate women, and Old Main, the four original faculty homes, and the surrounding section of the campus were designated as a National Historic District.

It was at this time that the college's trustees appointed a task force to spend the year studying the admission of women as resident students, benchmarking other liberal arts colleges. Balancing the question of expense against the legal and moral imperative of providing equal facilities and opportunities for women, the task force also had to weigh the consequences of a shrinking applicant pool across the state and nation. Projections showed that the number of in-state high school graduates might soon decline by as many as 14,000 (from 62,000 in 1974 to 48,000 in 1985). In the fall of 1969, the average SAT at Wofford was 1038, compared to a national average of 956. By the fall of 1974, the average SAT at Wofford had dropped to 941, closing in on the national average of 924. In just a few years, the number of freshmen at Wofford who had finished in the bottom two-fifths of their high school classes increased from just 3 percent to 19 percent, though that alarming figure had fallen back to 11 percent by 1974. College leaders hoped that admitting women as resident students would double the pool of well qualified applicants.

In October 1975, the Board of Trustees

approved the faculty's recommendation to institute full, residential coeducation at Wofford even though the student body voted against allowing women to live on campus. By the fall of 1978, the entering freshman class had 221 men and 79 women.

Whether holding their own in class or on the Homecoming court, Wofford's first resident women more than proved their place at the college. For a short period of time, their admission standards were higher than those of men's because the trustees wanted their enrollment to grow gradually. Women also fought for playing time in Andrews Field House and survived life on the top floor of Wightman Hall, a building since demolished. Still, Carol Brasington Wilson '81 and Roberta Hurley Bigger '81 felt more than a drive to succeed; they also felt a welcome. "There was a place for us at Wofford," said Wilson, who was elected vice president of the student body her sophomore year. That same year, Bigger held the office of secretary, and Kim Maloney Hasseldon '81 served as treasurer. Thus, three of the four Campus Union officers were

women. Women in leadership and faculty positions, however, remained scarce. Dr. Vivian Fisher was the first woman hired to a tenure-track position in 1973. In 1980, Dr. Susan Griswold came to the college to head the foreign language department. She took the title of chairman after her male counterparts declined to adopt a gender-neutral alternative; she felt it was crucial to be perceived as their equal. Other early women on the faculty included Constance Armitage Antonsen, Marie Gagarine and Linda Powers Bilanchone. In addition to teaching, they immediately became role models and sometimes counselors for Wofford's first women residents.

By 1981, the college was no longer operating at a budget deficit, and just in time. Bargain-savvy consumers began shopping for colleges the way they shopped for cars. In November 1983, *U.S. News & World Report* published the first in its series of higher education rankings, placing Wofford among "America's Best Colleges." (Other publications have since joined the college rating frenzy, and Wofford continues to do well in these annual surveys.) Increasing the endowment became a priority in the 1980s, as did positioning the college for national recognitions. Joining the NCAA, adding unique programs such as the Presidential International Scholar program and accepting leadership roles in national organizations helped Wofford make this transition.

In 1964, when the first wave of Baby Boomers lapped against Wofford's campus, they did what they've done to every institution since—they changed it. The second wave of Boomers (1975-1985) took those changes, adapted and began nurturing the Wofford of today. If the generations before had been about rooting tradition firmly within Wofford's Upstate clay, then the generations between 1964 and 1985 were about altering some of that tradition and reseeding the campus consciousness with a new, progressive Wofford Way.

President Paul Hardin *(left)* and President Joe Lesesne during their transitional period in 1972.

By the end of the 1970s, once-prosperous Morgan Square was cluttered with abandoned buildings and vacant lots. The urban blight around the campus presented a serious challenge in recruiting and retaining students.

Interim 1968: A Seminar in Orbit

This article by Lewis P. Jones '38, in a somewhat longer and more detailed version, first appeared in the September 1968 issue of Sandlapper *magazine.*

Mules are not supposed to panic at the sight of a hound. One did in January. Deputy sheriffs are not supposed to panic at the sight of a bus. One did in January. Young men are supposed to go to school in the winter. Thirty-two did not in January 1968.

The mule was pulling a wagon along the ancient towpath of the Santee Canal, dug by hand in the 1790s; the foresaid animal hardly expected to encounter this "hound"—specifically, a Greyhound bus apparently lost deep in the woods of Berkeley County, almost as if it had made an emergency landing.

As for the deputy, he was going along a sandy back road deep in a Lowcountry swamp, minding the sheriff's business, where he most

The late Dr. J.M. Lesesne '19, a leading South Carolina historian and president of Erskine College, leads "orbiting seminar" students through a church cemetery near Donalds.

obviously did not expect to encounter this same Greyhound bus barreling along at a good clip in those wilds. When last seen, this gendarme was heading for a broker to buy Trailways stock.

The young men involved were 32 Wofford students aboard that erratic bus, traveling 3,200 miles without leaving South Carolina as they visited 36 of the 46 counties.

The odyssey, labeled "South Carolina: A Seminar in Orbit," was a history department project and one of the Interims made possible by the new 4-1-4 curriculum of Wofford College. In this program, two weeks are cut off each of the regular semesters (putting first semester exams before Christmas) and combined for the January Interim. During that month, each student and faculty member devotes himself fully to only one project. It must be something other than a regular

semester course telescoped into 30 days. Many special seminars (some interdepartmental), independent study and research projects, and several trips kept the student body busy. Some were kept hopping—in this case 32 were hopping around the Palmetto State. (Other tours: Mexico, Switzerland, Italy and the United Nations).

The South Carolina project was tied to history—sites and sights of historical significance. Each participant had some small topics to study during the few days on the Spartanburg campus, and oral reports were frequent (usually on the bus as it approached the subject matter of the report). Each student had maps and kept a daily journal—some ending with masterpieces consisting of huge packets that could dwarf an encyclopedia. One group plotted ancient roads and trails on modern maps—a task of both research and detective work that ultimately made the whole group more alert to the Buncombe Road, Keowee Path, Blackstock Road and others when they saw them. A photographic record of the state was made for the history department—more than 1,000 slides.

In all, the students were on the road 23 days. Eleven of these were one-day trips, one was overnight, and the coastal swing lasted 10 days.

A typical one-day tour began with a 7:15 departure from the campus (some of the travelers got a rude introduction to the sun's winter habits) and a run to Greenville with two stops en route. There the perambulating historians met their guide, Miss Laura Ebaugh, professor emeritus of Furman. She tolerated no foolishness from laggards as they toured the older homes of the town, went into Christ Church (1852, with congregation from 1820) and the old Beatty home (1834), and then journeyed out the Old Buncombe Road to the Rock House of the late 18th century, where the students were soon smitten by another lady, their hostess Mrs. Harry Haynesworth III. Departure was delayed while two souls were recovered from the attic that they were exploring.

Lunch at Furman University was followed by a visit to the Bob Jones University Museum of Religious Art and then to the Greenville Art Museum. Then another house: the handsome Victorian mansion of Mr. and Mrs. Sapp

Funderburk, two good Furman people who royally entertained the Wofford delegation at a tea. Next stop: Perone's restaurant for spaghetti supper, and then to Southern Railway's centralized train control room to watch in fascination the remote control of trains and tracks from Atlanta to Salisbury. The Greyhound headed to Spartanburg about 10 p.m., with the weary collegians aware that it rolled again next morning at 7:30 for a Chester-York area tour.

During the 3,200-mile trip, the bus was never as much as 30 minutes late. This feat was made possible by local guides and local "providers" who were as keenly conscious of a loaded, tight schedule as was the bus driver. Methodist churches literally stuffed the students—especially in smaller towns, where the lone restaurant or two would have been swamped with 32 hungry young men in a hurry. Holly Hill is an example—here the Wesleyans fetched forth mountains of barbecue. Three hours later the company of scholars was stuffing again at Harrietta Plantation, and two hours later at the Methodist Church in Georgetown. It was not only a historical tour but also a gastronomical expedition.

Can just anybody go into an orbit like the Wofford Interim? Yes. Judging from the number of requests for the condensed itinerary, a large number are so disposed. Begin by reading South Carolina history. Write county historical societies for available maps and brochures. Write chambers of commerce; some have especially helpful maps, guides and booklets. Many have historical trails and maps that permit traveling students to do their own guiding and studying. Obviously, individuals or families cannot get into all the places the Wofford orbiters did, but nearly all of the most intriguing places periodically do have tours of some homes and plantations.

What will you get from the experience? Maybe no more facts of history than you can get from the library, but you can get the feel and flavor of it—and enjoy it as much as a trip to Europe. It might even convert you. After all, one request for the Wofford itinerary came from the father of a bridegroom who was taking unto himself a Texan as wife. The purpose? To provide travel directions for a honeymoon-in-orbit in South Carolina that might perhaps dim some of the Texas talk! If you see one of these Wofford orbiters, he may ask you if you have ever been to Sedalia, or whether you think Mulberry Plantation in Kershaw is better than Mulberry Plantation in Berkeley. He's been there.

Prague 1969: Witness to History

In January 1969, an Interim trip made it possible for 16 Wofford students to be eyewitnesses to history. As originally conceived, their project was to explore the interface between science and government in Czechoslovakia, a Communist country where liberal reforms were in progress. Then, in August 1968, 600,000 Soviet troops moved into the country and replaced the government with a hardline regime. When faculty members B.G. Stephens '57 and James D. Bass learned that their trip would still be possible, they decided to go ahead and observe the volatile situation firsthand. The decision to go to Prague attracted wide attention.

Marion Peavey '65, the college's news media relations director, joined the trip and a crew was dispatched from the South Carolina Educational Television Network. When the Wofford group landed in Prague, they walked to the terminal between rows of heavily armed Communist soldiers. Then, on January 16, Czech student Jan Palach protested the invasion by self-immolation at the St. Wenceslas monument. Several Wofford travelers were present during the fiery incident, and the entire group witnessed the days of national mourning and protest that followed. The Prague Interim of 1969 proved to be a unique and life-changing experience.

Don Woodward '72 and Peter Larson '70 in Prague.

Joe Lesesne: *A Good Man and a Good President*

In an age with few heroes, it becomes even more important to honor those who stand above the crowd. Several years ago, Furman University had the privilege of bestowing an honorary doctoral degree on Joab Lesesne on the occasion of his retirement as president of Wofford College. He had led

to earn his master's and doctoral degrees in history from the University of South Carolina. He began his career at Wofford in 1964 as an assistant professor of history, and he soon distinguished himself in the classroom. Lesesne was a luminous teacher who made the past shine with interest and significance.

Professor Lesesne was appointed assistant dean in 1967. Soon thereafter, he implemented the college's Interim term, a four-week winter learning program that has become an indispensable part of a Wofford education. He later became director of development and then dean of the college. In 1972, at the ripe age of 34, he was named Wofford's ninth president. Lesesne quickly realized that going from the faculty to the presidency meant abandoning righteousness for pragmatism. He also discovered that a college president needs the endurance of an athlete, the wisdom of a Solomon, and the courage of a lion. But perhaps most important is to have the stomach of a goat in order to accommodate all of the civic club luncheons, campus banquets and meals-on-the-run.

As a resolute champion of the distinctive virtues of residential liberal arts colleges, Lesesne led Wofford through a remarkable era of progress, change and achievement. The college's endowment soared during his long tenure, new buildings were constructed, and he helped attract a stronger, more diverse faculty and student body. Along the way, President Lesesne displayed extraordinary composure and resilience. Hard to surprise and even harder to shock, he displayed the magnanimity of a saint in dealing with complaints and crises.

President Lesesne became a leader of national prominence within the higher education community. He was the first southerner to chair the board of the National Association of Independent Colleges and Universities, and he headed the council of presidents of South Carolina's private colleges.

In addition, he is a retired major general in the South Carolina Army National Guard, and he has chaired the South Carolina Commission on Natural Resources.

Yet the real value of a career can sometimes be better gauged by a person's character than by a public portfolio. Joe Lesesne is a genial representative of a fast vanishing world of grace, civility, loyalty, faith and moral rectitude. A warm man with a big heart, he has no

President Lesesne enjoys being roasted by the Salvation Army at a benefit in 1995. ~ Courtesy of the Spartanburg *Herald-Journal*

the Methodist college for 28 years. And he served it well—with a special genius that everyone observed yet no one can define.

Joe Lesesne was raised on a college campus. His father, a Wofford graduate, served as president of Erskine College. After graduating from Erskine, the younger Lesesne went on

enemies—even among those who disagree with him. Known for his casual intensity and refreshing humility, he loves to tell stories and to catch fish.

For almost 30 years as a college president, Joe Lesesne manifested unshaken nerve, rescuing wit, and, above all, a love for Wofford that has never waned. He had a special affection for students. He teased them, entertained them, inspired them and guided them. They responded with equal affection.

It has been invigorating to be befriended by such a wise colleague. I cannot imagine anyone more effective at helping the people of this state appreciate the important role played by Wofford and the other private liberal arts colleges. Joe Lesesne is one of those refreshing people who prefers to grin rather than scowl, banter rather than pontificate. What a wonderful mentor he has been to me and many others.

In his compassionate awareness of others, in his instinctive respect for them, in his declared willingness to help, in his courtesy, tolerance and gentleness, Joe Lesesne demonstrated that the highest intelligence is at its most fertile and expressive when allied to the deepest humanity. As to all of these traits, he has provided us the great gift of his example.

Blessed are those who perform good works and earn our respect and admiration.

Thanks, Joe.

— *David Shi*
President, Furman University

This tribute first appeared in Dr. Shi's regular column in The Greenville News.

In his own words ...

from President Lesesne's Inaugural Address, April 12, 1973

"This is a living institution that prizes individual freedom of its people, and its methods of operation are more the result of history than design. The success of it depends upon cooperation and respect, which I believe can be expected because our own self-interest and the interest of our friends are so tightly bound. There is no more urgent responsibility than to help students develop a philosophy of life—or faith—which provides a fundamental understanding and purpose for life.

"We must continue to use our flexibility to develop new ideas and new techniques to better meet the needs of our students. Sensitivity to aesthetics is necessary to fully enjoy life. Therefore, we will provide opportunities for students to develop a basic understanding and appreciation of the beautiful.

"We are more convinced than ever that students will find a liberal arts education to be the most useful education for an information-centered world. Such a world will require ... an education that provides both the cultural background and the mental discipline and agility necessary for educational renewal and personal adaptability. We intend to put more conscious effort into the study of value questions, those motivating beliefs that establish our view of life and our basis for sound judgments.

"No distinguished institution can operate fully on student fees and the difference between those fees and full costs must be covered by someone. At a college like Wofford, that margin is paid for by alumni, parents, and friends, and the United Methodist Church. I believe Wofford has a bright future because of those of you who care enough to make it bright."

The Lesesne family portrait: Joe, Joey, Julie (a 1981 Wofford graduate), Harry, Lyle and Ruth

A *Library Retrospective*

The Whitefoord Smith Library (remodeled and renamed the Daniel Building in the 1970s) had been in service since the first decade of the 20th century. Even though the original building had been enlarged with the addition of wings on either end, the structure was too small even for the student body of the 1950s. Still, the building retained its 1910 Carnegie-style layout, with large reading rooms flanking an entrance with book stacks crowded behind the reading rooms. Students of the 1960s characterized the library as hot in both winter and summer, dusty from the furnace powering the heating system, and woefully crowded.

With the hiring of Frank J. Anderson as librarian in 1966, the college began planning for a new building. The draft of a Library Plan for Wofford College was submitted to President Charles F. Marsh in February 1966. In the document, the library planning committee addressed the physical requirements for a first-class library as well as other pressing deficiencies the members saw as holding the college back—the library's inadequate budget, the small staff, and the need for program space to enhance the academic program. A seminal statement declared, "The new library must create by its appearance the impression of a new possibility for education in a new pattern at Wofford. It must do so by defining the college's interest in having a place where books are readily available and attractively displayed, and where the primary concern is for a certain

relationship between students and learning."

In the new building, beautifully designed by Lyles, Bissett, Carlisle & Wolfe, those hopes were realized to a remarkable extent. An attractive open design encouraged studying, group work, recreational reading, browsing, and lounging. No walls or barriers separated the readers and the books. The building's neutral limestone walls and warm walnut paneling combined with large windows to open the interior space to the outside. The new building included a range of seating options, group study rooms, a gallery space, microfilm and index rooms, and, above all, three times the space of the old library.

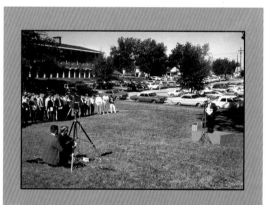

"*God of Wisdom, who dost call us from the darkness of ignorance into the light of understanding, we pray that this building for which we break ground may be a place where mental horizons are broadened and knowledge is deepened. Help us to find the joy that comes to those who seek after wisdom. May those who study here develop not only intellectual fitness, but also spiritual maturity. Thus may we carry forward to fulfillment the high vision of those whose dreams and sacrifices have led us to this day. We pray through Jesus Christ our Lord. Amen.*"

—*Donald S. Stanton, Chaplain*
Groundbreaking prayer, October 19, 1967

Much of the public architecture of the 1960s was undistinguished, but the design of the Sandor Teszler Library has withstood the test of time, inside and out. The late David James Edwards Jr. worked on the project while he was associated with the Columbia firm of Lyles, Bissett, Carlisle and Wolfe.

The new building opened on October 11, 1969, after 95,000 volumes had been carried across the campus drive from the old facility. On March 27, 1971, the building was dedicated as the Sandor Teszler Library. Mr. Teszler, whose portrait now hangs on the entrance floor, remained a regular visitor to the library named for him. A native of Hungary, he had fled Communism and come to the United States in 1948. In the 1960s he moved south and founded Olympia Mills. After his retirement, he continued to be a campus presence, taking two classes per term for 18 years, in effect becoming the campus grandfather until his death in 2000.

Under Frank Anderson's leadership (1966-1984) the library staff was enlarged to permit each department to be staffed by a professional librarian with an advanced degree. Impressive exhibitions were staged in the new gallery. During his tenure, Anderson operated the Wofford Library Press, a teaching press producing small editions of student-printed books during each January Interim term.

Many of the programs introduced during the building's early years continue to the present day, but with the advent of the technological revolution, both the building's requirements and the library programs have adapted and grown. In 1990, the old card catalog was replaced with a new automated library catalog. Simultaneously, the collection was reclassified from Dewey Decimal to the Library of Congress Classification System. The library went on to introduce its first CD-ROM electronic database in a stand-alone personal computer. Shortly thereafter a CD-ROM network was introduced, which made multiple databases available through a first-generation campus network. Eventually the growth in the amounts of electronic information made this system obsolete, and the library went on to offer dozens of World Wide Web databases and information services available across the much-expanded campus network.

At the end of 2004, the collection numbered 250,000 items (the holdings have diversified to the point that the librarians no longer count only books). In addition to the physical volumes on the shelves, the library provided access to nearly 40,000 electronic books and more than 9,000 electronic journals, as well as numerous encyclopedias, dictionaries, and specialized resources, such as databases of art slides and works of music. Catalog records were linked to library-produced Web pages, which provide more information and unique images, such as title pages from the rare books collection. Wireless access within the library was added during the 2004-2005 academic year. These current directions will continue to develop as information technology and innovation expand.

Within all these changes, the basic mission of the library has changed somewhat as well. The increasing complexity has meant that the need to teach students and faculty how to use the library has also increased, with two reference librarians now instructing every first-year student in the use of the library. These initial sessions are complemented by many upper-division courses and research components. The installation of the college Writing Center within the building has helped to further the integration of the library services into the educational mission of the college. No longer simply a repository for books, the Sandor Teszler Library is a laboratory where information is discovered and tested. Librarians no longer guard information within the walls of the library, but push access outside the doors and across the campus. They are no longer caretakers, but facilitators of what the planners of the building hoped for: "a certain relationship between students and learning."

—*Oakley H. Coburn*
Dean of the Library and Director of Academic Program Assessment

Groundbreaking for the Sandor Teszler Library was quickly followed by construction, and the new facility opened in 1969.

Under the leadership of Dean Oakley Coburn, the Sandor Teszler Library has a tradition of incorporating technological innovations into its operations.

Remembering Sandor Teszler

President Benjamin Dunlap wrote this tribute to Sandor Teszler for The Charlotte Observer, *where it first appeared in August 2000.*

Word of Sandor Teszler's death last week in Spartanburg brought back a wave a memories, including one that took place in a classroom five or six years ago. He was then a youthful 92.

We were screening the opening scene of Ingmar Bergman's "The Seventh Seal," in which a knight returned from the Crusades slumps wearily on a rocky Scandinavian shore. At that moment, a black-clad Death appears in classic theatrical guise, holding out his cloak to envelop the knight.

A tremulous Hungarian accent broke the heavy silence. "Uh-oh," it said, "this doesn't look so good."

But Mr. Teszler needn't have worried. He was still good for a number of years at that point, years full of the kindness and generosity that had marked his life for virtually all of the 20th century.

He had been born in the old Austro-Hungarian empire, where he was ostracized from childhood not so much because he was a Jew, but because he was afflicted with club feet that required many painful operations. From an early age he loved music, especially opera, and, later in life, he would befriend his fellow exile, the composer Bela Bartok.

Sandor Teszler

Extremely successful in the textile business, Mr. Teszler erred in supposing his contributions to society would protect him from the Nazis. He was wrong, almost fatally so, for he and his wife and two sons were taken to a death house on the Danube, where victims were systematically beaten to death. Midway through the beating, one of his sons pointed to the poison capsule each of them bore in a locket about his neck. "Is it time to take the pill now, Papa?" he asked.

Inexplicably, one of their tormentors leaned down to whisper in Mr. Teszler's ear, "Don't take the capsule. Help is on the way." Shortly afterwards, the family was rescued by an official from the Swiss embassy and taken to safety.

In Bergman's film, the knight stalls for time by challenging Death to a game of chess. If he wins, the knight will be spared. But the knight knows better than that. He merely seeks a reprieve that will allow him to commit a meaningful act.

Mr. Teszler's life had been full of meaningful acts. But after coming to this country and making another fortune, he set about improving the lives of everyone he met. In the aftermath of Brown v. the U.S. Board of Education—at about the time Ingmar Bergman was making his movie—Mr. Teszler noted the escalating rhetoric around him. "I have heard this talk before," he said. And, with a combination of shrewdness and saintliness worthy of Gandhi, he decided to integrate the workforce in his mills. He was the first in this region to do so.

Setting up heavy equipment in an unused high school gym, he took a group of workers for a prospective mill in Kings Mountain to live on the premises while learning the new operation. Half were white and half were black. After an initial tour of this temporary facility, he asked if there were any questions. Following an uneasy silence, one of the white workers raised his hand and said he was puzzled to find there was only one dormitory and one shower room.

"That is correct," Mr. Teszler answered. "You are being paid considerably more than other textile workers in this region, and this is how we do things. Are there any other questions?"

Picnic at the Lake, Endre Komáromi Katz (1880-1971), from Wofford's Teszler Collection of Hungarian art

"I guess not," the worker said.

Some weeks later when the new mill opened, workers of both races were greeted by a group of black and white foremen standing shoulder to shoulder.

"Are there any questions?" a black foreman asked.

After some shuffling about, one of the white workers raised his hand. "Let me get this straight," he queried. "Is this plant integrated?"

One of the white foremen stepped forward (he was the same man who had asked a similar question some weeks earlier). "That is correct," he said. "You're being paid a lot more than other textile workers in this region and this is how we do things. Any other questions?"

There were none.

For Mr. Teszler, such episodes served to confirm his faith that people are fundamentally good. And, in the company of this man with such persuasive cause for thinking otherwise, people did tend to discover their better selves.

In the last decade of his life, Sandor Teszler graced the campus of Wofford College, attending so many classes that the faculty, acknowledging a wisdom and experience greater than their own, honored themselves by making him an honorary professor. To hundreds of Wofford students he was simply "Opi," Hungarian for grandfather. The college library bears his name.

In the movie as in life, Death prevails in the end. But it doesn't win. Bergman's knight was a disillusioned Christian seeking some evidence for the existence of God in the human capacity for goodness.

Even his own determined act of charity leaves him somewhat unconvinced.

Had he met Sandor Teszler, he would have had no doubt.

Town Limits Landscape, Béla-Iványi Grünwald (1867-1940), from Wofford's Teszler Collection of Hungarian art

At Commencement 1987, President Joe Lesesne and Dr. Ross Bayard confer upon Sandor Teszler the honorary Doctor of Humanities degree.

Ab Can Do It

I have known Clarence "Ab" Abercrombie as long as I can remember. He and my father [Dean Dan Maultsby '61] used to teach in the sociology department at Wofford together. Our family sat near Ab at Wofford football games, and my brother, Alex, and I would visit with Ab when we went to Dad's office in the Daniel building. A Vietnam veteran who later gave my father a camouflage sweater for Christmas, Ab was and is, nonetheless, a gentle person—sort of like Mister Rogers in an Army jacket.

As a student at Wofford, I only took one course with Dr. Abercrombie. I steered clear of the mathematics and science courses he teaches. I went with his human ecology course, in the sociology department. It was a great class, all about the relationship between human beings and their natural surroundings. Dr. Abercrombie's travels throughout the world and time spent with remote cultures made strict use of a textbook unwarranted; we read selected books, but his firsthand accounts provided ample class content.

Ab has taken time away from Wofford throughout the years to concentrate on any number of academic pursuits. One is his study of crocodiles. He's a foremost expert on the fearsome reptiles. When "The Crocodile Hunter" became a TV hit in the late 1990s, my pal Peter Cooper '93 and I joked that the host, Steve Irwin, had stolen Ab's gig. Ab said he'd never seen the show but had been a guest at Irwin's crocodile zoo in Australia. "Terri (Irwin's wife) gave me a hug when I got there," I remember Ab saying.

Ab Abercrombie

Ab didn't get his TV show, but Peter and I thought he at least deserved a song. It's sort of a silly tune, probably one most appropriate for the very young. But we've had fun with it, Texas folk singer Eric Taylor heard it and liked it (Eric's approval is good enough for us), and as far as I can tell, Ab has taken it well.

—Baker Maultsby '92

"Ab Can Do It"
from the CD *Bingo=Sin*

Who can catch a crocodile?
Ab can do it
Has a pet reptile
Ab can do it
Makes the little children smile
Ab can do it
If Ab can do it, you can do it, too

Who knows the Africans?
Ab can do it
Been to the hinterland
Ab can do it
He's friends with a bushman
Ab can do it
If Ab can do it, you can do it, too

He's a good ole boy with a PhD
He's just the way that we want to be
He can do what he wants, so he does what he can
Clarence Abercrombie is a mighty, mighty man

Who can write a trucker song?
Ab can do it
Tell you 'bout the Amazon
Ab can do it
Sleeps with his boots on
Ab can do it
If Ab can do it, you can do it, too

He's a honky-tonk man with a PhD
He can cross a river, can climb up a tree
He can do what he wants, so he does what he can
Clarence Abercrombie is a mighty, mighty man

Who's a great American?
Ab can do it
A humanitarian
Ab can do it
Who's a big sports fan?
Ab can do it
Explains relativity
Ab can do it
Who can eat collard greens?
Ab can do it
Who can catch a crocodile?
Ab can do it

ENLIVENING THE ARTS

I n the mid-60s, Wofford College was described by President Charles Marsh as an "Oasis of Tranquility," suggesting that the community was isolated from the unrest of the real world. Perhaps the campus was an oasis, but for the fine arts, Wofford was more of a desert—the fine arts scene was pitifully underdeveloped. But the late 1960s and early 1970s were a time of change. Students became more socially conscious and aware of their intellectual energy. They wanted to express themselves in numerous ways, to find more outlets for their creativity. They were ready for energetic, artistic professors to harness their enthusiasm and begin building a foundation for a dynamic, vibrant fine arts program.

Fortunately, three pivotal faculty members came to the college convinced that everyone on campus should experience and enjoy the arts, and that, if challenged and motivated, Wofford students would rise to the challenge of doing work of high quality, even though majors in the arts were years away. These faculty members are profiled on the following three pages.

The Oasis of Tranquility did not survive the turbulent changes and unrest of the late '60s and '70s, but the fine arts found all the nourishment needed among Wofford faculty and students. The result was a vibrant campus fine arts environment that three college faculty members knew was no mirage.

—Tom Lentz '70
Vice President,
Broyhill Furniture Industries

Cast photo from a January
Interim production of *Grease*
in 1988 *(left)*; Dr. Victor
Bilanchone conducts a
community orchestra at a
holiday concert.

Constance Antonsen's Art History

D r. Constance Dean Armitage Antonsen joined the Wofford faculty in 1963. Having traveled the world extensively, she had her own impressive collection of Asian and Italian *l'objet d'art* including a full-sized statue of Hadrian from the Roman Empire in her backyard garden on Connecticut Avenue. In her art history lectures, Antonsen captivated students with her passion for her subject, particularly in the advanced courses covering the Italian Renaissance, Oriental and Greco-Roman art.

Few students forgot her descriptions of climbing through ruins and into tombs to see first-hand many of the ancient world's great art treasures. She brought to her classes not only compelling lectures, but a completely new perspective to the words "art history." A foundation of interest and enthusiasm for the visual arts was laid for what became an academic major, staffed by two full-time professors, Dr. Peter Schmunk and Dr. Karen Goodchild.

With the introduction of the first Interim in 1968, Antonsen was one of the pioneering faculty members who offered a foreign travel experience for Wofford students. In her Interim, students experienced the art and architecture treasures of Italy during January 1968.

Antonsen's career reflected the virtues of a true Renaissance woman She brought to her work at Wofford a reading or speaking knowledge of 13 languages. She competed internationally in fencing prior to beginning her academic career, and then she promoted and coached the sport on the intercollegiate level at Wofford for two decades. She served a term as president of the National Federation of Republican Women. During the Reagan administration, she chaired the White House Council on Aging.

—*Tom Lentz '70 with Doyle Boggs '70*

The *Music* of *Victor Bilanchone*

D r. Victor Bilanchone arrived at Wofford in 1972 as professor and director of music. He accepted a challenge different from the ones faced by his colleagues Antonsen and Gross, who had started programs from scratch.

"Dr. B" first had to revive Wofford's strong Men's Glee Club tradition; then, with the admission of women as students, he turned his attention to creating a mixed ensemble, the Concert Choir, which performed major works. He did all this with skill and gusto.

For years, Wofford concerts attracted standing-room-only audiences for performances of repertoire ranging from the Glee Club's crowd pleaser "Honey Brown" to Handel's *Messiah*, the Bach *Magnificat*, and the Vivaldi *Gloria* performed by the Concert Choir accompanied by a community orchestra with Bilanchone conducting. During this time, the character of Wofford's music program deepened and broadened in a way that was unexpected on a campus where there was no music major. Bilanchone initiated several ensembles, including a show choir, which he directed for several years, a string ensemble and a concert band.

In the 1970s and 1980s, Bilanchone renewed an aggressive performance schedule that took Wofford performers to international venues such as the 1980 Collegiate Choral Festival in Mexico City and the International Music Festival in Nassau. In the late 1980s and early 1990s, Bilanchone worked with Gross on a series of well-received Interim musical plays, beginning with *The Threepenny Opera*. The year 1993 saw the Concert Choir traveling to Carnegie Hall in New York City to perform *Magnificat* under the direction of John Rutter, the composer of the work. And, in 2000, the Concert Choir undertook a tour of Italy that included singing at Mass in St. Peter's Basilica in Vatican City.

Since then, numerous alliances among students in various fine arts disciplines have broadened the offerings available to Wofford and the community.

—Tom Lentz '70 with Doyle Boggs '70

J.R. Gross *and the* Wofford Theatre Workshop

In the fall of 1966, Dr. James R. Gross arrived as an assistant professor in the English department, and the performance arts received a personality who shaped a major intellectual and creative outlet for the remainder of the 20th century at Wofford.

Gross had taken numerous theater courses during his studies at Wake Forest, and his passion for the theater was obvious to his students. The new Interim term provided the ideal opportunity for Gross to unleash the pent-up creative energy of many Wofford students. In January 1968, the first Theatre Workshop Interim class was intrigued, challenged and energized by the opportunity of bringing theater to the campus. The students produced three plays that were

with limited experience.

Students inspired by these Interim productions encouraged Gross (who was becoming known affectionately as J.R. to his troupe of thespians) to produce more plays during the regular semesters with volunteer actors and staff. In 1969, Harold Pinter's *The Birthday Party* debuted to great acclaim in a makeshift theater environment created in the Montgomery Room of the Burwell Building. Barbara Ferguson, a local drama enthusiast who made many important contributions to Wofford theatre over the years, played the female lead. Several women commuting students were also involved in the production.

A grant from the National Endowment for the Humanities in the early 1970s provided

performed for the Wofford community at the conclusion of the first January term, and two more productions followed in the 1969 Interim. The reaction of the college community was pride and amazement that such professional productions could be coaxed from Wofford students in a very short time without the benefit of extensive academic offerings in theater. These Interim performances began to solidify Gross' reputation as a skillful director able to extract admirable performances from young actors

funds for a fine arts department with someone teaching full time in theater. Gross relinquished his English teaching responsibilities. In the spring of 1973, he was given a permanent, albeit humble, theater space in the old campus dining hall in the abandoned Carlisle Hall dormitory. A three-sided arena stage was designed, and the extra space at Carlisle provided dressing rooms, a lobby and offices. During the 1974 Interim, several plays were produced and performed at venues throughout South Carolina. In 1981,

The dedication ceremony of the J.R. Gross Cascading Steps

when the new Campus Life building was designed, the fully equipped, black box Tony White Theater was an integral feature.

When Gross retired after a 37-year teaching career at Wofford, alumni and friends of the college honored him with the dedication of the James R. Gross Cascading Steps, a water feature on the Liberty Trail between Wofford and the Spartanburg Regional Medical Center. Dr. Mark Ferguson '94 succeeded him on the faculty as the college began offering a major in theatre in 2003-2004.

Mark Ferguson '94, shown here *(far left)* as a student with Dr. Gross, went on to earn a doctorate at Washington University and returned to Wofford to head the theatre major after his mentor retired. In the early 1980s *(right)*, Gross appeared in a production of *Equus* with Jeff Bell '85.

Four Years is a Mighty Long Time

This essay by Peter Moore '69 first appeared in the 1968 Bohemian yearbook. Moore, now retired after 30 years service in the South Carolina Department of Vocational Rehabilitation, continues his close association with Wofford and the Wofford strings program.

I was the freshman …
With hope I came to see, to conquer a brave new world
of cuff-less trousers, dance and drink, of sleepless nights and long weekends
of football games, occasional books, of cutting class and damning food,
only to find this brave new world, while brave, while new—
was a shadowy exterior of the old game called Life that I had known before.
Little had I anticipated
amid the tumultuous insincerity of first back slaps
and suave, much-practiced smiles
that too often I must know the horror of finding myself alone
with only a scrap of assignment sheet
and a feeling of guilt as a guide to finding myself.
I turned to those near me, in the hum of midnight conversation,
with question in my eyes, yet did not ask
for fear of being singled out as a questioner,
as one who tried to pull back the veil of mediocrity.
Yet soon I did find that all of us
were tugging at the veil, while obeying
the silent scream within us that said,
"Don't blow it all—four years is a mighty long time."

Dr. Joe Killian and a history class in the mid-1970s; pool in old Wightman Hall; Homecoming morning on fraternity row

I was the sophomore …
A wise old man by now I called myself
for I had peered into those dark, intellectual realms and found
not much that I could not understand.
but every now and then, very seldom actually,
when I had cleared my mind of the drone of pealing bells
and shuffling feet and meaningless hellos
I sat there in the silence of that dark room
and reached out—desperately, frantically
I grasped for something
to close my hand around
and call right and call real and call good.
There had to be something there
besides the emptiness and complacent, cheerful nothingness
that clouds my mind by day
and putrefies my dreams by night.
I looked in the face of my brothers that night,
I watched them in the class, in gym, at drill, and as they talked
I looked beyond the eyes, the smiles,
the profane declarations of hate and disgust
over the now of Life.
And found that they were searching, too,
as I was searching, as many others before us had searched,
and I knew there was something real—a foundation for life,
a value, I couldn't quite verbalize, but something
that made all this worthwhile.

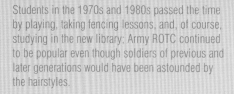

Students in the 1970s and 1980s passed the time by playing, taking fencing lessons, and, of course, studying in the new library; Army ROTC continued to be popular even though soldiers of previous and later generations would have been astounded by the hairstyles.

I was the junior …
Finding that I would have to leave
some things in this brave world to be conquered,
I took a deep breath and laughed long at Life
as I struggled toward a goal.
Mine were the joys of warm friendships and victory on the field.
And the sorrow of losing a friend and the agony of defeat
I suffered in solitude.
Sometimes the ludicrousness was overwhelming,
this constant drive toward something vague,
this constant search for a life to sink my teeth into,
but things were beginning to mean
and Life began to mean.
No longer was a book the despised reminder of tedious chore
but a friend—not my best friend, mind you—but a friend.
And questioning and finding out and damning food
and cuff-less trousers and long weekends
became the fringe of a tailored cloak I wore
with unpretentious hope.
Insincerity I found to be a mask that covered warmth.
And much-practiced smiles only hid an invitation
to a real bond.
I tossed aside the veil of mediocrity and established my selfness,
wanting to face the world and say,
"I am not afraid."
But fear was still a part of life, as I continued
to be judged by others' standards.
And I decided that four years was not
such a mighty long time.

The *Old Gold & Black* featured this cartoon about the "Big Streak" of 1974; The Gospel Choir entertained a range of audiences; Cats shared the campus home with the family of Dean of Students Mike Preston '63; Mark Olencki '75 looked this way as a campus photographer and yearbook editor in his student days. For three decades, he has captured the pulse of Wofford in his pictures.

OLD GOLD AND BLACK   March 5, 1974

"Well Dean, at least they're finally revealing their school spirit."

I am a senior …
An aborigine of the brave new world
and architect of awe-inspiring edifices of ideas.
I am a gazer into the future, and a rememberer of the past.
I look ahead and see another, even several brave new worlds,
waiting to be settled, to be conquered.
And I looked upon a place that taught me
that virtue is not obsolete,
that apathy cannot prevail
that integrity is earned, not bought.
And I looked back upon a place
where pleasure and pain are mixed to taste like life—
neither bitter nor sweet, but somehow good.
And I look back upon a place
where backslaps, books and long weekends
and toil and tears and hate and love
had weaned me on the milk of reality.
and I look back upon a place
I could call right
and call real
and call good
and I look back upon that place
with love.

Dr. Vincent Miller *(top)* thoroughly intimidated and inspired
several generations of students; cheerleaders looked like this
around 1980; D. J. Berard painted "Campus Life" in the mid-
1980s; the work now hangs in the Papadopoulos Building.

Student government leaders *(left)* Joe Patterson '69, George Corn
'69, Bill Harkey '69, Johnston Dantzler '69, Marvin Grooms '69
and John Bills '70 were hard at work on a Gulf Coast retreat when
this picture was snapped. The Vietnam War was raging at the
time; one way or another, Army service was the next stop for
many graduates of that era. ~Courtesy of George Corn

Remembering John Harrington

My true education began with a Wofford geology teacher, John Harrington, who died in 1986 at the age of 69.

I learned at least three good things from him: to read the land and discover in the dance of imagination and reason an intelligible world; to slide ideas against one another like sticks and delight in the sparks and smoke; and to see the connections that can be made in the world around me.

Harrington gave me a world where time moved in more than one direction, and no landscape holds steady for long. Because of him, I see children grind off benches the way glaciers slide down a mountain, lakes where they only once existed, and connections between grain sales and the paleoclimate of Russia.

In 1986, three weeks before his death from cancer, I had visited Harrington to confirm, once again, the magic of his teaching. I had been a student of his in the mid-1970s and an occasional correspondent since graduation. He was Wofford College's resident professor emeritus but had been confined to his bedroom since January. We could not walk the soapstone ridge near Lawson's Fork Creek as we had done many times in the past. The landscape of words and ideas would have to be a fitting field trip.

As we sat in his house on the outskirts of Spartanburg, he tried to convince me that he "was no Svengali." The magic he had worked for 20 years teaching geology at Wofford was nothing more than "having a little fun with rocks" he insisted. Harrington claimed he was just following in the field clothes of a few teachers who taught him to have a little fun. Just passing on a little understanding, he said.

When fresh out of graduate school, Harrington briefly worked for an oil company, but he found out in the first six months that he wasn't a corporation man. That's when he accepted a teaching post at Southern Methodist University. He taught the course designed to get rid of people who could not make it as geologists. He lasted seven years.

By the end, in 1955, he was spreading himself too thin: department head, in charge of a consulting firm downtown, trying to teach and write papers for geology journals. He also had trouble, as he put it, "being a lion tamer."

"The lion tamer doesn't actually tame anything," Harrington had said back then. "He gets in there with a chair and whip and gun, but really only stays within the genetic boundaries the cats establish. As a teacher, I felt the same way. I wasn't changing any of them. They were jumping on chairs because they knew it was safer there."

That year, while reading Rudyard Kipling's

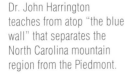

Dr. John Harrington teaches from atop "the blue wall" that separates the North Carolina mountain region from the Piedmont.

Just So Stories to his daughter, Harrington made a discovery that would change his life and teaching: "I realized you are not teaching students anything if they can't answer Kipling's 'why,' 'how' and 'which' questions." His students at SMU wanted to be taught "to be good technicians" so they could get jobs with oil companies. They did not see education as something they needed; graduation was what they needed. When Harrington tried to start teaching in a new way—a way he was not prepared for himself—he had a virtual riot on his hands.

A group of young geologists—one now a famous geologist with the space program—went to the dean and claimed that Harrington was incompetent. Their teacher gave the class a chance to vote on his methods. The students voted 28-2, with one abstaining vote, to uphold the charge of incompetence. Harrington admitted that, from the students' standpoint, they were right. He resigned from the university in the summer of 1956. "You don't always succeed," he said.

In his book, *Dance of the Continents*, Harrington described insight as the art of becoming personally aware. The insights of those Wednesday geology labs—in which Harrington taught me to see—are imprinted on my mind as clearly as the formula for the molecular structure of water, the multiplication tables or the parts of speech. In conversation, Harrington talked a great deal about genius. He suggested that genius was a field where anyone can stand. It was not some holy city populated only by people with high SAT scores or gifted and talented credentials or top-of-the-scale grade-point average.

One of the quickest ways to gain insight for Harrington was to open the door of time. He was once collecting on the cliffs at Lyme Regis on the southern coast of England. There he found an ancient ax head, a relic of paleo-Britain preserved among the cliff's rocks. Harrington could imagine the human being who made the ax so clearly that he was transported in time. "Separation in time was all that kept us from sharing my peanuts," he said about the moment. His genius may have been his pestering mind. No one was safe from the questions. Not college deans, freshmen or fellow travelers on airplanes or buses. When he got the answers, he let reason—what he called "least astonishment"—put them into context. "Follow me," Harrington told the class I was in. We boarded buses, and he took us out to see the world.

"I'm weak as water," Harrington said the

last time I saw him. I thought of rivers taking mountains down. As a teacher, I've begun to ask Kipling's (and Harrington's) questions of my students. As he taught me, I work daily to see life and death in context. Einstein once noted that "the example of the great and pure individual is the only thing that can lead us to noble thoughts and deeds." John Harrington hunted the pure paths of genius for much of his life. And what's more, he convinced a significant number more that they, too, could follow that path and discover genius in the context of every glistening stone.

—John Lane '77

The *NAIA Era*

It was the worst of times and the best of times: Wofford intercollegiate athletics in the 1970s and 1980s. During those decades, the college's investment in the program was insufficient to sustain the kind of success that would attract the best student-athletes, but greater than could be justified for "good time" sports. Facilities were unattractive and outdated. Though able and hard working, the coaching staffs were too small, and administrative support was minimal. In many sports, the Terriers competed with fewer scholarships than their opponents.

Still, competing with South Carolina colleges and universities of different types and missions in District 6 of the National

On June 8, 1973, at Gramling, South Carolina, Wofford's golf team became the state's first national collegiate champion in any sport, winning the NAIA tournament by a margin of 14 strokes. The Terrier medallist was Marion Moore '75, with a score of 216, third best among 185 golfers. Vernon Hyman '73 placed fourth with 217, while Pat Crowley '73 tied for seventh at 220, and Stan Littlejohn '73 finished at 222. The head of this unique golfing family was the late Coach Earle Buice, who was inducted into the NAIA National Hall of Fame in 1984. Buice was thoroughly devoted to his volunteer coaching job, in terms of time, commitment and even his own money when the equipment budget ran low.

In the early 1980s, Coach Buddy Sasser led

Coach Earle Buice *(kneeling, left)* with his 1973 national golf champions

Association for Intercollegiate Athletics (NAIA), there were some significant achievements.

Running a triple-option wishbone offense, the 1969 and 1970 football teams won 20 consecutive games against some tough opposition that included Davidson's 1969 Southern Conference champions. Coach Jim Brakefield's Terriers were ranked first in the NAIA for most of the 1971 season before losing to Texas A&I in the national championship game.

Wofford to a series of successful football campaigns, including an 8-3 season in 1982 that ended in controversy when the Terriers were left out of the NAIA playoff field. The most memorable afternoon of that era was probably a trip to Clemson for the season's opener in 1981. The Tigers finished the year as the undefeated NCAA national champions, but the Terriers played well in the first half and actually led at one point before losing 45-10.

Men's basketball teams won more than 20 games in 1974-75 under the legendary Coach Gene Alexander and in 1984-85 under Coach Wayne Earhardt. Hall of Fame players during those years were Doug Lowe '75, James Blair '83, Robert Mickle '85 and Wayne Rice '87. In 1985, Richard Johnson began his tenure of 17 successful seasons as the Terrier basketball coach.

Baseball Coach Mark Line, who had a 210-158 career record from 1986-95, won NAIA District Coach of the Year honors as the 1987 squad put together a 23-11 mark. Wofford then set a college record for victories the following year with a 27-12 season.

Men's soccer began as a club sport in 1968 and became a varsity program in 1975. Even without scholarships, Terrier soccer teams gradually became competitive at the NAIA level, achieving the program's first winning season at 9-6-1 in 1978.

Movement in a positive direction began in 1981 with the opening of a new home court for Terrier basketball, the Benjamin Johnson Arena in the Campus Life Building. An even more important step forward came in 1985, when the commitment was made to employ a senior administrator as a full-time director of athletics. Danny Morrison '75 accepted this challenge. By the end of the decade, it was easy to see improvements both in the caliber of student-athletes choosing Wofford and in the financial health of the program.

—Doyle Boggs '70
compiled from Wofford Today

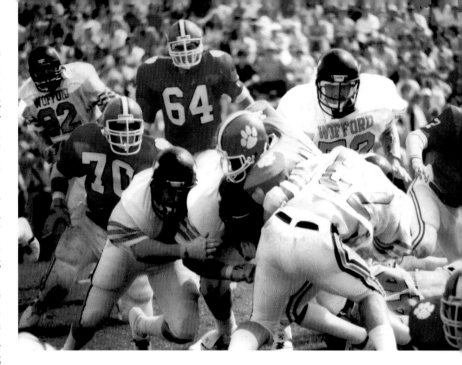

Wofford fielded its first men's varsity soccer teams in the early 1970s after several years of club-level competition; a scrappy Terrier football team put up a good fight in the 1981 season opener with eventual NCAA national champion Clemson University.

The Story of Stymie

A strong candidate for the title of the all-time Terrier mascot is Stymie, who was active in the 1972 and 1973 seasons. One fall afternoon in 1972 when the Terriers were sporting an 0-2 record, Stymie strayed into the dormitory room where football standouts Ed Wile and Tom Bower were watching television. She turned over their trash can and began nuzzling the remnants of their fast food lunch. The little dog adopted Bower on the spot, and the Terriers' luck changed immediately—they went on to upset Presbyterian and finished the year with six wins in the last eight games. In May 1974, Bower and Stymie walked across the commencement stage together, and Stymie received a miniature Wofford diploma to wear on her collar.

Women's Athletics: The Early Years

When the Wofford women's basketball team traveled in 2004, players rode in a chartered bus and dressed in classy uniforms. They played in the same Southern Conference arenas and stayed in the same hotels as the men's team.

What a difference a generation makes.

Although Wofford began admitting women resident students in 1976, it wasn't until 1980-81 that the college fielded intercollegiate women's athletics teams. In those early years, the men's and women's programs did not receive equal support or attention.

Karen Rhodes Cable '82 was a pioneer women's student-athlete at Wofford. "I had played ball all my life," she recalled. "When I

Meg Hunt '84 was the first woman to attend Wofford on an athletics scholarship. A member of the Wofford Athletics Hall of Fame, she later became an editor for the Spartanburg *Herald-Journal* and president of the National Federation of Press Women. She is pictured with Brad Eppley '84, captain of the men's team.

went to college, I didn't think I wanted to play varsity sports. But during my freshman year, 1978-79, I began to miss competing." Cable first looked into club sports because she remembered college brochures stating women's athletics teams were being planned, but she found that none were yet available. As a result, she played with a fraternity's intramural teams.

In 1979, Patricia Gainey was hired to direct the women's athletics programs and to move the Terriers into varsity status by 1980-81. She coached both the volleyball and basketball teams through 1983-84.

Karen Weishuhn Harris '83 was the captain for both the volleyball and basketball teams during her time at Wofford. She had received an academic scholarship, and basketball at the club and later intercollegiate level was an added attraction. "I was already coming to Wofford, so my attitude was, 'I play ball. Do you offer it?'"

Meg Hunt '84, the first woman to receive a Wofford athletics scholarship, averaged 23 points in her first five games as a Terrier. Amy Harrison '85 was the only other scholarship player on the 1980-81 squad.

Hunt and Harris both recalled some unusual challenges as well as initial resistance. "Nothing vicious was ever said to our faces," says Hunt. "Any resistance we felt was much more subtle. Professors didn't always want to let us out of lab for games or practice. And sometimes we would hear snide comments about our being women athletes."

The most serious problem stemmed from the fact that there was only one full-sized court on campus, in Andrews Field House. The scheduling of it was so difficult that women often had to practice at 6 a.m. Hunt recalled having to work around the men's practice and game schedule. "We even had to surrender the gym floor to the fencing team and intramural tournaments at times."

"Once women entered Wofford," she said, "there was more of a sense of inevitability [regarding athletics opportunities]. What I do recall was the sense that we were an afterthought—that Wofford would do this as cheaply and as simply as possible."

Hunt recalled, "We had to sell programs at the football games to raise money to buy warm-up suits. We rode in vans rather than buses, and the food on road trips wasn't great either. [A good meal was a box lunch with a

piece of chicken in it instead of a sandwich.]
Sometimes we would forego food altogether
on a shorter trip so we could have more money
for food on the longer road trips."

Although the women endured less-than-
attractive conditions, Hunt noted, "We never
did think about quitting."

There were some students and faculty who
actively supported the women in their new
venture. Hunt recalled Dr. Dennis Wiseman,
Dr. Lee Hagglund, Dr. Philip Racine and Dr.
Deno Trakas coming out and scrimmaging
with them, because the team did not have
enough players for five-on-five practice
sessions.

"I remember several varsity athletes,
including James Blair, Mike Howard and Tim
Renfro, who really supported us," said Hunt.
"They would practice with us and come to our
games. Only occasionally did we have to
remind any of them that their role wasn't to
win, but to help us improve."

"We didn't have depth, height or skill,"
concluded Cable of that 1980-81 squad. "Our
center, Janet Nixon, was 5 feet, 8 inches, and
she was a fashion model. Teams like Winthrop
had players well over six feet tall. One of our
teammates didn't even play high school ball.
She played church league. But we finished
with a winning record."

Despite the many obstacles they faced, the
1980-81 women finished with a 12-10 record.
In their sixth game of the season, Wofford and
Converse met in athletics for the first time.
Pam Parnell and Amy Harrison carried the
team with a 27-point combined first-half
scoring performance, and Hunt scored 15

second-half points as the Lady Terriers
defeated the All-Stars 64-48.

Those first years had less tangible positive
outcomes, added Harris. "I remember a lot of
camaraderie, a lot of silliness," she said. Harris
recalled that, as one home game approached,
it became public that Winthrop intended to
score 100 points on the Lady Terriers. Wofford
held the Eagles to 90-odd points. The women
received windbreakers as a reward. "Our
uniforms that year were Wofford shorts and
T-shirts from the bookstore, so getting
windbreakers was a big deal."

The women's volleyball team endured a
similar beginning. Roberta Hurley Bigger '81
played with Harris and Cable on the college's
first volleyball team, a club team, in 1979-80.
The men's basketball coach did not want to
adjust his team's practice schedule,
so the women ended up practicing at
6 a.m.," recalled Bigger. "The only
people who came to the games were
friends and boyfriends." Still, she said,
"It was fun to be one of the first
women athletes."

—*Sarah Ross Cohen '88*

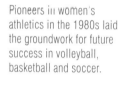

Pioneers in women's
athletics in the 1980s laid
the groundwork for future
success in volleyball,
basketball and soccer.

The Douglas Wood Story

For the better part of 50 years, my family has been associated with this fine college. My grandfather, the late Russell Arthur Miller, was a groundskeeper here and worked from President Walter K. Greene all the way to President Joe Lesesne. He was my first teacher of Wofford history, and in my youth regaled me with stories of Wofford's presidents, professors and students. His historical accounts of Wofford instilled within me an intense pride in this college's many contributions to humanity. Because of him, I became convinced that in order to understand and comprehend the moral and philosophical complexities of the mission and future of this college, one must at once become learned in its history.

— Douglas E. Wood '90
Receiving the Young Alumnus of the Year Award, 2001

In 2004, Dr. Douglas Wood was named the founding director and principal director of the National Academy for Excellent Teaching at Columbia University's Teachers College in New York City. His assignment was to work with teachers and administrators across the country to establish a new national model for high school teachers.

to help teachers install technology, and inspired teachers and administrators with his sense of humor and risk-taking. "I love bringing people to the table—whether they are legislators, teachers or parents—to focus on doing the right things for young people," said Wood.

After graduation from Wofford, Wood became a classroom teacher in Columbia, South Carolina. He also participated in a yearlong telecommunications and cultural exchange with counterparts in Japan. After completing a master's degree at Middlebury College, Wood earned his doctorate at the Harvard University Graduate School of Education. Faculty honored him for outstanding academic achievement during the 1996-97 and 1997-98 school terms. His research also won Harvard's John E. Thayer Academic Prize, a university-wide award, for "meritorious scholarship."

Dr. Douglas Wood '90 with his grandfather and President Lesesne at graduation, and as a Columbia University faculty member in 2004.

Wood was selected for this position because of his work as executive director of the Tennessee State Board of Education. During his tenure (2000-2004), Wood expanded the state's reading, teacher quality and early childhood education programs. He also championed English as a Second Language programs in the schools. Described as fresh thinking, energetic, charismatic and progressive, Wood visited all of Tennessee's counties without once checking into a hotel, preferring instead to stay in the homes of educators or parents. He crawled under desks

The *Laura Griffin Story*

Historic Charleston hardly ever closes—except on one mid-winter Saturday morning. Since January 1997, the city has held the annual Laura Griffin Memorial 5-K Run to honor a 1983 Wofford graduate. Griffin's phenomenal accomplishments and dedication to helping others prompted the city and the College of Charleston to organize the event.

Laura Griffin was struck and killed by an automobile as she jogged along The Battery on the evening of January 17, 1996. The driver of the vehicle was intoxicated, and, ironically, at the time of her death, Griffin was serving as the director of the College of Charleston's Office of Substance Abuse Prevention.

"Wofford took a timid little girl, gave her a scholarship and molded her into a beautiful, caring leader," her mother recalled. During her college years, Griffin was active in student government, participated in Kappa Delta social sorority, and was the 1982 Wofford Homecoming Queen. She was inducted into Phi Beta Kappa and Blue Key. Majoring in French and psychology, Griffin studied abroad in Rennes, France. She started on the men's tennis team before there was a comparable program for women players. Later, she served as an active director of the Wofford National Alumni Association.

Laura Griffin began her life after graduation as a marketing analyst and training specialist for Sonoco Products Company, an international packaging corporation with operations in almost 100 nations around the world. She took a year's leave of absence, beginning in October 1985, to accept a Rotary International Scholarship for study in Manchester, England. There she completed a master's degree in industrial and organizational psychology.

A year after her return from England, Griffin moved to Charleston, where she counseled young people between the ages of 18 and 25 and eventually found her professional niche at the College of Charleston. She soon began work on a doctoral degree in clinical and community psychology at the University of South Carolina. She was completing a dissertation at the time of her death. The doctoral degree was awarded posthumously.

—Kristin Sams '05

President Joe Lesesne crowns the late Laura Griffin '83 at halftime of the 1982 Homecoming game.

If You've Got Wings, Fly

Professor of Philosophy Walt Hudgins joined the Wofford faculty in 1972 and served actively until his death on May 30, 1986. He was known as someone who made students think. He also encouraged them to explore a variety of interests, as he had. An ordained minister, Hudgins also wrote plays and had worked as an accountant. At his death, Hudgins left money to the college. Several of his friends also made gifts in his memory. A faculty committee formed and created an award to recognize students outside of the mainstream who dared to be different and had a sense of adventure. Recipients are encouraged to use the monetary award given along with a plaque to travel or do something interesting that they might not normally do. The following is from a speech he gave at Wofford College Scholars Day in 1980. This excerpt was edited by Linda Powers Bilanchone of the Wofford faculty.

When I was asked to make this speech, I told them I was not funny and could not tell jokes. They said I was funny-looking, and that was good enough. But I was not always funny looking. I once looked like Robert Redford.

Does your hometown have a phony place that makes phony promises? One such place in Spartanburg is our health spa with plastic Greek statues and appropriate plastic fig leaves in appropriate plastic places. My wife gave me a guest pass to the health spa for my birthday. I think that she was trying to tell me something. When I went into this plastic health resort, the man-in-charge spent much time trying to sell me a membership, telling me how I could look like Robert Redford. I spent an enjoyable hour with machines that can mold and melt you, push and pull you into anybody you want to be. I looked into the mirrors—the room is covered with mirrors—and I begin to think, "I am … I am beginning to look like Robert Redford." …

Aren't you Wofford Scholars the Robert Redfords of the world—handsome, beautiful, gifted, talented? … Several years ago the man who won the Nobel Prize for Literature was García Márquez, who loved to tell fanciful stories about the price one has to pay to live in this world. One such story is about a couple named Pelayo and his wife, Elisendra, who dig for crabs. One day while crabbing they found an old man lying face down in the mud by the sea. I guess he was like all old men lying face down in the mud except he had enormous buzzard wings, and they were dirty and half-plucked and filled with lice.

Pelayo didn't know what to do with the old man so he put him in a chicken coop, and the people came to look at this strange creature that had washed up on the shore. The local priest knew he wasn't an angel because he couldn't speak Latin. And the people knew he wasn't an angel because a blind man went to see him. Rather than recovering his sight, he grew 18 extra teeth. But nonetheless they were willing to pay five cents to see this special man with grimy wings. Pelayo built him a special nest and fed him eggplant mush.

Some people thought the old man should be named mayor of the world. Those of sterner stuff thought he should be named a seven-star general. And though they talked, all they could think to do was to keep him in a coop and charge five cents a look. And though the old man with wings was smarter than the rest of them and more decent than the rest of them, they could not see he was special for that. Only that he was a funny old man with buzzard wings. They knew they didn't have Robert Redford on their hands. Well, one day the old man just flew away from his own special hell—the chicken coop. …

Soon it will be time for you to fly away, not to become Robert Redford, but to sharpen

Dr. Walt Hudgins

your wings so that from your heights you can get a better sight of things? … It is a widespread belief that bright students can get by on their own. After all, you have wings. After all, you are the Robert Redfords of the academic world. The educational system has cheated you if it has allowed you just to get along—if it has put you into a chicken coop.

But the past is prologue. Your high school days—your days when you grew up protected by loving parents and relatives—the day when someone else controlled your destiny and the money spent on your destiny and the hours you kept and the hours you threw away—all that is prologue. A prologue to a special hell— called college—where you will be held accountable for your own destiny. Are your hopes and your visions more deserving of a destiny than most? I would not be foolish enough to call you geniuses—nor look upon you as pure vessels of virtue set down in this land of Babylon—but I hope that I would be bright enough to know that perhaps you are a little more keen, a little more acute, a little more astute than many of your fellow students. Some of you perhaps sitting here tonight— will end up in a chicken coop of a world, never being able to fly. … All too many do. And Wofford is trying to say by this scholarship program—"If you got wings—darn it—fly!"

Commencement exercises throughout the 1970s, 80s and 90s were held at Spartanburg Memorial Auditorium, but the classes did enjoy a traditional processional across the campus and through the front gate to North Church Street. As faculty marshal, Dr. Dennis Dooley led the graduates for many of those years.

Sixth
Generation
1987-2004

GLOWING YEARS
OF MOMENTUM, 1984-2004

by Larry T. McGehee

In the decades after World War II, Wofford's claim to fame was that it preserved liberal arts in South Carolina while operating financially in the black year after year and maintaining an enrollment right around 1,000.

President Joe Lesesne, left, celebrates a "New Track Record in Annual Giving" with Mark Christian '90, J.E. Reeves Jr., the late Marshall Chapman, Rob Gregory '64, and Steve Powell '63.

In a universe of 3,700 American colleges and universities, it was a twinkle in the eye, not very sturdy in resource underpinnings but steady in its focused orbiting.

All of that changed one day in 1985. That was the year that the F. W. Olin Foundation rejected Wofford College.

In 1984, the administration had asked the New York-based foundation to fund a high-tech classroom building designed to permit a 33 percent increase in the number of faculty members. One of 92 colleges seeking an Olin grant, Wofford learned in early 1985 that it was one of five finalists. But, when the smoke had cleared from intensive building design and documentations and a foundation site visit, Olin President Lawrence W. Milas wrote that

the college would not receive the grant. The date was August 22, 1985.

Sometime after the rejection, as the college sought to find out what had gone amiss in its application, someone at the F. W. Olin Foundation said that Wofford, although a fine candidate, was, by comparison with the winner that year, "stunted." At the October 1985 Board of Trustees meeting, the coffee break discussions all revolved around that word. It carried subsidiary negative connotations and indictments: retarded, apathetic, provincial, non-aggressive and shoddy.

The October 1985 bubbling among trustees reached volcanic dimensions in February 1986, when President Joe Lesesne informed the board that the foundation was willing to accept another application from Wofford if it could demonstrate more progressive energy in its planning and program building. The board, headed by its first woman chair, Anne Springs Close, approved changing its forthcoming May meeting to a major three-day retreat. Its aim was to get Wofford up and moving, into the major league of American higher education.

A growing number of endowed professorships and faculty chairs enabled Wofford to attract additional nationally recognized scholars and teachers. In 1993, Dr. Benjamin B. Dunlap was appointed the first Chapman Professor of the Humanities at Wofford. Seven years later, he became the college's 10th president.

In 1986, Wofford's trustees went into retreat for three days at Springmaid Beach, analyzed "where the college was, where it should want to be, and how to get there." Then, it formed a task force of more than 100 trustees, alumni, faculty, staff and students that met monthly as committees for a year, with President Lesesne and new Board Chairman Russell C. King '56 as co-chairs and Vice President Larry McGehee as planning coordinator.

With its Masterplan, the college had established a planning process it had never had before. Since that time, Wofford has operated in a planning mode, with regular retreats to review and update the college's progress and goals and with subsequent task forces on athletics, technology networks, sciences enhancement, curricular reforms and development campaigns. At least a thousand alumni, faculty, students, donors, trustees and consultants have provided thousands of hours of planning to the work of the college since May 1986. Subsequent board chairs—Walt Sessoms '56, Rob Gregory '64, Russell King again, and Minor Shaw—all have been committed to the Wofford planning process.

The planners themselves became investors in, or solicitors for, the college. In 1981-82, a national fundraising consulting firm, asked to study Wofford's prospects for raising $30 million in a campaign, sadly reported the goal was not feasible, and that Wofford could probably raise only $6 million, perhaps $9 million with some luck. For the first 12 years of the Masterplan (1988-99), Wofford was asked to raise $100 million in gifts; when 1999 ended, it had raised $108.6 million. In Phase I of the 1987 Masterplan, the college sought $30 million in new personnel, program and capital funds, and secured more than $33 million. In Phase II, the college sought $75 million and secured more than $90 million. In a campaign coinciding with the college's 150th anniversary celebration, Wofford set a goal of more than $100 million again, primarily for endowed professorships and endowed scholarships, and for some capital improvements such as renovation of Main Building.

Almost every American college in the 19th century was the shadow of one person, whether president or primary donor, but Wofford College in 2004 represented the collective enterprise of many otherwise individualistic women and men possessing varied interests and talents. Just as the *Mayflower* brought a whole community to

Plymouth Rock, Wofford College's year of planning was a voyage of many, not just of a few. Ever since, the support infrastructure for Wofford has expanded exponentially. Expanded ownership has been the key to the college's momentum.

Wofford constituencies have taken justifiable pride in Wofford's age, admissions applications, academic standards, fiscal efficiency and effectiveness, student performance, faculty excellence, physical appearance, peer-college approval, singularly undergraduate mission, donor support,

alumni and trustee distinctions, Phi Beta Kappa status and classical liberal arts model. Wofford College has done things well. Effective planning did not change Wofford's classical college commitment—*well-selected students working with well-selected professors in liberal learning, in-residence and round-the-clock*—but it improved the internal programs and external visibility that are the servants of that commitment. As the college's plans have been implemented, Wofford has gained improved quality control and wider geographical marketing and recognition.

By turning rejection into opportunity, Wofford College moved in less than two decades from being "stunted" to being "stunning."

To the naked eye, the physical transformation of Wofford was most evident. Wofford property has expanded north and east, growing from 90 acres when planning began to nearly 150 acres today. The Spartanburg

Graduation rates are perhaps the single most important measure of quality in an undergraduate college. Eighty percent of the students entering the college in the fall of 1988 earned degrees within six years

Regional Medical Center and Wofford College moved toward each other, connected by a health walkway, Liberty Trail, and the J. R. Gross Cascading Steps of boulders and brook. Meanwhile, more than 5,000 trees have been planted, sprinkler systems installed for lawns, roads and walks moved about, and the campus has become a national arboretum, complete with labeled "noble trees" and walking tours. A sophisticated underground fiber optic network connects the entire campus. Impressive new facilities (pictured and described on following pages) have been added.

Beneath the physical surface of the campus, other changes were taking place as well in the two decades. Applicants for admission increased from fewer than 1,000 in 1986 to more than 1,600 in 2004. By 2004, more than half the first-year class ranked in the top 10 percent of their high school graduating classes. The average entering SAT score increased from 1042 in 1986 to 1249 in 2004. Out-of-state enrollment increased from 22 percent in 1986 to 37 percent in 2004. The women-to-men enrollment ratio remained steady at a healthy 50-50. Minority enrollment stood at 11.6 percent.

Retention of the first-year class increased from 77 percent in 1976 to 92 percent in 2004. The faculty-student ratio improved from 1:19 in 1986 to 1:12 in 2004. Wofford had 57 full-time faculty in 1986, and in 2004, it had 82 full-time teaching faculty, with 90 percent of them holding doctoral or equivalent terminal degrees. The number of majors available to Wofford students grew from 16 in 1986 to 24 by 2003. A creative writing program, art history and theatre majors, and a string ensemble program represented special emphasis on the arts. Chinese was added to the curriculum. Wofford ranked year after year among the top ten U.S. campuses in percentage of students studying abroad for credit. The graduation rate improved from 71 percent in 1986 to 76.6 percent in 2003. Over 45 percent of the graduates went on for advanced study within two years. In a flurry of curricular study and change, faculty from disparate disciplines created first-year learning communities that have been cited nationally for their impact and innovativeness.

The college's endowment funds (fair market value) multiplied 12 times, from $9 million in 1986 to $111 million in 2004. The educational & general budget (revenue enterprises excluded) increased from $6 million in 1986 to $23 million in 2003. Giving to the college for the 20 years from 1984 through 2003 was $154.8 million, six-plus times the previous 20-year (1964-1986) total of $24.5 million. Prestigious national grants were received from the Kresge Foundation, the Howard Hughes Medical Institute, and the Andrew Mellon Foundation.

U.S. News & World Report ranked Wofford

in the top 30 percent of 217 liberal arts colleges in its *Best Colleges 2004* book. The *Princeton Review College Guide* featured Wofford in its book, *The Best 351 Colleges for 2004*. The Fiske *Guide to Colleges 2004* hailed Wofford for its "rigorous academics" and in 2003 listed it as one of the nation's 22 private-college "best buys." The *Yale Daily News Insider's Guide to the Colleges 2004* sang Wofford's praises, as did the *2002 Barron's Best Buys in College Education*.

Wofford did not become a rich kid's college. Student comprehensive fees remained close to the College Board national average for four-year independent campuses. Over 82 percent of the students received financial aid (including loans and work-study) from all sources, and three-fifths of them received aid from college funds.

To call these 20 years since the Olin Foundation rejection "Wofford's Golden Years" would be a misnomer. That phrase implies that "the best years are in the past," and that certainly is not the case for Wofford. The years since 1984 have been "Glowing Years," not "Golden Years," in which the tiny Wofford star in the galaxy of higher education shone brightly and was visible to alumni and to strangers alike as worth watching.

And what of the Olin grant? That saga has a very happy ending. In 1988, Wofford was one of 75 applicants and was not chosen as a finalist. But in 1989, Wofford was one of five finalists from among 58 applicants. In June 1989, Foundation President Lawrence W. Milas notified the college that it had received a grant of $5.5 million for a high-tech classroom building. The grant subsequently was increased to $5.9 million, and the F. W. Olin Building, overlooking the entrance pool and fountain, crests the campus proudly, dedicated with pomp and circumstance in May 1992.

Magnificent and useful as the Olin Building has been, its impact pales beside the impact of that 1985 Olin rejection, from which flowed countless blessings of momentum, flowing even today because the processes of planning and funding have been perpetuated. "Shining with untarnished honor," Wofford is a singular star of celestial clarity in higher education's expanding universe. Bright years lie ahead for this shining star—Wofford: Stunning, Not Stunted.

Dr. Natalie Grinnell *(center)* teaches a class on the steps of Main Building.

The *Daniel Legacy: Power* of *Philanthropy*

Overnight, a 44 percent increase in Wofford's endowment! That was thrilling news to the college community in July 1992, when officials announced bequests from Homozel Daniel totaling almost $15 million. While Mrs. Daniel

Homozel Mickel Daniel

had no personal ties to Wofford, she had come to admire the college through Roger Milliken, Dr. Larry McCalla '43 and other friends. Mrs. Daniel's great-niece, Minor Mickel Shaw, later served with great distinction as a Wofford trustee.

Daniel family generosity to Wofford extended back to the early 1960s. During the reconstruction of Main Building, Charles and Homozel Daniel made a gift for Mickel Chapel, an intimate space with the advantage of ground-floor accessibility. Later, Wofford sought funds to remodel another historic structure, the old Whitefoord Smith Library.

This classroom and music building was renamed in honor of Mr. Daniel.

The prestigious Charles E. Daniel Endowed Scholarship program began in the mid-1970s. By the time of Mrs. Daniel's death, this scholarship program had a long record of success. Wofford trustees immediately allocated additional support for the eight Daniel scholarships, which provided full comprehensive fees for two first-year students annually. The trustees also voted to use some of the new dollars to encourage other contributions for endowed scholarship funds. Here's how the plan worked: Suppose Jane Smith, an alumna of the college, wanted to support outstanding students who also might be women's soccer players or participants in the theatre major. When a commitment to begin the Jane Smith Endowed Scholarship Fund at the $250,000 level was made, a second scholarship matched it, the Daniel/Smith Endowed Scholarship Fund.

A second great impact of the Daniel bequest at Wofford was felt on the faculty through the creation of endowed chairs named in honor of Dr. Larry H. McCalla and his wife, Rachel. One chair each was designated for mathematics, chemistry and biology. The availability of the McCalla chairs accelerated the college's plan to improve a faculty-student ratio of 1-to-14 and also made it easier for Wofford to attract bright scholars and able teachers from around the country and the world.

President Lesesne knew of Mrs. Daniel's bequest long before her death, but he had no idea how large it was. "She was a very private person," he said. "She never told anyone how much to expect. Perhaps even Mrs. Daniel would have been pleasantly surprised at how effective her estate planning had been, and the tremendous impact her generosity has had on independent higher education in South Carolina."

—Doyle Boggs '70

Walt W. Sessoms '56 and his wife, Harriet, of Atlanta, have twice participated in the Daniel matching scholarship program.

Head football coach Mike Ayers *(right)* thanks Jim Switzer '80 and his mother, Toccoa Switzer, for their participation in the Daniel Legacy Program. Jim's daughter, Lizzie Switzer '07, represents the fifth generation of this family to attend Wofford.

Daniel Legacy Scholarships

- *Daniel/Avant Family Endowed Scholarship Fund*
- *Daniel/BB&T Endowed Scholarship Fund*
- *Daniel/Bank of America Endowed Scholarship Fund*
- *Daniel/J. Harold Chandler Endowed Scholarship Fund*
- *Daniel/Jack Peterson Endowed Scholarship Fund*
- *Daniel/LaFon C. and Winston C. Dees Family Endowed Scholarship Fund*
- *Daniel/Michael E. Edens Endowed Scholarship Fund*
- *Daniel/Harvey Stafford Floyd Endowed Scholarship Fund*
- *Daniel/Robert E. Gregory Family Endowed Scholarship Fund*
- *Daniel/Cleveland S. and Curtis H. Harley Endowed Scholarship Fund*
- *Daniel/Elmore G. and Dorothy C. Herbert Endowed Scholarship Fund*
- *Daniel/Douglas H. Joyce Endowed Scholarship Fund*
- *Daniel/Russell C. King Sr. Endowed Scholarship Fund*
- *Daniel/Ruth O. and Joab M. Lesesne Jr. Endowed Scholarship Fund*
- *Daniel/Robert W. McCully Endowed Scholarship Fund*
- *Daniel/Harold M. McLeod Sr. Endowed Scholarship Fund*
- *Daniel/Joseph B. Miller Endowed Scholarship Fund*
- *Daniel/Walter S. Montgomery Endowed Scholarship Fund*
- *Daniel/J. E. Reeves Jr. and Family Endowed Scholarship Fund*
- *Daniel/M. Stewart and Steven W. Mungo Endowed Scholarship Fund*
- *Daniel/Switzer Endowed Athletic Scholarship Fund*
- *Daniel/Molly Sessoms Endowed Scholarship Fund*
- *Daniel/Walter W. Sessoms Endowed Scholarship Fund*
- *Daniel/Joe E. Taylor Family Endowed Scholarship Fund*

Roger Milliken: *Five Decades* of *Service*

Except for three brief periods when a hiatus was required under the bylaws, Roger Milliken served continuously on the Wofford Board of Trustees from the mid-1950s into the third millennium. Milliken's passion and commitment for Wofford College and its community has been remarkable throughout that half-century.

Francis Pendleton Gaines *(right)* was the first of five Wofford presidents to benefit from Roger Milliken's leadership on the Board of Trustees.

In 1994, The Association of Governing Boards of Universities and Colleges honored Milliken with its annual Distinguished Service Award in Trusteeship. Shortly after receiving this prestigious award, Milliken granted an interview to the college magazine, *Wofford Today.*

When you first were offered the chance to become a trustee of Wofford, why did you accept?

In the 1950s, the college had many strengths, but it also had some significant weaknesses, particularly in its financial situation and its physical plant.

I started learning about the college from President Pendleton Gaines. We first met so-

cially, and then I visited him on the campus. I got more and more excited about the possibilities of what could be done on a campus that was smaller than my alma mater, Yale. I decided that I wanted to help a very worthy institution (Wofford specifically) to grow itself into the ranks of the most prestigious small liberal arts colleges. I felt then, and I feel now, that the Wofford constituency shares that dream. It has been a pleasure to serve with dedicated trustees, including many alumni and representatives of the South Carolina Conference of the United Methodist Church. They are very proud of their college, as they should be.

When you came on the board, there were almost immediately a number of significant reforms in the management of the college. Could we talk about those?

It has been my experience that in many nonprofit institutions, trustees have a tendency to feel that they can budget an increase in expenditures and then hope that somehow there will be an increase in giving over the course of the fiscal year to offset these increases. I thought it would be better to raise the money before making a commitment to spend it; in other words, the Annual Fund for 1993 should support the operating budget for the 1994-1995 academic year. I was able to make a gift that permitted Wofford to put "forward funding" into effect. I believe that this policy has enormously helped the college in operating a continuously balanced budget. When Wofford goes out to raise money, it is not going out to cover a deficit or pay off a

After the opening of the Roger Milliken Science Center, Mr. Milliken himself led students on a tour of the new facilities.

mortgage, but to actually create new opportunities for its students. Several times in those early years, I promised to match and give money to the extent that alumni increased their giving levels. That incentive helped the college put into place an effective organization for appealing to its graduates for financial support. I believe that this effort would probably have happened anyway, but perhaps it came earlier than otherwise would have been the case.

Could you share your vision with us about what Wofford and liberal arts education will be like in the future?

I am the product of a liberal arts education, having majored in French history at Yale. I believe in this approach to education, because it lays the groundwork for a lifetime commitment to continuous learning and receptiveness to positive change. Potential Nobel Prize winners have failed to be recognized because they had not developed the written and oral communications skills that a liberal arts curriculum teaches and inculcates. Of course, I would add immediately that any complete liberal arts education includes the requirement to take courses in the sciences and mathematics.

Good facilities and good programs will attract the best students. The best students will attract the best faculty members. We are on that road, and that is very exciting to me. The challenge to the Board of Trustees is to inspire Wofford's constituency to come up with the financial resources necessary to support the comprehensive plan that we now have in place.

In the spring of 2001, Milliken participated in formal ceremonies marking both the inauguration of President Benjamin Dunlap and the dedication of the new science center.

"What's right with college football, personified"

When Shawn Graves came to Wofford in 1989, he was a marquee football recruit. When he graduated four years later, he had left his mark on not only the football program but also on the college and NCAA record books. He has the remarkable distinction of being the Most Valuable Player in all four of his varsity seasons, and he was the first Terrier football player in the modern era to have his jersey retired.

As a 5-foot-8-inch, 152-pound high school senior, Graves was recruited by a number of NCAA Division I-A programs as a wide receiver or defensive back, but he chose to play his college football at Wofford. His decision was based on academic considerations and the opportunity to play quarterback in a wishbone offense, the same system that had made him a star in his hometown high school in Marion, South Carolina.

Graves' record-breaking career began with an incredible first-year performance. In 1989, he rushed for 134.8 yards per game and 24 touchdowns. Those 24 touchdowns quickly put him in the Wofford and NCAA record books, earning him four national records: most rushing TDs by a freshman in a season, most touchdowns by a freshman in a season, most rushing touchdowns by a quarterback in a season, and total touchdowns by a quarterback in a season.

Graves continued his record-setting ways during his sophomore year. In a game against Lenoir-Rhyne College at Snyder Field on September 15, 1990, Graves ran for 323 yards, breaking the NCAA and Wofford records for single-game rushing yards. The 1990 season ended prematurely for Graves when he suffered a broken arm in a wild 64-46 victory over East Tennessee State. Even so, he scored 17 touchdowns and averaged 147.1 yards per game. Wofford finished the regular season 9-2, earning a berth in the national Division II playoffs.

Early in his junior year, Graves enjoyed one of his memorable performances at The

Citadel's Johnson Hagood Stadium. Although the two teams had not played every year, the Terriers had not beaten the Bulldogs since 1958. In talking with a Charleston *Post-Courier* reporter leading up to the game, Graves referred in passing to the vintage dress uniforms worn by cadets as "monkey suits." Emphasized out of context by the newspaper, the quote became a battle cry for The Citadel fans, but Graves had the last laugh. Near the end of the third quarter, Wofford was down 12-0, but then the Terriers got on the scoreboard with a Graves touchdown. In the fourth quarter, with ball in hand and seemingly surrounded, Graves made a zigzag midway down field, leaving everybody in his wake. It was, as Sports Information Director Mark Cohen recalled, "a run only Graves could make." Wofford held off the Bulldogs in the final minutes and went home with an important 15-12 victory. Those 1991 Terriers were improved on defense and ended the season with their second consecutive 9-2 record and another appearance in the NCAA Division II playoffs, this time at Snyder Field.

Injuries plagued Graves in 1992, forcing him to sit out two games. Nevertheless, he rushed for 990 yards and 11 touchdowns, averaging 110 yards per game. He fell 10 yards shy of becoming only the eighth player in NCAA history to post four 1,000-yard rushing seasons. By the end of his senior year, he had rushed for 5,128 yards, smashing the old

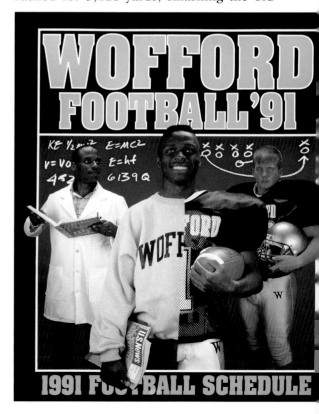

On the field and off, Shawn Graves '93 was an ideal personification of the Wofford student-athlete.

record for career yards rushing by a quarterback, previously held by Dee Dowis of the Air Force Academy.

Though his on-the-field accomplishments stood on their own merits, many people did not realize until his final seasons that football was just part of Shawn Graves' very special life story. They did not know Graves was missing the right pectoral muscle. They did not know he suffered from asthma and severe allergies when he was born. They did not know he had to have blood transfusions as an infant. They did not know he hadn't been expected to live to see his first birthday. Gradually, though, people at Wofford and far beyond began to learn about Graves' start in life, especially when veteran radio newsman Paul Harvey featured the Wofford quarterback on his daily radio broadcast. People now truly knew, as Harvey says, "the rest of the story." Graves also addressed viewers in a nationally televised anti-drugs "Just Say No" public service announcement for the NCAA.

In August 1992, Graves was featured in the *Sports Illustrated* college football preview issue. The story, "Options Aplenty" noted Graves' personable demeanor as well as his athletic achievements. Writer Ed Hinton, who spent a day on campus with Graves, opened the story with, "What's right with college football, personified, approaches in the corridor. College Football As It Should Be, embodied, extends a hand." The story featured a full-page photo of a shirtless Graves running toward the camera, providing a vivid illustration of the missing pectoral muscle that made his achievements seem that much more incredible.

"Shawn brought a lot of attention to the college through his athletic exploits, but equally impressive was how he handled the attention," said Danny Morrison '75, director of athletics during the Graves era. "Whether he was speaking to elementary school children or members of the South Carolina Athletics Hall of Fame, Shawn was able to read his audience and comment appropriately."

After graduation in 1993, Graves played briefly (though not at quarterback, as he had been promised) with Saskatchewan of the Canadian Football League. He returned home in 1994 and started a successful business career. He has been a member of the Wofford Alumni Executive Council.

—Sara Ross Cohen '88

Mike Ayers, below, ranks as Wofford's all-time winningest football coach, and his intensity, character and pride are mirrored in his teams. Since taking over the head-coaching duties at Wofford in January 1988, he has seen the Terriers grow from NAIA membership to NCAA Division II, Division I-AA Independent in 1995 and the Southern Conference in 1997. In seven years as a Division II member, Ayers' teams made the national playoffs twice and posted six wins and a tie against Division I-AA competition. In 2003, Ayers was the recipient of the Sports Network's Eddie Robinson Award as the national coach of the year. The Terriers were picked to finish fifth in a preseason poll by the league coaches, but Wofford went 8-0 for the SoCon's first perfect mark since 1998 and won two games in the Division I-AA playoffs.

The Panthers' New Summer Home

When Jerry Richardson '59 first came to Wofford as a student-athlete, most people thought he was too slow for college football. By his senior season, he had made himself into a Little All-American offensive end. He signed a professional contract with the Baltimore Colts and caught a touchdown pass from Johnny Unitas in an NFL championship game.

In 1961, Richardson joined his Wofford quarterback, Charles Bradshaw '59, in investing his savings ($4,000) to open the first franchised Hardee's Restaurant, on Kennedy Street in Spartanburg. During a highly successful career as a food service executive, Richardson was very active in revitalization efforts in downtown Spartanburg.

As he left the restaurant business to become owner and founder of the NFL's Carolina Panthers, Richardson was approached by Dr. Joe Lesesne, then Wofford's president, about the prospect of holding summer training at the college. Wofford was attractive: It was the right distance from the team's home in Charlotte so that players would be away from home and its distractions, but fans could easily visit the camp; the campus's size and arrangement were ideal, with adequate residence halls and dining

Key players in the drive to bring Panthers training to Spartanburg: George Dean Johnson '64 and his wife, Susu; Jerry Richardson '59 and his wife, Rosalind; Jimmy Gibbs and his wife, Marsha.

facilities; and Spartanburg offered lodging, restaurants and news media outlets.

The public-private partnership of the local business community, the Spartanburg Area Chamber of Commerce, the city of Spartanburg, the county of Spartanburg and the college was successful. The fund-raising campaign, "Let's Make Spartanburg the Summer Home of the Carolina Panthers," headed by local businessman Bobby Pinson, was bolstered by a $1 million lead gift from George Dean Johnson Jr. '64 for a new physical activities building; and a $500,000 gift from Jimmy Gibbs and his wife, Marsha, for stadium improvements. The need for NFL-quality athletics facilities was met with the construction of the Richardson Physical Activities Building and Gibbs Stadium.

The Carolina Panthers held their first summer training camp at Wofford College in 1995. Tourism and the community's exposure to the outside world helped drive economic development and growth.

Construction of Gibbs Stadium benefited not only Wofford, but also Spartanburg County School District 7, which contributed $750,000 in exchange for a 15-year license-to-use granted to the Spartanburg High School football team. Ultimately, the entire community enjoyed Gibbs Stadium as a venue for other major events, such as the Franklin Graham Crusade in 2001 and the Shrine Bowl of the Carolinas in 2004 and 2005.

—*Laura H. Corbin*

A City Transformed

Spartanburg's "new" central city that emerged after 1985 reflected a population and business community of exuberance and vitality. It resulted in a distinctive blend of shops, apartments and condos, some built in strikingly refurbished period structures. New restaurants provided lunches for the returning downtown workforce, as well as dinner and nightlife. Within a five-minute walk of the central business district rose the attractive, state-of-the-art Spartanburg County Public Libraries Headquarters, a totally renovated and expanded Spartanburg Memorial Auditorium, and the headquarters offices of several national and international companies—Denny's Restaurants, Advance America, Extended Stay America and QS/1 Data Systems, among the latest arrivals.

The ambitious Renaissance Park Project passed a milestone when the four-star, 250-room Marriott hotel and conference center opened in late 2003. Along the Renaissance Park's planned "promenade" will be areas for downtown community festivals and events, leading toward the proposed Center for Arts, History and Science to be located adjacent to Barnet Park. The park itself became home to the multimillion-dollar Zimmerli Amphitheatre, an outdoor stage that has brought concerts—from symphonic performances to popular rock bands—to the community.

Division I, Here We Come!

Sitting down to prepare tomorrow's lessons for my high school classes one night in December 2002, I remembered the men's basketball team was playing at Virginia Tech, at that time a member of the Big East Conference. Tuning into the game and hearing excitement in the voice of longtime play-by-play announcer Mark Hauser, I realized that the Terriers were clinging to a one-point advantage late in the second half. Wofford began trading baskets with the Hokies, regaining composure after losing a 20-point advantage. With each lead change, I felt the tension build, recalling my experiences as a Wofford student-athlete and avid fan of Terrier basketball.

After Wofford nailed down the victory with free throws, I had a sudden realization. The college had established itself as a competitive force within the Division I ranks. With this victory in 2002, sandwiched between wins over Clemson in 2001 and Auburn in 2004, the Terriers had come a long way since the days when I played on NAIA and NCAA Division II men's basketball teams.

Facing traditional rivals from both the Southern and Carolinas Conferences in the 1950s and 1960s, and blessed with legendary coaching from Joel Robertson '41 and Gene Alexander, the Terrier program thrived. However, by the early 1980s, Wofford faced severe recruiting and scheduling disadvantages under vague and unenforceable NAIA academic guidelines.

At the same time, the Terriers often faced humorous and sometimes eerie settings, according to former coach Richard Johnson. Upon arriving at a high school gym to play an NAIA District 6 foe, coaches saw officials taping down the three-point arc without the use of any visible measuring device. Referees sometimes wore stopwatches around their necks as a substitute for the 45-second shot clock. One visiting gym had three rows of bleachers, one scoreboard and a dressing room that doubled as the public restroom. On another road trip, the Wofford men watched in disbelief during a women's game as fans chased down and assaulted the official who had thrown out the home team's coach. And during one opening round of the District 6 playoffs, an oversized jazz band rocked the house from a catwalk directly behind the basket, intimidating the freshmen and sophomores on the last Wofford team to play NAIA basketball.

The college addressed the dilemma in the Masterplan of 1987, which recommended a move from the NAIA to NCAA, Division II. From that time until 1995, Wofford athletes endured long road trips to face Division II foes. Going to an Alabama campus meant an eight-hour bus ride (with coaches tossing out fast-food hamburgers as the post-game meal) and arriving back on campus at 6 a.m. Once, the men traveled to the Tangerine Tourney in central Florida, played two straight nights, and rode straight back to make Monday classes. The goal simply was to win as many games as possible. The Wofford men looked forward to the traditional Little Four tournament and a big Division I game here and there, but it was difficult to remain focused without the opportunity to vie for a conference crown or a playoff berth.

Again, looking for a better identity, Wofford

Ian Chadwick '01

Before becoming director of athletics in December 2001, Richard Johnson coached Terrier men's basketball teams for 17 years, steering the program to NCAA Division I status and posting a 236-230 career record.

created an Athletics Task Force in 1992, attempting to view various alternatives. These options included giving up athletics scholarships and moving to Division III, keeping the status quo as a Division II independent, or upgrading to Division I and seeking a conference affiliation. After a careful cost-benefit analysis and much deliberation, Wofford opted for the latter course, allowing itself a 10-year window to find a conference. Fortunately, an opening occurred almost immediately in the Southern Conference in 1995. The Terriers played as a Division I independent for two seasons, and in due time, they became eligible for the post-season SoCon and NCAA tournaments.

After the Terriers defeated Davidson and Furman twice during this era and earned a trip to the Division II playoffs with a 21-6 record in 1993-94, it came time to make the jump to Division I in 1995. Encountering more talented and better-funded teams, Wofford needed to play perfectly to compete at the higher level. Gaining experience from a very long 4-22 season, the Terriers defeated Navy, Patriot League champions and an NCAA tournament team, and improved to seven wins in 1996-97. According to center Chris Arp '97, who felt the initial impact of change, this season provided a turning point for the program, which had gained respect from opponents. Playing Colorado close and limiting Wake Forest's Tim Duncan of later NBA fame, players realized their sacrifices had laid the foundation for future success. In the third season in Division I (1997-98), Wofford defeated Chattanooga, an NCAA "Sweet-16" team in the previous year, and earned a second place regular-season finish in the South Division of the SoCon.

Ian Chadwick '01, a shooting guard ideally suited to the Terriers' system, came on the scene as a freshman in 1997. He was a three-time All SoCon selection and, as of 2004, was the league's career three-point leader with 299. It was Chadwick who hit a basket at the buzzer to defeat Davidson 65-64 and put Wofford into the semifinals of the 2000 SoCon Tournament at the Bi-Lo Center in Greenville, South Carolina.

After that memorable game, transition time was over.

—*Stephen Jobe '91*

The Benjamin Johnson Arena in the Campus Life Building opened in 1981. Since that time, many outstanding players have represented Wofford and have made it one of the outstanding home courts in the Carolinas. During the 2004-2005 seasons, fans chose these players for the all-time "BenJo" team.

Women	Men
Meredith Denton '00	Greg O'Dell '92
Nancy Dubuisson '02	Matt Allen '95
Ricaye Harris '05	James Blair '83
Lucy Hines '01	Ian Chadwick '01
Meg Hunt '84	Seth Chadwick '97
Brenda Jackson '94	Mike Howard '83
Jenny Nett '02	Mike Lenzly '03
Judy Nwajiaku '90	Wayne Rice '87
Tori Quick '87	Antoine Saunders '87
	Howard Wilkerson '06

Southern Conference: *The First Decade*

Since 1921, the Southern Conference has been a comprehensive NCAA Division I athletics conference, ranking behind only the Big Ten (1896), the Missouri Valley (1907) and the PAC-10 (1915) in seniority. As of 2004, it offered championships in 19 sports that carry with them berths in the appropriate national playoffs.

On December 18, 1995, Wright Waters, then commissioner of the SoCon, announced the addition of three new members in the league: the University of North Carolina at Greensboro, the College of Charleston and Wofford.

"The SoCon is delighted with the addition of Wofford College to our league," Waters said. "Wofford fits the conference mold academically, athletically and geographically." Waters was correct in his analysis. A Phi Beta Kappa campus, Wofford came into the league with the full support of two similar liberal arts institutions, Davidson and Furman. While other SoCon members have higher enrollments and larger arena capacities, the facilities that Wofford was prepared to offer its own student-athletes and visiting competitors were second to none.

Wofford's symbolic debut in the SoCon, the opening game of the 1997 football season at Gibbs Stadium, attracted wide attention in Upstate South Carolina and a regional television audience (a first for the college). That day, the Terriers defeated the Keydets of Virginia Military Institute 23-13.

Over the next decade, Coach Mike Ayers and a staff that included Wofford alumni and former players Wade Lang '83, Nate Woody '84, Freddie Brown '91 and Eric Nash '02, in addition to veteran coaching professionals Lee Hanning, Bruce Lackey and Thomas Neel (not to mention President Emeritus Joe Lesesne), built the Terrier program into one of the best in what is usually regarded as the toughest NCAA Division I-AA football conference. In fact, during 2002-2004, Wofford was the SoCon's winningest football team with an 18-5 conference record. Equally outstanding was a 29-8 overall record (a winning percentage of .784—two of these defeats came at the Air Force Academy and the University of Maryland).

The 2003 football team marched through

Terrier football on a beautiful afternoon in Gibbs Stadium

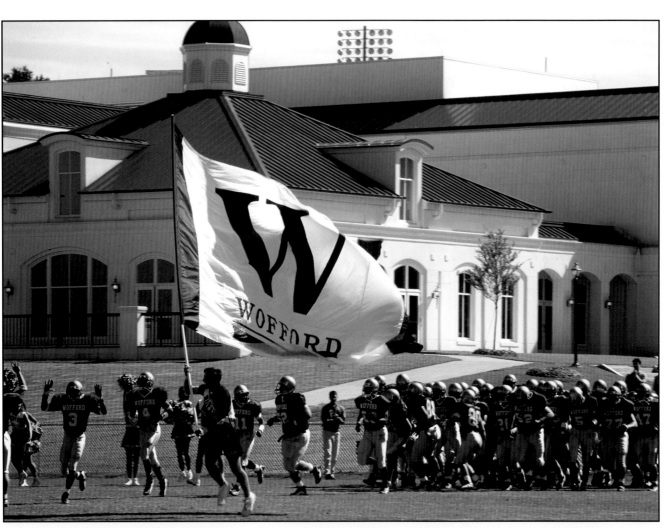

Ben Foster '02, Arthur Ashe Award winner

the Southern Conference undefeated and advanced to the national semifinals. Ayers received the 2003 Eddie Robinson Award as Division I-AA National Coach of the Year and was the SoCon Coach of the Year in 2000, 2002 and 2003. Ben Foster '02 won the national Arthur Ashe Award, which annually recognizes the male African-American athlete who most reflects the qualities of scholarship, athleticism and humanitarianism. Football All-American Matt Nelson '04 was named the SoCon Male Student-Athlete of the Year following his senior season.

Men's golf was another sport that could build on a strong tradition and several endowed scholarship funds to become competitive immediately at the higher level. Also important was experience at playing host to successful tournaments, including a Division II national championship event. Rion Moore '98 and William McGirt '01 reigned as SoCon individual tournament champions.

Basketball standout Adrien Borders '03 and Ugo Ihekweazu '04 won SoCon outdoor track and field championships.

SoCon membership challenged Wofford to support women's athletics at a higher level. Some conference universities did not field football teams but ranked as traditional powers in women's sports, funding and staffing their teams accordingly. However, Wofford women quickly demonstrated that they could compete at the Division I level. Louise Maynard '96 led the tennis program through the transitional years into Division I. She has been inducted into the Wofford Hall of Fame.

In their first year of competition in the SoCon, the women's soccer team finished the season with a 5-2 conference record and a 12-

7-3 mark overall. The Terriers were defeated in the conference championship match by the UNC Greensboro Spartans, a team that advanced to the national quarterfinals. Brigid Meadow '98, a Wofford Athletics Hall of Fame member, recorded 40 goals in her senior year. Keeper Illeana Moschos '98 posted 10 shutouts in 1996 and later had the thrill of competing for Greece in the 2004 Olympics in Athens. In basketball, Jenny Nett '02 was the 2001-02 SoCon Player of the Year in addition to being a first-team Academic All-American.

Wofford also provided outstanding leadership for the SoCon as a whole. Danny Morrison '75, a former director of athletics and senior vice president at Wofford, was named commissioner of the Southern Conference in December 2001. Dr. Ted Monroe ranked throughout the decade as one of the conference's most respected and knowledgeable faculty athletics representatives.

—Doyle Boggs '70, with assistance from the sports information staff

SoCon Members, 1995-2005

* Appalachian State University (1972-)
* University of Chattanooga (1976-)
* The Citadel (1936-)
College of Charleston (1998-)
Davidson College (1936-)
* East Tennessee State University (1978-2004)
* Elon University (2003-)
* Furman University (1936-)
* Georgia Southern University (1991-)
University of North Carolina Greensboro (1997-)
* Virginia Military Institute (1924-2003)
* Western Carolina University (1976-)
* Wofford College (1997-)

* Division I-AA Football programs

Danny Morrison '75, former senior vice president at Wofford and Southern Conference Commissioner, became director of athletics at Texas Christian University in June 2005. He is shown here *(left)* with Jerry Richardson '59.

A *Campus Transformed*

When the Wofford College National Historic District was recognized in 1974, the campus projected a distinctive charm that South Carolinians often call "shabby gentility." To insiders, it seemed like home. Celebrating a passage from the poet James Joyce, Dr. Dennis Dooley and his students planted and nurtured cuttings from a green rose bush they had discovered at Walnut Grove plantation. Vehicles were permitted to park almost everywhere, even if shrubbery, lawns and pavement sustained unnecessary damage. Dan DuPré's orderly canopy of oak trees was aging, even as hundreds of birds and squirrels shared it joyfully with those who lived and worked underneath.

The authors of the 1987 Masterplan did not seek to change what was distinctive about the campus environment. However, they wanted Wofford to return the historic district to the original concept of a pedestrian park overlooking Spartanburg from the city's northern border. They argued that in the absence of sound planning and professional attention to landscaping details, an opportunity to reach out to prospective students, townspeople and visitors was being overlooked.

General recommendations soon were translated into specific projects. For example, the Neofytos D. Papadopoulos Building and the Franklin W. Olin Building, both employing classical design using white stucco, were hailed as comprising the college's new front door. Butler Circle, with its distinctive trident fountain, and Charles Parks' sculpture "Light" in the front of the Sandor Teszler Library were other attractive additions. Outside the historic district, in the vicinity of the new Gibbs Stadium and the Richardson Physical Activities Building, great efforts were made to cultivate a variety of trees and shrubs that offered four-season appeal.

Some other projects completed between 1987 and 2004 included:

(1) Rerouting the vehicular drive through the heart of the campus to make it more direct, and eliminating parking places that blocked campus vistas. A particular effort was made to remove obstructions from views of Old Main and to reaffirm it as the emotional and physical center of the campus.

(2) Redesigning and replacing worn out and cracked pavement, curbs and sidewalks and installing state-of-the-art drainage and irrigation systems.

(3) Applying a white coating to the brick-veneer exteriors of the Burwell Building, Andrews Field House and the Campus Life Building to bring them into more harmony with neighboring structures.

(4) Developing and implementing comprehensive plans for landscaping and outdoor gathering spaces.

—*Doyle Boggs '70*

A Charles Parks sculpture, "Light," stands in front of the Sandor Teszler Library. It was commissioned for the college by the family of the late William Light Kinney III '91, who died in an automobile accident in July 1989. He represented the fourth generation of his family to attend Wofford. The inscription on the base of the sculpture comes from Psalm 43: "Send out thy light and thy truth, let them lead me."

Standing at the top of the steps of Main Building, the observer of 2001 could not fail to be impressed with the beauty of the Wofford landscape. Compare this view to a photograph on pages 80-81, made from exactly the same spot 40 years before.

The Campus Life Building *(above)*, the Burwell Building and Andrews Field House turned white almost overnight.

Outdoor gathering spaces, such as Players' Corner, were important additions to the campus.

The *Wofford Arboretum*

In November 2002, the entire 150-acre Wofford campus was designated as an arboretum, and Wofford became a member of the American Association of Botanical Gardens and Arboreta.

With species ranging from the American Yellowwood to the Yoshino Cryptomeria, a spreading canopy of more than 5,000 trees, all identified and catalogued, shelters the members of the Wofford community. The Emily Brunner Holly brightens dark, winter days with its red berries, while the red-tinged flowers of the Coral Bark Japanese Maple beautify early summer days. Students find comfort studying under the Eastern Redcedar and the Willow Oak on the main lawn, and a walk through Liberty Trail and Park refreshes members of both the Spartanburg and Wofford communities.

Instrumental in planning and creating the landscape and arboretum design for Wofford were nationally renowned horticulturalist Dr. Michael Dirr, formerly of the University of Georgia; famed landscape architect Rick Webel of Innocenti & Webel; and Trustee Roger Milliken, chairman of the board of Milliken & Company. Wofford students Matt Borders '03, Ryan Gilreath '03 and Steve Olejnik '07 assisted in research for and production of the first brochures and guidebooks. Dr. Doug Rayner of the biology faculty and a capable groundskeeping team headed by Bill Littlefield provided staff support.

In November 2004, the addition of the Liberty Trail and Cascading Steps, a tribute from former students to the longtime theatre and fine arts professor Dr. James R. Gross, expanded the arboretum both in size and in splendor. This trail north of the historic district links Wofford's campus to the Spartanburg Regional Medical Center arboretum, forming part of the Hub City Connector of the Palmetto Trail.

—Kristin Sams '05

The Mary Black Phillips Walk *(right)* connects the Olin Building to the historic district.

Michael Dirr *(left)* and Rick Webel, are nationally known authorities on trees and landscaping whose talent is reflected in the Wofford Arboretum

President Dunlap used this poem to dedicate the Wofford Arboretum in November 2002. The audience was asked to fill in the blanks and did so with great enthusiasm.

O Muse, let's get a little smarter
And sing of this city named for ——— (Sparta),
How a galaxy of botanical knowledge
Descended one day at Wofford ——— (College)
With noble trees and plans to treat 'em
Not just as woods, but an ——— (arboretum).
The first of the legends to confer
Was a passionate gardener, Michael ——— (Dirr).
The next was deft with every pebble,
Golf balls and greens, zealous Rick ——— (Webel).
But as each adds every frill he can,
He relies on Roger ——— (Milliken),
The master builder whose ideas stamp us
As more than a Bradford-pear-ridden ——— (campus).
For them we've gathered here on these banks
To offer our most horticultural ——— (thanks).
Let us do that now, in the Wofford way:
For Mike, Rick and Roger, hip hip ——— (HOORAY!)
            hip hip ——— (HOORAY!)
            hip hip ——— (HOORAY!)

Neofytos D. Papadopoulos Building (1987)

The Neofytos D. Papadopoulos Building is dedicated to the memory of the father of Dr. C.N. "Gus" Papadopoulos '54. At the east-side entrance to the building is Butler Circle, which features a stainless steel trident fountain designed by Harold Krisel of Bridgehampton, New York. Inside, the reception room is furnished from the Irish Georgian and Winterthur collections of the Kindel Furniture Co. of Grand Rapids, Michigan, which is owned and operated by Robert S. Fogarty '59 and his daughter, Paula S. Fogarty '86.

Reeves Tennis Center (1992)

From the date of its completion, the Reeves Tennis Center has ranked as one of the finest college facilities in the nation. There are 11 courts, plus a building with dressing rooms, a reception room and an observation deck. The late John E. Reeves was a textile executive, philanthropist and Wofford trustee and several members of his family have been important trustees, friends and benefactors of the college.

Franklin W. Olin Building (1992)

After fierce nationwide competition, the New York-based F.W. Olin Foundation selected Wofford as the recipient of a $5.9 million grant for this outstanding academic building. Features include model classrooms with computer, video and audio technology; the campus media center; and student study and workstations. An 80-seat teaching theater is well designed for film, video and other on-screen presentations and provides an ideal setting for public speaking and foreign language interpretation exercises. The Olin Building became the hub of a campus-wide technology network linking almost all classrooms, offices and residence hall rooms with computer, video and library resources. The network became operational in February 1999, and Wofford subsequently was selected as one of *Yahoo/Internet Life's* 100 Most Wired Campuses.

A computer science class, taught by Dr. Angela Shiflet

Richardson Physical Activities Building (1995)

The Physical Activities Building is named to honor the family of Jerry Richardson '59, a business leader and founder of the Carolina Panthers of the NFL. The building's upper level was designed as the Wofford community's wellness and physical fitness center. It features an aerobic dance studio, four racquetball courts, and the latest fitness and weight-training equipment. There are also offices for coaches and athletics department staff. The Verandah reception room and patio offer an impressive view of the surrounding playing fields.

New Residence Halls (1990s)

Wofford added two new residence halls, Carlisle and Wightman, in the 1990s, and construction on other residence halls was planned for the following decade. Students in these newer buildings occupy small suites in various configurations that allow a measure of privacy unimagined in the college's first century. All the rooms are wired into the campus technology network and feature computer and television service.

Gibbs Stadium (1996)

Wofford's football stadium (shared with Spartanburg High School) was named in honor of Jimmy and Marsha Gibbs, recognizing their contributions to Spartanburg and their lead gift in the stadium project. The late Melvin "Razor" Gibbs '46, an outstanding athlete in several sports at Wofford, was the father of Jimmy Gibbs, a Spartanburg businessman.

Roger Milliken Science Center (2001)

At a cost of more than $15 million, Wofford celebrated the new millennium by adding magnificent new science facilities and renovating an abutting building from the 1960s. As President Dunlap said in his inaugural address, "The Milliken Science Center is more than offices and labs—it is, in effect, the intellectual crossroads of the college, where students from every discipline gather to study and compare ideas." The building houses the departments of biology, chemistry, physics and psychology. The Great Oaks Hall, Acorn Café and Players' Corner are popular gathering places for faculty, staff and students.

Russell C. King Field (2004)

Russell C. King '56, a member of a three-generation family at Wofford, made it possible for NCAA baseball to return to the campus after an eight-year absence when he made a commitment in excess of $1 million for a new facility on campus. Toccoa Switzer and her family made a gift for the construction of the seating area, which provided 900 permanent seats located behind home plate. Grass banks behind each dugout bring the total capacity to 2,500.

The Restoration of Main Building

Another page in the history of Old Main was turned in December 2004, when a major interior renovation began. The comprehensive Sesquicentennial revitalization project represented a carefully planned combination of historic preservation and modernization to allow the building to continue to serve its original purposes.

Even before interior work began, $2 million was spent correcting serious moisture problems in the exterior walls, creating a critical central campus infrastructure loop (heating, ventilation and air conditioning), and landscaping.

Construction crews focused initially on the west wing academic section of Old Main, which traditionally had been assigned to the departments of history, religion and economics, as well as on the central section that included Leonard Auditorium. Similar renovations in the east wing, which had been assigned to the departments of English and sociology, were scheduled for the fall of 2006.

In addition to recreating many of the historical architectural features of the Leonard Auditorium as it appeared a century ago, the interior phase of the Old Main project called for adding an elevator in the west tower, greatly improving accessibility for those with disabilities, remodeling all the restrooms, and installing the latest instructional technology in the auditorium, classrooms and seminar rooms.

Gifts totaling $6 million for the interior phase of the Main Building project had been raised by October 21, 2003, when the Watson-Brown Foundation of Thomson, Georgia, announced a $1.4 million grant for renovations in Leonard Auditorium. Donnie Love, an historic preservation architect with McMillan Smith & Partners Architects in Spartanburg, directed the auditorium project. He completed a very similar project at Walker Hall at the South Carolina School for the Deaf and the Blind in Spartanburg, a building of the same vintage designed by the same architect, Edward C. Jones.

—Doyle Boggs '70

Wofford *as* Summer Camp

"There was the little girl who didn't want to go to the Sunday worship service; she said she was an amethyst."

—Dr. Richard Robinson '61

The Summer Program for Academically Talented Students was a Wofford tradition for 20 years, bringing young people to live on campus, take classes with Wofford faculty and interact with other students from around the South. I was involved with the "gifted camp" as a camper for three summers and a counselor for one summer. Others had longer relationships. Pat Patterson '92 spent five years as a camper, four years as a counselor, and two years as assistant director.

Dr. B.G. Stephens '57 started the pilot project in 1980. McCalla Professor of Mathematics Dr. Richard Robinson '61 directed the camp from 1981 to 1993, followed by Meri Eubanks Lynch '88.

The gifted camp for 5th through 9th graders operated in three two-week sessions. For us campers, it did not matter if you were attending other camps, visiting relatives or traveling abroad that same year, Wofford was the centerpiece of the summer. No matter what session, campers shared similar feelings and nearly always left with a special love for Wofford.

Dr. Erin Bentrim-Tapio '91 was introduced to Wofford as a camper during its inaugural year. She returned four more summers and still keeps in touch with one of her counselors, Dr. Brian Odom '83. Bentrim-Tapio reminisced how she became friends with camper Chanin McClurkin '91 when counselors caught them moving mattresses down the hall so they could become camp roommates. The two former campers began a long friendship and roomed together in their first year at Wofford.

In the 1990s, the camp was expanded to include "Brainstorm!," a program for 4th through 6th graders, and SummerSCAPE, a college preparatory program for 10th and 11th graders. Campers took classes outside a normal curriculum such as Other Places, Other Times; Media vs. Reality: Fact or Fiction; and

Scott Cunningham and a young friend work intensely on a summer art project.

Dr. Richard Robinson, McCalla Professor of Mathematics, directed the Summer Program for Academically Talented Students from 1981 through 1993.

Prides & Prejudices: Ethics in Society. Recreation time included sports as well as a popular shag dancing class. Afternoons were spent in enrichment classes such as youth theatre, "On Broadway" musicals and slide-show yearbook, while evening programs included the talent show, game show night, line dancing lessons and theme parties.

After attending camp, many of us knew we wanted to come to Wofford for college. We felt the comfortable community that made camp a meaningful experience. As Wofford students, we realized that the feeling had not changed. One former camper remarked, "Gifted camp introduced me to Wofford, a place that I have come to love and consider a part of me."

Wofford's first-year class included former campers for many years. Sixteen former campers entered Wofford with me in 1998. Some of us became counselors and found out that not much had changed since we first lived in Shipp Hall. We adjusted to the fact that going onto the opposite gender hall would not result in being sent home and that "lights out" didn't apply to us. Yet, our camper background was helpful since we already knew which rules we had tried to bend (or break) years before.

As a freshman, it was amusing to tell Dr. Ted Monroe that I called him "Dr. Ted" in a camp class and to remind Dr. Talmage Skinner how I met him when practicing on the piano for the camp's church service. At Homecoming, it is still fun to see former counselors and recapture memories.

Former campers will continue to have a different perspective of Wofford because we first came as curious children looking to explore a college campus. Each summer we discovered a welcoming atmosphere that invited us to learn more about our own individualism, our similarities with others, and interesting subject matter. As students, we found out why our counselors told us Wofford was a special place with an uncommon atmosphere filled with extraordinary people.

—*Lucas McMillan '02*

One of the most popular offerings in the summer program involved television production and videography.

Student Life *the* Millennial Generation

The day I moved into Wofford in the fall of 1985, my mom, four siblings (ranging in age from 4 to 16) and I loaded all of my stuff into the trunk of our well-used beige Oldsmobile and made the trip to Spartanburg. I began unpacking while my little sisters and brother tested the bed, climbed under the desks, and discovered the musty recesses of a closet that hadn't been used in three months. In less than an hour, my mom was handing me a plate of home-baked, chocolate-chip cookies, giving me a kiss and telling me to share and make friends with the girls on the hall. They were gone and college was mine to handle—for better and sometimes worse. Still, it was mine for the next four years.

It was in that culture that Dean of Students Mike Preston '63 thrived. Preston likened his philosophy of managing student life to teaching a child to bake cookies. "It's easier to say 'get out of my way,' but it's better for them if they do it for themselves," said Preston. "I made sure the important stuff got done, and that they didn't get hurt, but I stayed out of their way."

Unless, of course, someone broke Preston's cardinal rule: "Do not violate the rights of someone else." On one legendary occasion the students in Greene Hall were having stereo wars into the wee hours of the morning. After numerous complaints, Preston walked from the Carlisle-Wallace House across the campus drive carrying a chainsaw and mask. At around 4 a.m. he cranked up the chainsaw and walked the halls billowing smoke and creating more

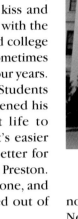

Dean Roberta Hurley Bigger '81

noise than an entire campus full of stereos. Needless to say the music stopped, and the remainder of the night (and the remainder of the semester, for that matter) passed peacefully.

Preston was dean from 1973 until 1995. During his tenure, the drinking age changed from 18 to 21 (something he lobbied and spoke against at the State House in Columbia), and women joined the college community as full-time resident students. As dean of students, Preston discovered that "the father of a son was dramatically different from the father of a daughter, even if he was the same person."

Still the parents of the 1970s and 1980s were, for the most part, under the belief that college meant hearing from their children when they needed a home-cooked meal, clean clothes or money. Parents were relatively unconcerned with student life programming.

Nationwide, several factors began to change that. Couples were postponing the decision to have children until they were in their late 30s or early 40s. These older parents did not have several other children back at home to divide their attention from their college-age offspring. Tuition costs also began to rise, making this group of investment-savvy parents want to monitor the use of their money more closely. In addition, these "helicopter parents" (so labeled for hovering above

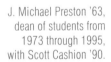

J. Michael Preston '63, dean of students from 1973 through 1995, with Scott Cashion '90.

the campus) had been programming their children's social lives since they first enrolled them in Dynamite Soccer or Kindermusik as preschoolers.

New technologies affected student life as much as they did the classroom. When Angela Thomas first began working in the student affairs office years ago, contacting students meant sending them a note in the mail or waiting outside of their classroom to give them a message. It was the era of the hall phone. Hall phones were replaced by personal room phones, then by college-owned room phones and answering systems, and yet again by mobile phones. In 2004, according to Thomas, contacting a student across campus meant making a long-distance call to a cell phone that might be answered in the next room.

Dr. Will Willimon '68, a United Methodist bishop who has been a Wofford parent and trustee, studied college student life for several decades when he was a professor of religion and Dean of the Chapel at Duke University. According to Willimon, "Students [of the Millennial Generation] admire their parents, like their parents, and would be happy to see more of them." When Willimon was in college in the late 1960s, only 8 percent of his peer group grew up in divorced families. "A couple of years ago, 38 percent of the first-year class nationally came from separated or divorced homes. That made a huge difference in the type of students we have, and in their needs," said Willimon. "Today's students are the most attached generation of adults yet, with cell phones and e-mail."

In 1995, when Roberta Bigger '81 became

A future career Army officer, Willie Witherspoon '89, as he looked at ROTC Summer Camp, Fort Bragg, North Carolina

Wofford's dean of students, the pendulum was swinging in this direction. The Parents Advisory Council wanted to see improvements to the residence halls and sought alternative activities to weekends on Fraternity Row. The college's revised Masterplan (1989) outlined eight areas for adapting the student life program to the millennial generation of parents and students.

In response, Wofford:

(1) Expanded the student life staff to include an associate dean of students, a director of volunteer services, a director of Greek life, a counselor and a director of multicultural affairs

(2) Increased the student life budget to bring additional cultural, educational and social programming to the campus

(3) Improved campus safety with increased numbers of officers and better equipment, the use of technology, the installation of blue call boxes across campus, exterior phones on the residence halls and partial fencing of the campus

(4) Improved residence life through

When leading a group to China, Professor Philip Keenan and his wife, Mary Kay Keenan, usually arranged for a photo in the Forbidden City.

Student Body President and Homecoming Queen Wendi Nix '96 with President Lesesne. She went on to a major television market sportscasting career.

One of several new community events developed in the early years of the Dunlap presidency, the annual Winter Lighting after Thanksgiving became a major campus celebration.

increased funding of regular maintenance in the residence halls and key card technology, improved training of residence assistants and additional residence life staff members

(5) Constructed several residence halls to accommodate more students in on-campus housing

(6) Developed new areas on campus for student gatherings and meetings

(7) Revamped health services by creating a campus emphasis on wellness, working to reduce alcohol risks and revising the beverage alcohol and drug policy

(8) Streamlined the judicial system and added an honor code.

All these reflected a renewal of the commitment Wofford made during the administration of Paul Hardin to interpret residential life as a contract between the individual student and the academy. "We made changes in order to be proactive, not reactive," said Bigger. "The programmatic additions such as the honor code and the judicial system helped Wofford define the value of our community. The facility improvements were enhancements that demonstrated that we were evolving into a better, stronger community prepared for the future."

—*JoAnn Mitchell Brasington '89*

Before the Benjamin Wofford Ball on Saturday night, both men and women looked forward to "Greek Games" during Spring Weekend.

Mary Beth Knight *(left)* '95 and Susan Harris Worley '96 sent this photo to Tim Allen, star of the popular television comedy *Home Improvement*, and asked him to wear a Wofford sweatshirt on the air. Sure enough, it happened on October 15, 1996.

Since 1990, "Bid Day" for the fraternities at Wofford traditionally ends with a plunge into the fountain and pool at the Church Street entrance to the campus.

A *Ministry of Presence*

Dr. Talmage Skinner '56 served as the Perkins-Prothro Chaplain at Wofford from 1986 through his retirement in 2003. During his career in the South Carolina Conference of the United Methodist Church, he pastored several Upstate congregations in addition to serving for 10 years as chaplain and instructor at Spartanburg Methodist College. Here is a conversation he had with the staff of *Wofford Today* in 1996.

It may seem strange to start by asking for a job description, but you've commented repeatedly that the church-related college is a unique form of ministry. Why do you say that?

I am grateful to God for this moment in time to live and work with these people—the faculty, staff and particularly the students of Wofford. As they live lives of service and go their separate ways, I have a unique and ultimate opportunity to live up to John Wesley's ideal—the world is my parish.

Our colleges ideally are communities like the old village parish, where all the neighbors know and care about each other. They are all involved in the same calling, the pursuit of

knowledge and personal growth. Not surprisingly, some members of this community are very interested in worship experiences; some are dubious or indifferent. Others may come from different Christian or non-Christian traditions than our own. Nevertheless, we endeavor, as John Wesley would say, to find the link between knowledge and vital piety. The Campus Ministry tries to keep that goal in focus by working closely with the trustees, faculty and staff as well as the student body.

I might add that this approach to education is part of the heritage not only of Wofford, but also of Methodism. As of 1990, there were 124 educational institutions across the country affiliated with our church that enroll more than 200,000 students. On the average, Methodist colleges and universities allocated almost 19 percent of their annual budgets to institutional financial aid, and a good portion of that investment in individual students was made possible because of dollars given by church members.

Dr. Talmage Skinner '56 conducted ecunmenical Holy Communion services in Mickel Chapel and made sure the space was available for individuals and religious fellowships.

How does the Campus Ministry at Wofford apply these principles?

At good church-related colleges, Campus Ministry takes many different forms, but it can never be something tucked away in a building on the edge of the campus, or simply trotted out on special occasions.

A Christian ministry of presence is at the heart of Wofford life. Perhaps the most important role of the chaplain is to be involved with the life of the campus in every way possible, from the athletics teams to the musical groups. The key word is available— available for counseling, friendship and support, whether in the privacy of an office, at halftime of the volleyball game, or even outside under an oak tree.

There are many and varied worship opportunities. The religious life council coordinates the activities of six chartered religious organizations representing Catholics, Episcopalians, Presbyterians, Methodists and Baptists as well as several nondenominational fellowships.

Today's Wofford students think globally

Premarital counseling is one of the important duties of a college chaplain. Through the years, Dr. Skinner officiated at almost 80 weddings involving members of the Wofford community.

Dr. Skinner inspired and led a tradition of frequent singing of the alma mater.

and act locally through the Twin Towers program that helps young men and women find a volunteer niche in the community. Our students have worked in Spartanburg human service agencies like the Boys & Girls Clubs, Habitat for Humanity, the St. Luke's Free Medical Clinic, a neighborhood soup kitchen, the South Carolina School for the Deaf and the Blind and others. With this experience behind them, Wofford graduates will become great assets to the churches and communities where they pursue careers and establish families. This may be the partial answer to the question, "What does the church get back for its investment in Wofford students through the Senior College Scholarship Fund?"

What do you see as the greatest challenge in the relationship between the church and the college?

The mood in the United States is mirrored in the life of the church and the colleges: reorganization, downsizing, more accountability. I think the church and its colleges need to be very careful during this period. It would be easy to start thinking like a married couple that has become a bit too comfortable in a long, happy and productive relationship. They start to ask themselves questions: What's in it for me? What does the college get out of its relationship with the church? Or, what does the church get out of its relationship to the college?

These are the wrong questions. We should be asking: What kind of people do we want our children and grandchildren to be? What kind of world do we want them to live in? How can we best shape our institutions to nurture those kinds of people and that kind of society?

Wofford is doing a lot of soul searching about those questions. We hope our churches will do so as well.

Wofford in the Community

Wofford's tradition of volunteer students goes back to the early 1950s. The Gas Bottom Project, which emerged under student leadership provided by Farrell Cox '54, was a pioneering biracial effort to provide recreational activities for children in this disadvantaged neighborhood near the campus.

In the late '60s, Happy Saturday volunteers met neighborhood children every week at a designated telephone pole for recreational activities. Henry Freeman '71 recalled asking for and receiving a $50 stipend from the college to buy peanut butter and jelly sandwiches for his guests.

In 1982, Dr. Larry McGehee, vice president of the college, worked with the Kettering Foundation on an important national project on civic engagement. The discussions led to the establishment of a number of formal and organizational volunteer services at Wofford and other institutions of higher education.

Over the two decades between 1984 and 2004, Wofford students provided more than 1,000 hours of weekly support to Spartanburg area human service programs during the academic year. A few of the agencies receiving support included the Boys & Girls Club, the Bethlehem Center, the St. Luke's Free Medical Clinic, "Just Say No" and a range of literacy programs. Many agency heads have said that they simply could not function without their Wofford students.

The Twin Towers volunteer service organization, formed in 1989, has been involved in many projects. For example, the annual Halloween Carnival and Terrier Play Day bring

Spartanburg's chapter of Habitat for Humanity, directed by Ben DeLuca '49, frequently partnered with college volunteers.

Winner of a Thomas Jefferson Award (WYFF-TV) for outstanding leadership and commitment to public affairs through community service, Samie Clowney '01 attended the Candler School of Theology at Emory University after graduation.

Advanced Spanish students of Dr. Laura Barbas Rhoden participated in a tutoring project in Spartanburg's Latino community, earning a 2003 South Carolina Commission on Higher Education Service Learning Award. Other projects brought children from central city neighborhoods onto the Wofford campus for a variety of activities.

a host of children from community service agencies to the campus to interact with Wofford students.

The Bonner Scholars Program began at Wofford during the 1991-1992 school year. It was among the first of 25 collegiate service scholarship programs nurtured by the Corella and Bertram F. Bonner Foundation in Princeton, New Jersey. In exchange for a scholarship commitment, Wofford's Bonner Scholars serve 300 hours during the school year and 240 hours during the summer in local and national service agencies. Students engage in a range of service issues and focus areas including literacy and education, children and mentoring, senior services, hunger and homelessness, medical service and environmental action.

In 2003, the Campus Ministry Center under the leadership of Dr. Ron Robinson '78 and the Rev. Lyn Pace '99 began offering expanded programming devoted to the concept of service learning, a four-fold mission that seeks to *inspire* participation in the spiritual journey, *motivate* commitment to Christian practices, *engage* in vocational discernment, and *build* social and spiritual assets in the culture.

In his first address to the South Carolina Methodist Annual Conference, Chaplain Robinson said, "We at Wofford want you to send us your finest students, formed in the Christian faith. We will send back to you young women and men who are prepared to be leaders in the church and community."

—*Doyle Boggs '70 with Lyn Pace '99*

Dr. Ron Robinson '78

Into *the* *Future:*
Engaged, Integrative Learning

In July 2000, Benjamin Bernard Dunlap became Wofford's 10th president. After the highly successful decade of the 1990s, many in the college community wondered whether the new administration would be characterized by continuity or change. The answer to that question proved to be "both."

The 2005 Presidential Seminar, led by Joe Lesesne and Benjamin Dunlap

The continuity was best reflected in Wofford's scores on a new instrument for institutional effectiveness. The National Survey of Student Engagement (NSSE) benchmarked institutions based on five comparative attributes: the level of academic challenge; active and collaborative learning; student-faculty interaction; enriching educational experiences; and a supportive campus environment.

Wofford scored so well on NSSE that it was selected for Project DEEP (Documenting Effective Educational Practices), which sent teams of educators to 20 campuses of various types and missions across the country. The project concluded in 2005 with a 348-page published report titled *Student Success in College*. Wofford, it was found, works as well as it does because people trust each other and want to do better tomorrow than they did today. The spirit of collaboration evidenced in administrative matters, among students working on group projects and engaging in group study in and outside of class, and via community events, provides rich conditions for active and collaborative learning.

As the new millennium approached, however, the Wofford community set out to move beyond its traditional strengths through ambitious curriculum reform. President Dunlap challenged each individual member of a growing, diverse and energetic faculty: "If you had the assurance of sufficient time and institutional support to teach the sort of course you've always dreamed of, what would you do?"

The response, outlined in the next few pages, suggests that the faculty took to heart Dunlap's call.

—Doyle Boggs '70

Dr. Charles Bass, McCalla Professor of Chemistry, is respected for the individual work he does with the students in his laboratories.

A *Fine Teacher* and a *Great Dean*

For a quarter century, Dan Maultsby has been the academic leader of Wofford College. Few academic deans have such a long tenure; far fewer yet have the admiration, respect and trust of their faculty that Dan has earned.

Dan's association with Wofford began in 1957 when he enrolled as a freshman. His undergraduate career was characterized by academic excellence and student leadership, both of the highest caliber. It was clear to all who knew him that Dan possessed personal characteristics that would make him a leader. After earning a doctorate in sociology at the University of Tennessee and serving two years as an Army officer, Dan returned to his alma mater in 1969 to begin a long and distinguished academic career, first as a professor, then as director of financial aid, and finally as senior vice president and dean of the college, the position he held in 2004.

I have had the privilege of knowing Dan since we were classmates at Wofford. I have worked with him during his entire academic career, and I have observed the ways he has shaped the character of Wofford College. Foremost among these has been his successful effort to perpetuate and enhance a spirit of trust, collegiality, cooperation and respect among students, faculty, administrators and alumni. This spirit, which virtually defines Wofford, is rare in academia. It has resulted in an atmosphere in which undergraduate liberal education thrives and in which both teachers and students feel challenged, supported and encouraged. Dan's success in enhancing this atmosphere can be measured by the low turnover rate among faculty and the low attrition among students. People who come to Wofford tend to stay.

Dan Maultsby has also shaped the character of Wofford through his efforts to recruit the very best faculty and students. I am convinced that the current faculty and students are the best in the nearly 50 years since I first came to Wofford. Such excellence is surely due in large measure to Dan's commitment to the recruitment of faculty and students who are well matched to the goals and character of the college.

As dean of the college, Dan has been unusually open and sympathetic to faculty. He gives patient and careful consideration to faculty ideas and concerns, and he is a faithful advocate for the faculty to other constituencies

Dean Dan B. Maultsby '61

of the college. Faculty recognize Dan Maultsby as a dean who can be trusted to do the best he can with the resources available to him to help them be the best teachers and scholars possible.

I have counted Dan Maultsby as my friend since we were freshmen at Wofford a long time ago. We have both spent our entire career at Wofford. For most of my teaching career Dan Maultsby was my dean, and it was a great privilege to have worked with him. He did not, of course, *bring* commitment, dignity and integrity to an office that lacked them; previous deans had those qualities in abundance. He did, however, bring his own version of those characteristics, a version that most others at the college and I have grown increasingly to appreciate. Dan has provided steadying guidance to Wofford, embracing innovation when it seems appropriate while remaining faithful to the goal of making Wofford a superior undergraduate liberal arts college. In a succession of fine academic administrators at Wofford, Dan Maultsby is surely one of the very best.

Dan Maultsby was a fine teacher, and he is a great dean. Even more important, he is a good man. He is what Wofford hopes its graduates will be. My favorite image of Dan is of him and his wife, Kit, walking home following the 2004 graduation, Dan still in his academic robe, holding one of his grandchildren.

—*Richard L. Robinson '61*

Opening Doors to Programs Abroad

In the early 1980s, when Dr. Susan Griswold became the chair of the foreign language department, Wofford offered group-travel experiences during the Interim, and students occasionally spent time in traditional European university settings. Given the rapidly changing world around them, the faculty wanted to lower the barriers that had restricted student interest in programs abroad. They knew Wofford would benefit enormously from having a cadre of seniors with experience in international universities and proficiency in foreign languages.

In 1987, Dr. Ana María Wiseman was named to the newly created position of study abroad advisor and, several years later, she was promoted to assistant dean of the college and director of programs abroad. Wofford previously had become affiliated with The Council for International Educational Exchange (CIEE), the Institute for the International Education of Students (IES), and several other consortia. Students who desired to study overseas were permitted to draw on funds from their financial aid packages. All grades and credits earned abroad carried full acceptance into the Wofford academic program, so there would be no delay in graduation.

Dean Ana María Wiseman

Wiseman also developed a set of preparatory and re-entry activities and resources including pre-departure student advising and a pre-departure family orientation. While abroad, students received sustained support from the college, including pre-registration for the semester in which they returned to

During her time in Paris, art history major Margaret Grimsley '05 took advantage of the opportunity to do freehand sketching in the Galley of Greek and Italian Sculpture at the Louvre. As a senior, she presented a paper titled, "Cennini and Alberti: The Late Medieval and Early Renaissance Theoretical Influences on the Practice and Painting of Fra Angelico at San Marco," at the National Conference for Undergraduate Research.

The global nature of Wofford studies abroad is reflected in the experience of Will Sloan '06 in Amman, Jordan *(left)*, and Rachel Doboney '05 in Copenhagen, Denmark.

Wofford. A student employee of the Office of Programs Abroad maintained communication with students, welcoming e-mail and photos as well as short commentaries about experiences overseas. Upon their return, the students attended welcome-home events, where they shared photos and stories with their fellow travelers, faculty and staff.

By the fall of 1991 participation in Programs Abroad at Wofford had soared. According to annual "Open Doors" studies reported in the *Chronicle for Higher Education*, Wofford consistently ranked in the top ten of all U.S. colleges and universities in percentage of students earning credit in foreign study. During the January Interim, Wofford students pursued intensive language and culture courses in Quebec, Italy, Spain and Germany.

The Programs Abroad concept continued to flourish and reached maturity as an integral part of the Wofford experience. In order to major or double-major in a foreign language, students in the 2000s planned on at least one semester studying overseas where their language is spoken and written. Also, majors wishing to be certified to teach a foreign language in public schools spent at least a semester overseas working to improve their oral proficiency. Other academic departments routinely encouraged their students to participate in foreign study. For example, majors in art history usually spent an Interim or a semester abroad, and government majors opting for the world politics concentration were required to study overseas.

In 1999, the department of foreign languages and the department of accounting and

finance integrated their offerings to create the exciting intercultural studies for business major. ISB majors were expected to complete a core of courses in accounting and finance, in the appropriate language track (French, German or Spanish), and they were required to spend at least one semester in a foreign study program.

—Doyle Boggs '70,
with Ana María Wiseman

The *Art* of *Mending:*
A *Presidential Scholar's Journey*

Seest thou not that the ships sail through the Ocean by the grace of Allah? ...
Verily in this are Signs for all who constantly persevere and give thanks.

—The Koran

As a rising senior at Wofford College in 2000, I was selected to serve as the 16th Presidential International Scholar. A scholar is invited to travel into countries that are usually considered "underdeveloped" from an occidental angle. The burden disguised in the accolade is outlined by the stated criteria for selection. The president of Wofford College selects the single student he or she deems "best fit to serve humanity."

President Dunlap poses with three of the scholars he has chosen: Allyn Steele '05, Thomas Pierce '06 and Dawna Quick '04.

By accepting the scholarship, a scholar assumes a lifelong obligation to serve humankind. With concept of service whittled in a Boy Scout troop, I knew the ideals of selflessness and leadership by example. When I traveled, the need for service unfolded like an infinite bolt of cloth that could not be returned to its spool. I lived intimately with water shortages, ecological questions, political debates, riots, disease, war, crime and socio-economic tensions. Every location broadened the awareness of my blind acceptance of the burden to serve. Most situations seemed desperate at best, if not beyond repair.

Halfway through my journey, I was aboard a felucca on the Nile River, conversing with its captain. Captain Awad was teaching me about Islam. As he spoke, he pointed to his tattered sail, worn from constant use.

"Kristofer," he said, "every day I thought Allah had to give me a new sail. If my sail does not survive, I cannot survive."

I expected a begging hand. So often, I had been requested to give money to support good causes. The Presidential Scholar is not allowed to give any money for charitable causes, which made the credit card always seem heavy in my pocket. I am ashamed of my assumption that his conversation was listing toward funding. Instead the captain of this small wooden vessel handed me a nugget of wisdom.

"I realized that if each person I meet gives me one small piece of cloth, I can mend the sail I have," Captain Awad smiled, "Allah is providing the new sail, one piece at a time." I had Awad's philosophy of mending as a boon for my return.

Kristofer Neely in northeast India near Guwahati

The Presidential International Scholarship was founded and funded by an anonymous donor who does not attempt to hide his identity from the scholar. In fact, the benefactor makes a point to contact the scholar quickly. I found him to be intense and forthright, with no hesitation in sharing his perspectives on the journey that he hopes will stir up the core of the driven and directed student who is blessed with this distinction.

Dr. Bill Mount, my major advisor, pulled me aside when I accepted this prize and asked, "Do you think it is wise to accept an award that promises one free year of dysentery?"

The journey is dysentery by design. It is a year of gut-wrenching, soul-shaking loneliness that opens the eyes of the scholar to the reality of the world in which we live. The boundlessness of the opportunity only adds

To my knowledge, even today just below the Aswan High Dam, Captain Awad steers his vessel with a patchwork sail. Into that off-white triangle is sewn the thin navy blue bandana that I gave him. The handkerchief once belonged to my brother, Erik. He passed away after my trip began. My journey was ripped at one edge by his unexpected death; I returned home to mourn before I ventured on.

When I left home for the second time, I carried that worn piece of cloth with me in my backpack. My trail went forward from the Dominican Republic, up the Amazon River on hammock boats, through the Andes Mountains, into South African prisons, and through the deserts of Jordan. I left the bandana as a scrap with Captain Awad on the Nile. I continued my journey through Israel, along the Ganges River system, and into the

to the stark contrast by providing a fanfare from the community before and after the journey begins. The donor wants every scholar to have "a combat experience that leaves you cold, wet, alone and missing your momma."

All of the condescending do-gooders in the world will not change the world as much as the world will change the individual scholar. The Presidential International Scholarship is not a fantasy tour, though the trip is mythic in its grand proportions and expectations. The lessons are simple. Meet a few more good people and learn about them. Enjoy the beauty of the earth. The donor's charge is to "return to Wofford with both of your thumbs." He knows that is the key to getting another student to sign up for the experience.

mountains of Nepal. I returned to America when my grandmother passed away.

Formally bookended by personal grief experiences, my trip is not really over. I carry the charge of service for humanity. It is heavier than my threadbare backpack ever was. Life is not without rough edges, but I, like Captain Awad, accept the patches I can collect. I still have some scraps to give in return. One Wofford student is given the chance each year to go all the way around the world to learn that the heroic dream of youth is passing, but the collective human spirit can triumph over all manner of human suffering, if we bother to look each other in the eye.

—*Kristofer Neely '02*

Furman Buchanan '88 took Wofford pennants with him on his journey as a Presidential International Scholar and shared them with Chinese children.

The *Novel Experience*

In 2002, Wofford inaugurated "The Novel Experience," to introduce first-year students both to the humanities and to the city of Spartanburg.

In this unique program, each freshman is asked to read a selected novel over the summer and write an essay of 250 to 500 words on a specified topic related to the novel. During the first week of class, all the freshman humanities classes report to Leonard Auditorium, where one representative of each class pulls the name of a Spartanburg restaurant out of a bucket. The restaurants have ranged from fine dining establishments to The Beacon and have included such establishments such as Abby's, Taco Dog and Longhorn Steakhouse. Then, during a true "town and gown evening," professors lead their students to the restaurants for discussions of the novel and an introduction to the Spartanburg community.

During the fall semester, the author of the book is invited to campus for a special convocation and a public reading later in the evening. The best first-year essays are published in an attractive booklet, and the author makes use of them in the convocation lecture and enjoys lunch with the published essayists.

In 2002, Charles Johnson's *Middle Passage* was selected, and "The Novel Experience" was mentioned in *USA Today*. The essay topics were "I am Rutherford Calhoun," or "I am not Rutherford Calhoun." For 2003, Geraldine Brooks' *Year of Wonders* was selected, and students wrote essays responding to the question, "Why is this a year of wonder?" For 2004, Orson Scott Card's *Ender's Game* was the novel of choice, and students wrote on the topic, "Is the War of the Third Invasion justified? Why or why not?"

The early development of The Novel Experience was largely the work of the late Dr. John Cobb '76, who was the coordinator of the Wofford humanities program and also taught in the college's Presidential Seminar. After his death in an automobile accident in the summer of 2004, Dr. Cobb's sister, Ann Cobb Johnson of Spartanburg, made a gift of $2.5 million to establish an endowed chair in his memory.

"Dr. Cobb was an exemplary member of the Wofford faculty, a gifted teacher who was respected and admired by colleagues, students, alumni and all others who knew him," said President Dunlap in announcing the gift. "The recipient of this major endowed chair must be an excellent, energetic and caring teacher-scholar with a passion for teaching students in and out of the classroom. The holder of this chair should be a person who excites and inspires students to excel."

—*Doyle Boggs '70 with Laura H. Corbin*

"The Novel Experience" author Charles Johnson speaks in Leonard Auditorium, while Dr. John Cobb looks on.

Learning Communities

"Students have so much to contribute and create, and they seem to learn more than in a traditional setting. There are no classroom walls, and we're learning from each other."

—Dr. Ellen Goldey, 2001-2002 United Methodist Foundation National Educator of the Year and first recipient of Wofford's Roger Milliken Award for Excellence in the Teaching of Science.

Jacob Smith '07 described "Meet the Creek Day" as "one of the biggest learning experiences in my life." Meg Morrison '07 wrote: "All of our best qualities shined through ... and enabled the schoolchildren to have respect for us and, more importantly, see us as role models."

These first-year students, both participants in a Wofford Learning Community, wrote these comments in their journals about the day in 2003 they hosted dozens of elementary school children in an outing to Lawson's Fork Creek. That class, called "the Nature and Culture of Water," explored connections between the sciences and the humanities—sometimes-isolated disciplines. The Wofford students studied the chemical and physical properties of water and the ecology of fresh water ecosystems. They also surveyed poetry, short stories and novels with themes linked to rivers, lakes and the natural world. With their professors, John Lane '77 and Dr. Ellen Goldey, and guests from a wide range of ages and backgrounds, they discussed value issues and the role that water plays in the religious, historical and social makeup of a community. Then they shared it with area children.

The success of this pilot project led to Goldey's applying for and the college receiving grants from the National Science Foundation and the Andrew Mellon Foundation to develop other learning communities combining science and the humanities.

Among the classes that resulted were: "The

The "Nature and Culture of Water" learning community meets at Lawson's Fork Creek near Spartanburg.

Science of Science Fiction," taught by Dr. Deno Trakas and Steven Zides; "Did You See That?—The Senses, the Mind and our Perception of Reality," taught by Dr. Clayton Whisnant and Dr. Dave Pittman '94; "Scientific and Literary Perspectives on Madness: Reality's Dark Dream," taught by Dr. Sally Hitchmough and Dr. Cecile McAninch; and "Thinking Like a Mountain: Conserving our Natural Heritage," taught by Dr. Gerald Thurmond and Dr. Doug Rayner.

Wofford was chosen along with 18 colleges and universities to participate in a National Learning Communities Project aimed at strengthening innovative approaches to college teaching and learning. In November 2003, Wofford and NLCP co-hosted a daylong event, which drew faculty from throughout the region who were interested in learning communities. A number of learning communities at Wofford were featured in the presentation.

—Doyle Boggs' 70 with
JoAnn Mitchell Brasington '89

Computational Science

Frank Seelos '99 performed computational science research at NASA's Jet Propulsion Laboratory (JPL) in Pasadena, California, during the summer of 1998. There, he worked with the Near Earth Asteroid Tracking (NEAT) team and developed software (HAVANA) to quickly access images of specific moving objects from JPL's extensive observational archive. In mid-July, NEAT observed a previously unknown asteroid for 12 days but needed earlier photographs to determine the object's exact path through space. Using HAVANA and careful mathematical computations, Seelos and another scientist found that the asteroid, previously undetected, had been captured on film from 1993. This archival discovery made it possible to calculate the asteroid's orbit with minimal error. Seelos' mentor at JPL, Dr. Eleanor Helin, recognized his contribution by naming an asteroid in his honor.

Computational Science is a fast-growing interdisciplinary field that is at the intersection of the sciences, computer science and mathematics. Many interesting and important scientific problems require its interdisciplinary approaches. Massive amounts of information in Web-acccssed databases (such as those for the human genome project) present to scientists daunting challenges in storage, retrieval, processing and visualization. Moreover, large, open-ended scientific problems (such as those for predicting hurricanes) often require the algorithms and techniques of computational modeling and simulation.

"Computers have become fast and cheap enough, networks have become sophisticated enough, scientific visualization has become mature enough, and the Internet has become pervasive and friendly enough so that a meaningful undergraduate computational science program is not only desirable but possible," said Dr. Angela Shiflet, chair of the computer science department. "Individual software applications are available, but we have been slow to organize the pieces into a suggested set of tools for undergraduates. We are working to fill that gap."

—Doyle Boggs '70

Frank Seelos '99

The *Write Stuff*

Emphasis on creative writing is a century-old tradition at Wofford, going back to the first issues of *The Journal* in 1889 and works by the students of Kenneth Coates from the 1930s through the 1960s. That tradition was enhanced in 1981 with the establishment of the Wofford Writers Series, then later with prizes for best student novel and the addition of a new program in creative writing.

Dr. Dennis Dooley was responsible for the creation of a series that has brought dozens of writers to the Wofford Campus. "I received a phone call from a literary agent in New York who was putting together an American tour by a promising Irish poet named Seamus Heaney [a future Nobel laureate]," recalled Dooley. "He was going to be in Columbia and two days later at a college in Virginia, and the agent needed a stop in between.

"She wanted to know if we were interested. She needed $500 to $700 for the visit, and I said yes without hesitating. I didn't know if the college had the money. I had heard about Seamus Heaney and read his poetry, and I figured I would pay out of my pocket if necessary. So Seamus came, and his visit was an enormous success."

Dooley and Dr. Deno Trakas received college funds to bring three writers to the campus in 1984-85. By then, the successful format for the Writers Series was established. An informal afternoon session in the Shipp Hall Lounge allowed audience members to question the writers about their motivation, their style and their publications. In the evening the writer gave a formal reading in what is now the McMillan Theater in the Campus Life Building. Over the years, the list of distinguished writers and poets has lengthened to a Who's Who in contemporary Southern literature, including Lee Smith, Larry Brown, Jill McCorkle, Dave Smith, James Dickey and Harry Crews.

In the 1990s, drawing upon faculty success in both the teaching and practice of writing fiction, poetry, plays and non-fiction, the Wofford creative writing program was organized into a formal sequences of courses, led by Trakas and John Lane '77 and augmented by other Wofford faculty and visiting professors, including novelist Rosa Shand. Among these new offerings was an advanced course that requires every student enrolled to write a novel. Between 1995 and 2004, more than 50 Wofford students wrote

novels in the course, offered every other year.

The best novels, selected in competitions, receive the Benjamin Wofford Prize and are published professionally for wider audiences. Occasionally a work of book-length nonfiction also receives the prize. Two thousand copies of each book, in paperback, are distributed to the campus community, English teachers and honors students in high schools, book review editors, and creative writing professors at other campuses.

Rucht Lilavivat's novel, *The Stars of Canaan*, received the first award, published in 1995, followed by Travis Wheeler's novel, *The Joshua Requiem* in 1997; Mac Leaphart's novel, *Strange Light* in 1999; Josh Hudson's *When You Fall* in 2001; Liz Scarborough's *Tangle* in 2003; and Thomas Pierce's *said the dark fishes* in 2005. In 2000, Scott Neely's *A Good Road to Walk* became the first winner of the Benjamin Wofford Prize for Nonfiction.

In addition to the novels, student works in poetry, short fiction and personal essay are regularly published in limited editions in-house. Wofford creative writing students have moved on to pursue graduate study at the University of Virginia, Bennington College, the University of North Carolina at Wilmington, Johns Hopkins University, Columbia University and Warren Wilson College, among others.

—Sarah Ross Cohen '88
and Lucas McMillan '02

Visiting writers traditionally meet informally with students for a question-and-answer period.

A KINGDOM OF THE JUST

by Benjamin B. Dunlap

I first came to Wofford in the early 1980s to address its faculty as part of a speakers' series sponsored by the South Carolina Committee for the Humanities. I remember gathering in the downstairs of Burwell, in the Montgomery Room. The event was well attended, and I got the general impression that Wofford professors were as affable and collegial as I knew its President Joe Lesesne to be. Joe and I had served together for some years on the South Carolina Rhodes Scholarship selection committee. Joe was the longtime chair of that committee, and I had come to admire the generous-spirited manner in which he presided over the competition, putting every candidate at ease and making sure they all felt like winners—as indeed they were. Joe had not been with me on the district committee when a brilliant young pre-med student named Eddie Coffey represented Wofford in the Rhodes competition and won. But I was there, in Atlanta, and I vividly remember thinking Eddie was a lot like Joe Lesesne in his unassuming eagerness to do what needed doing without any fuss about himself or his own accomplishments. For anyone old enough to recall the folksy wisdom and integrity of Sam Ervin during the Watergate hearings, it was a characteristic with powerful appeal.

I came back to Wofford in 1984 as a convocation speaker. This time, I spoke in "Old Main," in Leonard Auditorium, and,

presumably because attendance was required, that venerable hall was nearly full—suggesting to a jaded visitor from a state university that Wofford was full of students like Eddie Coffey, hungry for liberal learning. As it happens, my talk was a lighthearted and partly autobiographical paean to the liberal arts, and it got the sort of response that prompts a speaker to believe his audience must be remarkably enlightened. That conclusion was confirmed by the luncheon that followed, for I sat at a table with Joe Lesesne, Lewis Jones, B.G. Stephens, Dan Maultsby and Larry McGehee. There were giants in the earth in those days.

That same audience whose receptiveness had been so welcoming the year before invited me back as its commencement speaker in 1985. Perhaps to reassure me, Joe told me that the students who attended my previous appearance had petitioned to have me return for their graduation. Evidently, they wanted more of the humorous anecdotage that made them feel by contrast so confident in their own abilities. My life had been full of misadventures, so I had plenty of material. But this time I dwelt a bit more on the value—I believe I said "necessity"—for the sort of liberal arts education that places like Wofford afforded. And I witnessed something new: the extraordinary affection Wofford students and faculty felt for each other and for the experiences they had shared.

Everyone who chooses an academic career yearns to belong to such a place at such a time in its institutional history. It was obvious to me that Joe Lesesne and Dan Maultsby had created and sustained at Wofford an environment in which, as Joe himself once observed, they took what they did seriously without taking themselves seriously. It was a place where true community flourished, where collegiality was real, and the things that all admissions-office brochures purport to offer were truly to be found. The besetting sins of the academic world are envy and resentment, and internecine squabbles tend to be all the more vicious because, as Henry Kissinger once observed, the stakes are so small. But, in making that statement, Dr. Kissinger had assumed the stakes were merely a matter of status and remuneration where

Dr. C. Edward Coffey '74 was the college's fifth Rhodes Scholar and went on to a distinguished career in psychiatry. He also has the distinction of being one of the first of many Wofford men to marry a classmate, Kathleen Seegars '74.

rewards systems were askew and status was measured by how little one taught. At Wofford, I could see quite clearly, the stakes were vastly higher, involving an assurance that one's colleagues were just as hard working and just as committed to the essential task of teaching and learning as oneself. Nobody stood on his dignity, and everyone had the satisfaction of being part of something they loved and served. I had always supposed such an academic utopia must exist, but I had begun to despair of finding it. I left the Wofford campus almost reluctant to return, for fear my naïve enthusiasm might be dispelled.

But I did return … for the dedication of the new Franklin Olin Building in 1992. There was to be a televised roundtable discussion followed by a banquet in the new building itself, and, for both events, I was seated next to Roger Milliken who, as chairman of the facilities committee of the Wofford Board of Trustees, presided like Gandalf over festivities in the Shire. In the course of our feast, I had the temerity to tell Mr. Milliken that, given its state-of-the-art technology and design, "anyone would be delighted to teach in such a place." Shortly afterwards, I was visited in

Columbia by a delegation including Joe Lesesne, Dan Maultsby and Larry McGehee. They were there to offer me the new Chapman Family Professorship in the Humanities.

That was a life-changing moment for me. For the next seven years, I taught full time at Wofford, offering interdisciplinary courses in the arts and humanities, teaching British, American and European literature as well as Asian studies, film history and creative writing. Together, Joe Lesesne and I launched the Presidential Seminar, offered to graduating seniors every spring—Joe being the initial president in question and the late John Cobb serving as my collaborator when spring football and other commitments took Coach Joe away from campus. During those years, I also traveled with Wofford students on Interim trips to India, Indonesia, Europe and the South Pacific, and, as much as my students and I went out to the world, the world came back to us each semester in the person of Sandor Teszler, who audited classes at Wofford into his 97th year. We voted unanimously to make the wise and good Mr. Teszler an honorary member of our faculty. It was typical of him that Mr. Teszler, as modestly self-effacing as

Sweet tea on the front porch of the president's house is a Friday afternoon tradition at Wofford.

Joe Lesesne himself, was so pleased by this gesture, whereas, in point of fact, we had honored ourselves by honoring him.

In the spring of my seventh year, I was unexpectedly and improbably catapulted into the presidency of Wofford College. I write in my fifth year as president, and, though it is too soon to comment on changes that are taking place around me, it is reassuringly clear that, as legendary faculty and staff retire, they are being replaced by gifted successors who feel the same gratitude I did when, late in my career, I stumbled into this little Kingdom of the Just.

Under the continuing aegis of Roger Milliken, there have been stunning additions to the campus. Continuing the momentum established by the Olin Building a decade before, the Roger Milliken Science Center is surely the most significant new facility since Old Main itself. Russell C. King Field and Switzer Stadium have been built along with Wightman Hall, and dramatic renovations have transformed Andrews Field House, the Campus Life Building, the Burwell dining facility, and, yes, even Old Main, which, as I write, is having its antique splendor restored. The first of two new housing facilities is already under construction, keeping pace with the needs of a changing student body. Land acquisition has expanded the campus itself by over 50 percent in the past decade, and its designation as a national arboretum merely confirms the obvious for any visitor: Wofford is one of the most beautiful college campuses in America.

During this same period, Wofford's faculty has continued a steady expansion, offering

Dr. Ingrid Geer Shick '98 poses in front of the mural she created for the biology department suite in the Roger Milliken Science Center. After graduation, she began her practice of veterinary medicine and married classmate Bryan Shick.

new courses of study and earning a well-deserved national reputation for curriculum innovation. Students get better and more diverse every year, although Wofford remains true to its essential mission of educating the future leaders of our state and region.

The authentic, if somewhat fatuous, enthusiasm of William Wordsworth in the aftermath of the French Revolution is often quoted to students of romantic literature: "Bliss was it in that dawn to be alive, but to be young was very heaven." I was not young when I first came to Wofford, and I have grown considerably older since that first visit. But I can report that, more than 11 years into my time here, it has been for me a time of unrelenting bliss. I can only imagine and envy what Wofford must be like today for students, but I have a good opportunity to learn more about that perspective from my grand-daughter, who came as a first-year student in the fall of 2004. I readily confess to my own infatuation with Wofford, but this college is, I am altogether confident, a more reliable source of meaning and satisfaction than any revolution. For, from Ben Wofford to Joe Lesesne and onward to those who will come after us, Wofford has been in its essential characteristics a constant and unchanging star, shining untarnished. So it was, so it will be.

Wofford College, now and forever!

The interior of the Campus Life Building was spruced up and greatly enhanced during the college's sesquicentennial with projects related to the McMillan Theater (formerly the lecture-cinema room) and the Commons (below).

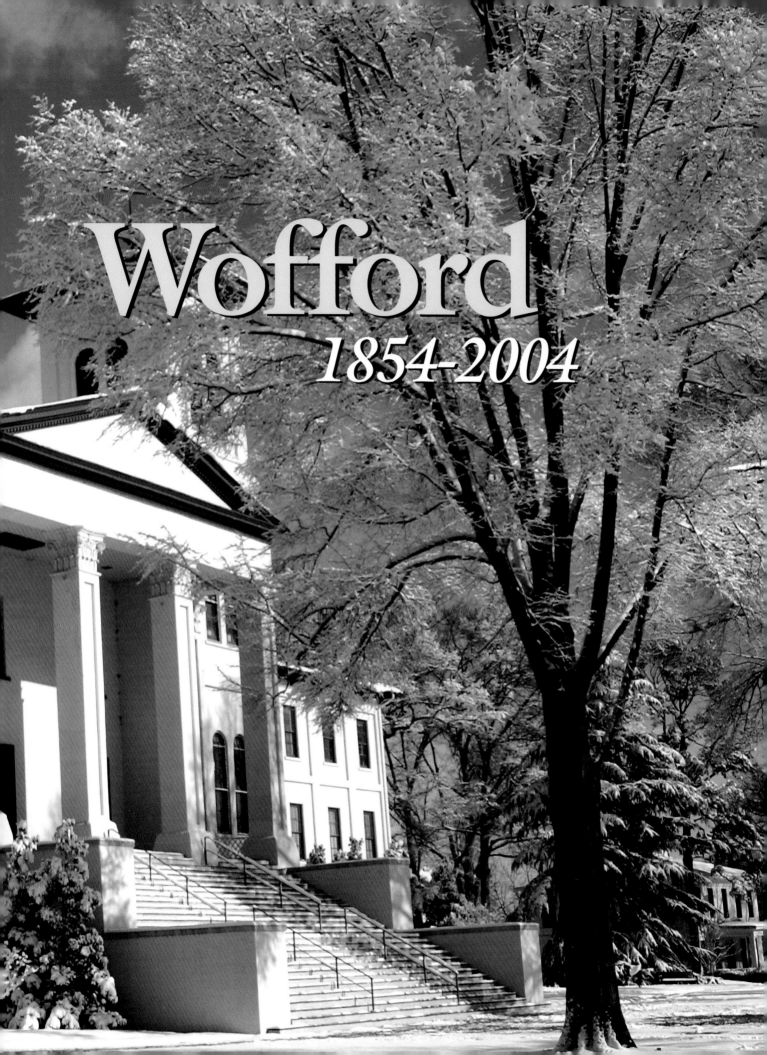

Wofford
1854-2004

A WOFFORD COLLEGE CHRONOLOGY

December 2, 1850 — The Rev. Benjamin Wofford of Spartanburg dies, leaving a bequest of $100,000 to found a college "for literary, classical and scientific education in his native district." Trustees are to be elected by the appropriate Annual Conference of the Methodist Church.

August 1, 1854 — The college opens for its first session with an enrollment of seven students. A future Methodist bishop, William Wightman, is the first president.

July 1856 — Wofford confers its first degree. The recipient, Samuel Dibble, goes on to enjoy a distinguished business and civic career in Orangeburg, South Carolina, and, in the 1880s, serves in the US House of Representatives.

July 12, 1859 — With Charles Petty as the first president, a Wofford alumni association is organized. The motto, originally in Greek, is "We, the adopted, honor the mother who nourished us."

May 1864 — Trustees invest virtually all of the college's endowment in Confederate currency, bonds, and other soon-to-be-worthless securities.

1869 — The first Greek-letter social fraternities, including a still-active chapter of Kappa Alpha, are founded on the campus.

1875 — James H. Carlisle becomes president, serving through 1902. Sometimes called the "greatest South Carolinian of his day," Carlisle was known throughout the region as an inspirational teacher of ethics and morals.

January 1889 — The first issue of the Wofford *Journal* appears; it is thought to be the oldest continuously published college literary magazine in the South.

"In heaven above, where all is love,
There'll be no faculty there;
But down below, where all is woe,
The faculty, they'll be there.
W-o-f-f-o-r-d, W-o-f-f-o-r-d,
W-o-f-f-o-r-d.
Hang the faculty!"

—Student yell of the 1890s

December 14, 1889 — Wofford and Furman play South Carolina's first intercollegiate football game.

November 6, 1895 — Professors Henry Nelson Snyder and A.G. Rembert represent Wofford as 10 leading colleges and universities meet in Atlanta to form the Southern Association of Colleges and Schools, a regional accrediting agency. Chancellor James H. Kirkland of Vanderbilt University, an 1877 Wofford graduate, is considered to be the association's founder.

1902 — Henry Nelson Snyder begins his 40-year administration as president. He is generally credited with establishing Wofford's academic reputation. In his first decade as president, he secures the funds needed to build a science hall, a library building and a large new residence hall.

1904 — Trustees decide to admit only men as students, ending a period when undergraduate women had studied at Wofford. (Between this date and 1975, a few faculty wives and daughters were accepted as commuting students, and women were admitted as graduate students during a period when master's degrees were offered.)

"Let him [the patriot] as Wofford did, spend a life of hardship and toil that he might found an institution, from which, as a foundation source, a triple stream of education, refinement and religion might flow forth, refreshing all the land. ... What must he be but a true patriot who contributes his wealth to the establishment of a well ordered college, blessing his country by the spread of education and the dissemination of the principles of honor, truth and virtue?"

—1857 graduate William Maxwell "Ruby" Martin,
delivering the 1860 commencement address.

December 29, 1919 — Wofford becomes one of the first church-related colleges in the United States to receive a unit of the infantry Reserve Officers' Training Corps. Approximately 2,000 Wofford graduates have received officers' commissions in the Army, Army Reserve or Army National Guard.

February 1928 — Twenty-one Wofford students, under the direction of Professor James A. "Graveyard" Chiles, form a club they call the *Deutscher Verein*. Seeing the need for an international honor society devoted to the study of German language and literature, the Wofford group goes on to form Delta Phi Alpha, which has grown to more than 30,000 living members with a headquarters at the University of Hawaii-Manoa. Wofford's alpha chapter is still active.

June 1933 — Faculty and staff finish a Depression year during which they work without pay for seven months. Wofford has accumulated an operating deficit approaching $187,000, and almost one-third of the $700,000 endowment is "non-productive." Emergency measures are necessary, but within four years, Wofford is relatively comfortable and again operating in the black. By 1942 and the coming of World War II, the college is debt-free.

January 14, 1941 — Wofford receives a chapter of Phi Beta Kappa, the prestigious liberal arts honor society. As of 2004, there are 270 of these chapters across the country. The independent Phi Beta Kappa colleges and universities in the Carolinas are Davidson (1923), Duke (1920), Furman (1973), Wake Forest (1941) and Wofford.

August 1942 — The only alumnus or alumna to serve as president of Wofford, Dr. Walter K. Greene '03, takes office as Snyder retires. Greene serves as president of both Wofford and Columbia Colleges for a brief period in the early 1950s as the Methodist Church tries to decide what do to with its colleges.

February 22, 1943 — Wofford classes move to Converse and Spartanburg Junior Colleges while the Army uses the campus to train "pre-flight" aviation cadets. Although most young men are in the armed services, some civilian classes resume on the campus in September 1944.

Spring 1948 — Wofford begins the "King Teen" program, one of the first merit scholarship competitions in the country. Its successor program, Wofford Scholars, continues into the 21st century.

September 1, 1952 — Dr. Francis Pendleton Gaines becomes president.

1953 — The Spartanburg County Foundation presents Wofford with a small planetarium for use by the college and youth groups in the community. For a generation, this is the only public planetarium in South Carolina.

September 1958 — Dr. Charles F. Marsh becomes president. During his administration, enrollment is allowed to rise gradually to a self-imposed ceiling of 1,000 men. Many new buildings are constructed, including the Milliken Science Building, the Sandor Teszler Library, the Burwell student and food service center, an°d three new residence halls.

May 12, 1964 — Wofford Trustees issue a formal statement that prospective students will be judged according to standards uniformly applied "regardless of race or creed." When Albert W. Gray of Spartanburg enrolls in the fall, Wofford becomes one of the first historically white independent colleges in the region to admit African Americans voluntarily.

"It has always been a source of pride to me to speak of the special quality of my Wofford education, and its unfailing service to me, in a multitude of tasks and projects over six decades. … My love and gratitude to Wofford endures and grows. Long may she flourish, as alma mater to new generations of young men and women, in their intellectual, moral and spiritual preparations for life."

—Albert C. Outler '28
Response to National
Alumni Association's
Distinguished Service
Award, 1987

January 1968 — Wofford adopts the 4-1-4 academic calendar, which allows students to spend the month of January working on a special "project." Many use this opportunity to do independent study or undertake travel-study tours with faculty.

September 1, 1968 — Paul Hardin III becomes president, serving for almost four years before leaving to become president of Southern Methodist University and, later, chancellor at the University of North Carolina at Chapel Hill. During a time of turmoil on college campuses, Hardin institutes a number of reforms, including "The Code of Student Rights and Responsibilities." Beverage alcohol is now permitted in certain places on campus, and compulsory "chapel" assemblies are abolished.

June 30, 1972 — Joab M. Lesesne Jr. becomes president.

1973 — The golf team, coached by Earle Buice, is host for the NAIA national championship tournament and wins it. This achievement is believed to represent the first national championship won by a South Carolina college or university in any sport.

June 1973 — Wofford receives $400,000 from the National Endowment for the Humanities to implement a revised and expanded humanities curriculum. The approved proposal provides for graduation requirement changes, two new majors, seminar-type humanities courses, and reading and writing laboratories.

September 1973 — South Carolina Tuition Grants program is implemented, providing financial assistance for deserving South Carolina students at independent colleges.

December 1973 — C. Edward Coffey '74 is selected as the fifth Rhodes Scholar from Wofford. (Dr. Coffey's subsequent career includes heading the department of psychiatry at Detroit's Henry Ford Medical Center.)

September 1974 — The South Carolina Conference of the United Methodist Church approves a plan to expand the Board of Trustees from 21 to 27 members and abandons a traditional quota of 11 lay members and 10 clergy Trustees. "Old Main" and the surrounding areas of the campus are designated as a National Historic District.

October 1975 — After a thorough study, the Board of Trustees approves the faculty's recommendation to institute residential coeducation at Wofford. By the fall of 1978, the first-year class is composed of 221 men and 79 women.

May 1977 — The Truman Scholars program begins, and Wade Ballard '79 is South Carolina's first winner.

March 1980 — Trustee "Gus" Papadopoulos '54 provides the funds for a weekend faculty/staff retreat to Fripp Island. Small groups discuss "The Essence of Wofford's Future." The concept is so successful that it becomes an (almost) annual event. Papadopoulos later becomes the first Wofford alumnus to pass the $1 million milestone in lifetime contributions to his alma mater.

June 1980 — First sessions of a Summer Program for Academically Talented Students (Grades 5-9) are held.

January 1981 — The $4.2 million Campus Life Building opens with a basketball game against The Citadel and a Wofford Theatre Workshop production of Shakespeare's *Twelfth Night*.

November 1983 — *U.S. News & World Report* publishes the first in its series of higher education ratings, placing Wofford among "America's Best Colleges." Wofford continues to do well in these annual surveys, ranking in the top three among "Southern regional liberal arts colleges" for five straight years before being promoted to a "national liberal arts college."

December 1983 — Wofford receives a $500,000 gift from The Abney Foundation of Greenwood, South Carolina, to establish the John Pope Abney Memorial Scholarship Fund. Subsequent contributions have continued to increase the endowment and scope of this program.

January 1985 — Danny Morrison '75 becomes Wofford's first full-time director of athletics, setting the stage for trustee approval of a plan for Wofford to join the NCAA. Morrison's administration of the athletics program continues through 1996, when he is promoted to senior vice president.

March 1985 — President Lesesne becomes the first Southerner to be chairman of the National Association of Independent Colleges and Universities (NAICU). During the '80s, he also serves on the board of directors of the prestigious American Council on Education, and as president of the Southern University Conference.

November 1985 — Collier Slade '87 travels around the world studying the problem of global deforestation as the first annual Presidential International Scholar.

June 1986 — Dr. Talmage Skinner '56 becomes the college's campus minister, improving spiritual life on the campus and developing student volunteer programs.

October 1986 — The Neofytos D. Papadopoulos Building opens and becomes "Wofford's New Front Door." The adjacent Hugh S. Black Building is extensively renovated for use by the admissions and financial aid offices in observance of its centennial in 1988.

May 1987 — Trustees approve the yearlong work of a planning task force chaired by President Lesesne and Trustee Chairman Russell King '56. Adoption of this Masterplan signals new momentum and sets dramatically higher goals for the college.

September 1989 — The F.W. Olin Foundation announces a $5.5 million gift to Wofford for a new academic building featuring first-rate computer and video teaching technology. The building is dedicated in May 1992, in colorful ceremonies.

June 1990 — College launches *The Campaign for Wofford: An Investment in People*, a $33.3 million drive to provide the first one-third of the funding for the 1987 Masterplan. Successful completion of this effort is announced in December 1991.

The Spires of Wofford

What say the spires of Wofford
That tower toward the sky?
One says, "Young man, stand firmly."
The other says, "Aim high."

What say the bells of Wofford
That call to wanton youth?
They plead, "Young man, speak surely
And always speak the truth."

What say the oaks of Wofford
Where robins nest and sing?
They say, young man drink deeply
Of the Pierian spring.

What say the sons of Wofford
On far-flung fields alone
They say, "Young man, you'll garner
As you have tilled and sown."

Though obviously inspired by a similar poem about Oxford University, these sentiments were well-received on the campus. For some years, "The Spires of Wofford" was memorized during orientation. The author, John Marvin Rast, was a Georgia native and an Emory graduate. A Methodist minister, he served a number of South Carolina pulpits before becoming editor of the Southern Christian Advocate. In 1941, he became president of Lander College and later served as executive secretary of the South Carolina Conference Board of Education. He received an honorary doctorate from Wofford in 1940.

September 1991 — Wofford has its first Goldwater Scholar, Jay E. Harris '93, and launches the Bonner Scholars Program to provide financial aid for deserving students and to encourage volunteerism.

May 1992 — The new John E. Reeves Tennis Center is dedicated, and the golf team plays host to the NCAA Division II national tournament.

July 1992 — Wofford shares in the estate of Mrs. Charles E. Daniel. Her will establishes three professorships ($2.25 million) and provides an additional $10 million for the general endowment.

May 1994 — Jerry Richardson '59 is the owner and founder of the Carolina Panthers of the NFL. To attract the team's summer training camp to Spartanburg, the people of the city and various agencies contribute the money needed to build the Richardson Physical Activities Building and Gibbs Stadium on newly acquired land north and east of the campus. The Panthers make their first visit to the college in July and August 1995.

September 1995 — Wofford becomes a member of NCAA Division I in athletics, competing at the I-AA level in football. Wofford fields additional women's sports teams in soccer, golf and track. In December, Wofford accepts an invitation to join the Southern Conference, effective with the 1997-98 academic year. The Terriers are very competitive in their first season and capture conference awards for sportsmanship and graduation rates among student-athletes.

December 1996 — A study by the Institute for International Education of Students reveals that Wofford leads the nation in sending students abroad to earn academic credit.

1997 — The distinguished historian of Southern politics, Dr. Dewey Grantham, comes to Wofford for the spring semester as the first Lewis P. Jones Visiting Professor in the department of history. The endowed chair had been established in April 1996 with a gift from Mr. and Mrs. George Dean Johnson Jr. In September, a $1 million gift from the Perkins-Prothro Foundation of Wichita Falls, Texas, creates an endowed chair in the department of religion for the chaplain of the college.

July 2000 — Benjamin B. Dunlap, Chapman P professor of Humanities, becomes Wofford's tenth president. He replaces Joab M. Lesesne Jr., who retires after serving since 1972.

April 2001 — The Roger Milliken Science Center opens, housing the departments of biology, chemistry, physics and psychology.

October 2001 — The "voice of Wofford," the original college bell cast by the famous Meneely Foundry in West Troy, New York, is restored and again rings out proudly from the west tower of "Old Main." It is part of an ongoing effort to preserve and modernize the historic academic building.

April 2002 — The United Methodist Education Foundation names Dr. Ellen Goldey of the biology department as the Outstanding Educator of the Year. Ben Foster '02 wins the Arthur Ashe Jr. Award as the outstanding male African-American College Athlete (*Black Issues in Higher Education* magazine).

September 2002 — First-year humanities classes enjoy a "Novel Experience" as part of their orientation. They read the novel *Middle Passage*, write essays for publication, and hear from the author, Charles Johnson.

"Wofford was where I met Thoreau and Lippmann, and Byron, Shelley and Keats; and where I found out the hard way that I could have known them far better had I not stayed out half the night chasing thrills and the other half trying to catch up. Weeding out empty distractions from the few basic rules worth living by did not come easy. It was here, too, in the late 1960s, where it became clear that war was real, hatred and racism were wrong, and scholarship and character went hand in hand. A lot of us learned these things back then … .

"And as I was leaving, I stood before the twin towers of Old Main, that magnificent classroom building at the heart of the campus where as an uneasy freshman I came face to face with growing up. The return to that spot renewed my strength, not as a young student away from home for the first time, but as a mortal man who prays a lot, and still wonders about what lies ahead.

And isn't this what a college is supposed to do?"

—John Burbage '70

November 2002 — The entire 150-acre campus is designated as the "Wofford Arboretum" in ceremonies featuring horticulturalist Michael Dirr and landscape architect Rick Webel. The college is a member of the American Association of Botanical Gardens and Arboreta. Nearly 4,500 trees were planted between 1992 and 2002, representing 97 native varieties.

November 2003 — The Terrier football team sweeps through its Southern Conference season undefeated and advances to the NCAA-Division I semifinals. Mike Ayers is the 2003 winner of The Sports Network's Eddie Robinson Award, signifying Division I-AA's National Coach of the Year.

February 2004 — Russell C. King Field opens, marking the return of Terrier baseball to a campus venue. Allyn Steele '05 is selected as a second team (top 40) member of *USA Today's* 2004 All-College Academic team.

2004 — The Anna Todd Wofford Center, in a renovated portion of Andrews Field House, provides additional office and meeting space for women's organizations and other student groups. Ongoing improvements to the Campus Life Building include a new Commons area and the McMillan Theater.

> *"Somehow, in spite of all the complexities, the individual student still manages to come in contact with the individual teacher. And occasionally, too, as in the old days, a student goes out and by his deeds and words makes an old professor remembered for his good intentions, and his college respected for the quality of its worksmanship."*
>
> —Professor K.D. Coates in the Spartanburg *Herald-Journal* Centennial Edition, 1954.

WOFFORD COLLEGE BOARD OF TRUSTEES

During a session in the mid-1970s, a group of newly elected members of the Wofford Board of Trustees was meeting for orientation to their new responsibilities. A member of the administrative team instructed the new board members: *"We hope that after today's session, you understand that you and your fellow trustees own Wofford College. Now, it is time that you all start paying for it!"*

It is the legal *ownership* of the college that resides with the Board of Trustees, collectively, according to the will of Benjamin Wofford and subsequent examinations of the college and its governance. How that ownership group has led and influenced the operation of the college over 150 years has evolved, much as the traditions and social practices have changed during the same time.

The 13 men named in the Wofford will as the original Board of Trustees were leaders of high moral character, religious training and good judgment. The will provided for trustee elections every two years through the "Conference of the Methodist Episcopal Church of the State of South Carolina." The number of trustees remained at 13 until the 1950s and only has been increased three times since, with a change in 2004 increasing the size of the board to 31 persons by 2007.

Through World War II, the presidents of Wofford and the other denominational colleges typically were recognized as key leaders in the Methodist Church in South Carolina. President Henry Nelson Snyder at one time actually chaired the conference committee responsible for selecting trustees. The trustees of that era, when the church directly funded almost one-third of the operating budget, were best described as overseers. Their job was to ensure that college officials were managing the modest assets of the institution soundly, and that no crisis reached to the point of being unmanageable. However, in the 1970s, tension developed, and it was actually possible for persons to be nominated by the authorized church committee—ultimately to be formally elected at the Annual Conference—who were *unknown* to the trustees and the administration. It also was theoretically possible for the conference to unseat the entire incumbent board in one session. In 1986, at the suggestion of accrediting agencies, a new system was devised to ensure advice and consent between church and college communities in trustee selection and to implement a system of electoral classes for the boards of Columbia and Wofford, with members serving staggered four-year terms.

Throughout their history, the trustees of Wofford College have been persons of keen interest in the college and its future, possessing outstanding character, a high level of business intelligence, and a willingness to work on behalf of the college. Their greatest responsibility is perhaps the selection of an able president to lead the day-to-day affairs of the institution, while at the same time offering guidance and financial support, as well as partnering with the chief executive and his cabinet to further the institutional vision.

The process begun in 1986 has continued, as has the momentum it generated. Of course, Wofford successfully secured the once-denied grant from the F. W. Olin Foundation, a result made possible in large part because the trustees stepped forward with greater leadership and financial support. The trustees also engaged in benchmarking other successful institutions, in studying marketing, and in raising funds and visibility. The number of standing committees has grown to eight, with each trustee serving on two, plus other key assignments. In the early 2000s, their meetings three times annually were spread over two days each, packed with discussion and information. The number of clergy trustees has decreased from a high of 11 to the present five, but the relationship with the United Methodist Church, and the presence of the church within the college program remains as strong as ever.

Former Wofford trustee and board chair Minor Mickel Shaw, whose term on the board ran from 1992 through 2004, was involved with and helped lead the transformation of Wofford and its board. Upon being elected chair in 2002, she was asked about trusteeship. "Perfect trustees need the best possible understanding of the larger picture. To take Wofford as an example, our trustees must understand how and why students and parents choose us over 3,000 other colleges. They need to know how college budgets are balanced and the financial aid process. They need to know a lot about peer institutions and competitors. That's the only way a trustee can develop a personal vision and participate wisely in the development of a corporate vision."

— *David Beacham '77*

At the February 2003 meeting, the trustees who were present participated in this group portrait. They are: President Dunlap, Minor Shaw, Will Willimon, and Gus Papadopoulos *(front row)* • Jack Meadors, Bernie Brooks, Jeannette Cooper Dicks, and Margaret Seymour *(second row)* • Hugh Lane, Katy Close, Tommy Brittain, Mike James, and Ed Reeves *(third row)* • Don Fowler, Paula Baker, Al Gray, Bob Stillwell, Russell King, Stewart Mungo, Julian Osbon, Roger Milliken, and Mike Brown *(fourth row)*

TRUSTEE HONOR ROLL

With grateful appreciation, the service of members of the Wofford College Board of Trustees from 1954 through 2004 is recognized.

R. Wright Spears
Herbert Lee Spell
Currie B. Spivey Jr.
W. Cantey Sprott
Agnes S. Stackhouse
Robert E. Stillwell
Hunter R. Stokes
Wallace A. Storey
Toccoa W. Switzer
Andrew Teszler
T. Reginald Thackston
Paul C. Thomas
E. H. Thomson
Robert P. Timmerman
James F. Trammell
Thomas T. Traywick
Benjamin R. Turner
Joella F. Utley
William J. Vines
Woodrow Ward
Joseph E. Wheeler
George W. Whitaker Jr.
J. Anthony White

FACULTY AND THE PRESIDENTIAL CABINET

With grateful appreciation, the following members of the Wofford community are recognized for their contributions to the college between 1954 and 2004. They are members of the full-time instructional faculty who attained tenured status (or who were to be considered for tenure after December 31, 2004). This list also includes a few faculty members who held special appointments, administrators serving in the president's cabinet, and professional librarians.

C. L. Abercrombie III
Fred T. Adams
George C. S. Adams
Jhon C. Akers
A. K. Anderson
Frank J. Anderson
Katerina Andrews
Nancy M. Arant
Constance A. Antonsen
Caleb A. Arrington
Hugh T. Arthur
Jack D. L. Ballance
Laura H. Barbas Rhoden
Charles D. Barrett
Charles G. Bass

James D. Bass
Ross H. Bayard
David M. Beacham
Curtis P. Bell
Camille L. Bethea
Roberta H. Bigger
Linda Powers Bilanchone
Victor Bilanchone
W. Raymond Bourne
Robert Arthur Brent
Timothy E. Brown
James R. Bruce
John M. Bullard
Mark S. Byrnes
Donald A. Castillo

Matthew E. Cathey
Charles E. Cauthen
William P. Cavin
L. Harris Chewning
Cermette J. Clardy
Kenneth D. Coates
John C. Cobb
Oakley H. Coburn
Alice H. Cochran
Jerome R. Cogdell
T. Keller Cogswell
John W. Coker
Lester H. Colloms
Philip S. Covington
Caroline A. Cunningham

Faculty at Opening
Convocation 2004

G. R. Davis Jr.
William E. DeMars
Joaquin F. DeVelasco
Christine S. Dinkins
H. Donald Dobbs
John T. Doby
Dennis M. Dooley
Benjamin B. Dunlap
Linton R. Dunson Jr.
Mark A. Ferguson
Terry A. Ferguson
Vivian B. Fisher
Jacques C. B. Forbes
John K. Fort
John G. Fulmer Jr.
Pendleton Gaines
Marie Gargarine
Daniel D. Gilbert
Susan E. Gilbert
Gerald A. Ginocchio
Ellen S. Goldey
Lillian E. Gonzalez
Karen H. Goodchild
R. Stephen Gowler
Boylston Green
Harold W. Green
Edward E. Greene
Walter K. Greene
Reese E. Griffin
Natalie S. Grinnell
Susan C. Griswold
J. R. Gross
Lee O. Hagglund
William W. Halligan Jr.
Ibrahim Hanif
Daniel H. Hank
Paul Hardin III
John W. Harrington
Barbara A. Heinick
Matthew A. Henderson
M. Elton Hendricks
Edmund Henry
Stacey R. Hettes
Jameica B. Hill
John Q. Hill
Sally A. Hitchmough
William B. Hubbard
Herbert Hucks

Walter E. Hudgins
Robert C. Jeffrey
Richard A. Johnson
Lewis P. Jones
Charles D. Kay
Robert L. Keasley
Philip S. Keenan
James A. Keller
Joseph H. Killian
Li Qing Kinnison
Charlotte A. Knotts-Zides
Kirsten A. Krick-Aigner
David I. Kusher
John E. Lane
John C. Lefebvre
J. Daniel Lejeune
W. Ray Leonard
Joab M. Lesesne Jr.
Ta-Tseng Ling
James C. Loftin
Paul S. Lofton Jr.
S. Frank Logan
Frank M. Machovec
C. Randolph Mahaffey
James P. Mahaffey
Nancy B. Mandlove
Charles F. Marsh
Esther M. Martin
George B. Martin
Dan B. Maultsby
Cecile B. McAninch
John R. McArthur
Byron R. McCane
W. Gary McCraw
Larry T. McGehee
Stephen A. Michelman
Vincent E. Miller
Edward R. Minus
Ted R. Monroe
Daniel B. Morrison Jr.
W. Scot Morrow
Robert F. Moss
William W. Mount
Samuel R. Moyer
James R. Neighbors
Charles F. Nesbitt
Roger O. Niles
C. C. Norton

Daniel W. Olds
Mark N. Packer
William A. Parker
Raymond A. Patterson
E. Gibbes Patton
Marion B. Peavey
Howard McI. Pegram
Charles S. Pettis
Russell C. Picton
John W. Pilley
David W. Pittman
Sally H. Plowden
J. Michael Preston
David Prince
James E. Proctor
Lucy B. Quinn
Philip N. Racine
Ramin Radfar
Douglas A. Rayner
Alliston K. Reid
Ricardo F. Remirez
Tracy J. Revels
Mary Margaret Richards
Wm. Eddie Richardson
Richard L. Robinson
Ron R. Robinson

Edward E. Greene was a
capable and dedicated senior
administrator from 1963
through 1996.

Faculty regalia reflects the diversity of the members' graduate universities: Dr. John Lefebvre (Duke University); Dr. Christine Dinkins (Johns Hopkins University); Dr. Mark Ferguson '94 (Washington University, St. Louis); Dr. David Pittman '94 (Florida State University).

Anne B. Rodrick
G. Mackay Salley
John L. Salmon
W. W. Scheerer
Catherine L. Schmitz
Timothy J. Schmitz
Peter L. Schmunk
Bates L. Scoggins
Donald M. Scott
Joseph Secondi
James E. Seegars
John L. Seitz
Christi L. Sellars
Angela B. Shiflet
George W. Shiflet
Edward H. Shuler

Talmage B. Skinner Jr.
Joseph D. Sloan
Harold S. Smithyman
Conley T. Snidow
Shelley H. Sperka
B. G. Stephens
Matthew A. Stephenson
Brand R. Stille
R. Phillip Stone
Christopher Strauber
Cynthia A. Suárez
Edward B. Sydnor
David A. Sykes
Timothy D. Terrell
Sandor Teszler
Ellen L. Tillett

Charlotte P. Tinsley
Thomas V. Thoroughman
Gerald T. Thurmond
Deno P. Trakas
David H. Tyner
Benjamin F. Varn Jr.
Richard M. Wallace
Virgil Scott Ward
Daniel W. Welch
Donald J. Welch
Martha E. Wharton
D. Edward Whelchel
Clayton J. Whisnant
David M. Whisnant
Susan M. Wiley
Josephine Williamson
Garoll Dee Willis
Carol B. Wilson
William M. Wilson
Sumter S. Wingfield
Ana María Wiseman
Dennis M. Wiseman
David S. Wood
Richard C. Wood
Margaret B. Wright
William W. Wright Jr.
Steven B. Zides

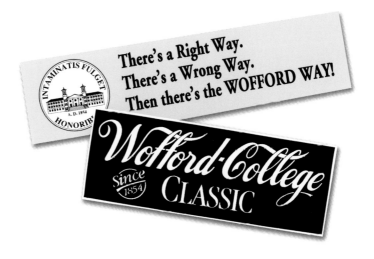

STAFF MEMORIES REACH BACK TO THE 1950S

When Doris Wade, Joyce Arthur and Lucy Quinn came to work at Wofford, students wore beanie caps for the first few weeks on campus, dressed up for Sunday dinner and attended required morning chapel twice a week. They reminisced with Nathaniel Coburn '06 for a sesquicentennial story that first appeared in Wofford Today.

Doris Wade recalled that her pay was lower, but the pace of work was quite a bit slower on her first day in the Wofford business office, March 1, 1954. Most offices were staffed with a director and a secretary. Her workday typically started at 8:30 a.m. and ended at 4 p.m., with a 90-minute lunch break and an occasional half-day of work on Saturdays. In the spring, work always was suspended so that everyone could go to Law Field to watch the afternoon baseball games. The highlight of the year was the annual Wofford vs. The Citadel football game at the state fair in Orangeburg. All the students, faculty and staff would travel downstate on chartered buses.

When asked how much she interacted with the students, Wade replied, "The students would come in with their parents to pay fees and fines. At that time, students could make tuition payments up until exam time. A long list of students who owed money was sent to the faculty before each exam, and the professors would tell a student if he or she had to make a payment before taking the test."

Wade even remembered trustees who once were students. "Seeing some whose grades weren't necessarily spectacular go on to become successful in life is very special," she said, "I like to think that the students have been my employer. We value long-lasting friendships as well as the financial support we get from alumni."

Wade says that a major transition came when Wofford began admitting women in the 1970s. "At first, women were only day students, and some of the men didn't really seem to want them on campus. But the competition for good grades became more intense. I think admitting women was healthy for all the students and improved Wofford."

✫   ✫   ✫

Joyce Arthur attended Cecil's Business College in the early 1960s. Her first job was as a secretary to G.W. Whitlock at Clifton Elementary School. She had wanted to be a nurse, but changed her mind while she worked at the school. She began working at Wofford on June 18, 1962, after being interviewed and hired by the late Herbert Hucks Jr. '34. Her weekly wages were $50. At the time, there were only two other staff members in the library besides Hucks and Arthur—the assistant librarian, Sumter Wingfield, and a cataloguer, Margaret Wright.

She had learned to type on an electric typewriter, but the library was equipped only with an ancient manual that she was unable to master. Eventually, she got an electric model, and she probably was not exaggerating in claiming to have prepared "millions of entries" for the card catalog.

In 1966, Frank Anderson became the new library director, and everything moved to the beautiful Sandor Teszler Library across the street. Arthur recalls organizing the student assistants who helped carry the books on carts across the street. In 1972, she started working in acquisitions, ordering books and videos and other materials for the library.

"I've loved working in a library all these years," she says. "I've always enjoyed seeing new books come in and being the first one to open them. I wish I could read them all." She also said that working with student library assistants has been a special pleasure and she hears from many of them on a regular basis.

✳   ✳   ✳

Lucy Quinn '83 has seen Wofford from a wide range of different perspectives since her first day on the job in October 1963. "The campus in those days was a lot like *Grease* (the play and movie). Everything seemed calmer and safer until the Kennedy and King assassinations made us realize that there was a world beyond Wofford and South Carolina."

In those days, everything from class rolls and grades to Selective Service reports had to be posted and filed by hand, so a number of young women worked on the clerical staff at various times. The registrar and director of admissions was the late Bates Scoggins Sr. '30, a man dedicated to the college who took great pride in his work. Quinn recalls that on snowy days, he would travel around town in his chain-equipped 1950 Ford, picking up staff so that no deadlines would be missed. In later years, when his eyesight was failing, he was known to cue everyone that he was too weary keep going with the phrase, "Let's stop and save something to do tomorrow."

To the staff, Scoggins was like a good faculty member working with inexperienced but promising students. "He always had time to explain everything," Quinn said, "Before too long we understood what we were doing and could take initiative ourselves."

Quinn said she was not necessarily looking for a career when she came to Wofford, but she soon overcame a bit of shyness and starting taking courses, one at a time on her lunch hour. Often, she was the only woman in a class with 25 men. She earned her Wofford bachelor's degree and later her master's. In 1987, after the retirement of Registrar Ned Sydnor '55, she was promoted to take his place.

Lucy Quinn always has been regarded as an effective administrator and a great friend to students, from first-year students struggling to adjust to academia to seniors nearing graduation with a problem or two to solve.

Martha Brewington, Mary Elizabeth Smith, Lucy Quinn, Joyce Arthur, Doris Wade *(left to right)*

THE COLLEGE STAFF

With grateful appreciation, the following members of the Wofford community are recognized for their contributions to the college between January 1, 1954, and December 31, 2004. They are members of the full-time academic and institutional support staff with ten or more years' service.

Betty J. Aldrich
Eugene F. Alexander
Shirley M. Alexander
Betty H. Anderson
J. Curtis Anderson
Warren G. Arial Jr.
Joyce D. Arthur
Mike W. Ayers
Irene Biggs Baker
B. Terrell Ball
Brenda Barnette
Kay B. Barry
Terry M. Belcher
Phyllis W. Bemelmans
Lynda H. Bennett
Virginia Bishop
Joyce G. Blackwell
John I. Blair
Doyle W. Boggs
Walter Booth
Faye Bowers
Arthur T. Boyd
James A. Brakefield
Ruth Brannon
Nell B. Brewer
Martha A. Brewington
Ted J. Bridges
W. Earle Buice
Tammie M. Burgess
J. Kenny Cabe
Michael Caldwell
Michael Calvert
Susan J. Calvert
Kaye B. Castillo
Jeanne C. Cheatham
Florrie Clark
Freddie Clements
Sarah Ross Cohen
Mark Cohen

Janice Croxdale
Ladson Cubbage
Susan M. Cummings
John R. Curry
Dennis Dandy
Lisa H. De Freitas
William D. Dill
Hattie M. Dogan
Joe L. Dominick
Archie Dominick, Jr.
Beverly J. Doster
Converse Draper
Larry F. Ellis
Reba O. Epton
Flora Bell Finger
Barbara Floyd
Elizabeth Forbes
Ellen Fowler
Patricia B. Fowler
David R. Friday
P. Diane Fuller
Mary Louise Gaines
Boyce L. Gilliam
Mae Sue Gory
Charles H. Gray
Glendora J. Green
Joe L. Greenlee
Elsie Greer
James W. Grice Jr.
Marcus K. Griffin
Ed Y. Hall
James A. Hall
Dorothy Halligan
Lee Hanning
Elizabeth S. Hardigree
Robert J. Hasson
Durwood F. Hatchell
K. Louise Hatchell
Donna D. Hawkins

Wallace B. Henderson
Kim E. Henry
W. Dean Hill
Hazel R. Holbert
Gail C. Holt
Mavis O. Horton
Lonnie J. Hosley
Ann Howard
Robert Huggin
Catherine Jeter
John Jones
Rebecca L. Jones
Lester E. Kennedy Sr.
F. André Kerr
David King
Franz H. Kop
Bruce H. Lackey
A. Wade Lang
Frances T. Lattimore
Marianna K. Leahy
M. Keith Ledford
Terri L. Lewitt
Mark D. Line
Joseph B. Littlefield
Addie M. Littlejohn
Hazel Littlejohn
Henry Littlejohn
Anna Jacie Long
Meri E. Lynch
Martha Mathews
Bill L. May
Guy S. McCombs
Susan S. McCrackin
Todd McCraw
Elsie B. McDowell
Mable McDowell
Brenda B. McGuire
Freddie L. Meadows
Jackie F. Means

Joanne V. Medlock	Clarence J. Reddick	Phyllis Sumner
Rush Arthur Miller	Joel E. Robertson	Jack L. Teachey
Arthur L. Miller	Fran Scott	Angela R. Thomas
M. Louise P. N. Miller	Richard W. Scudder	Kaiser Thomas Jr.
Mary Miller	Tony W. Self	Debbi N. Thompson
John W. Moore	E. L. Tina Shands	Mildred Thompson
Faith H. Morris	Crystal C. Sharpe	Helen Branyon Upton
Peggy B. Morrison	Billie Shaw	Jennic G. Vermillion
Mary Ann Morrow	M. Helen Smith	Kay S. Vipperman
Daniel R. O'Connell	Mary Elizabeth Smith	Ralph Voyles
J. J. Jack Owings	Pat A. Smith	Doris B. Wade
D. Smith Patterson	J. Warren Snead	Elizabeth D. Wallace
Connor Patton	Ray M. Southers	Dorothy Waters
J. D. Peninger	Ramoth Southern	Pam K. White
Gwen B. Pettit	Millie C. Steele	J. Ronald Wood
D. Elaine Pitts	Betty S. Stevens	Margaret Woodward
Janice M. Poole	Duane A. Stober	Nate W. Woody
Terri W. Putman	Edwin H. Story	Michael K. Young

These lists were compiled by Pat Smith and Doyle Boggs of the Wofford Communications Office in collaboration with appropriate administrators, senior faculty and staff, and the college human resources office. Every effort was made to ensure that these lists stand complete and accurate; however, there are gaps in certain college records. We at Wofford would, therefore, greatly appreciate receiving notice concerning needed corrections and additions.

As late as the 1980s, incoming calls to every campus extension passed through the college switchboard. The voice of Mary Miller– "WAAAH-ford College"–was familiar to all.

WHO'S WHO OF THIS PUBLICATION

Editors

Doyle Boggs '70 (editor-in-chief) is the executive director of communications at Wofford College. A member of Phi Beta Kappa, he earned his B.A. degree at Wofford and completed his M.A. and Ph.D. in history at the University of South Carolina. A contributor to several publications of the Hub City Writers Project, he is a past president of the Spartanburg County Historical Association and the South Carolina Confederation of Local Historical Societies. He retired from the South Carolina Army National Guard with the rank of lieutenant colonel.

JoAnn Mitchell Brasington '89 is a freelance writer, graphic designer and public relations consultant. She earned her B.A. in English at Wofford and her M.A. in journalism in 2000 at the University of South Carolina. Past historical research and narratives include *Textiles Go to War*, a master's thesis exploring the story of Spartanburg's mill villages during World War II, and the sesquicentennial history of the South Carolina School for the Deaf and the Blind. Since 1989, she has served as a designer, contributor and associate editor of *Wofford Today*.

Phillip Stone '94 has been archivist of Wofford College and South Carolina Methodism since 1999. He earned his B.A. at Wofford College and was elected to Phi Beta Kappa in 1994, and later earned his MA in history at the University of Georgia. He completed his Ph.D. at the University of South Carolina, studying the history of economic development in modern South Carolina and archives administration.

Book Designer and College Photographer

Mark Olencki '75 has designed over 30 books for the Hub City Writers Project and for Wofford College. In addition to more than three decades of photography work for Wofford College, his photographs have appeared recently in *Fourth Genre* magazine, *National Geographic's Heart of a Nation*, and *The Chattahoochee Review*. His photographs have been included in the permanent collection of the state of South Carolina, as well as the private collections of many businesses and individuals. Mark operates a photo/design business in Spartanburg, Olencki Graphics Inc.

Principal Essay Authors

Benjamin B. Dunlap, the 10th President of Wofford College, is a native of Columbia, S.C. After graduating summa cum laude from Sewanee, the University of the South, in 1959, he attended Oxford University as a Rhodes Scholar and Harvard University as a graduate student in English language and literature, receiving his Ph.D. in 1967. Since that time, he has held academic appointments at Harvard, the University of South Carolina and Wofford, where for seven years prior to becoming president he served as the Chapman Family Professor in the Humanities. A frequent moderator for the Aspen Institute's Executive and C.E.O. Seminars as well as its Crown Fellowship Program, he has lectured widely in this country and abroad, including time as a Fulbright professor in Thailand and a Japan

Society Leadership Fellow in Japan. His many publications include poems, essays, anthologies, guides and opera libretti. As a writer-producer for public television, he has been responsible for more than 200 programs, for which he has won numerous national and international awards.

Larry T. McGehee retired from Wofford in August 2005 after 23 years as a vice president and professor of religion. He holds a B.A. in English from Transylvania University, B.D., M.A., and Ph.D. degrees in religion from Yale University, and an honorary doctorate from Transylvania. Prior to arriving at Wofford in 1982, he was chancellor of the University of Tennessee at Martin for nine years. In retirement he continues to teach his senior seminar in American Religious History and write his weekly syndicated column, *Southern Seen*, for over 100 small-town newspapers. Selected columns appear in his book, *Southern Seen: Meditations on Past and Present* (UT Press, 2005).

Philip N. Racine is the William R. Kenan Professor of History and chair of the history department at Wofford. He is a graduate of Bowdoin College and earned his M.A. and Ph.D. degrees from Emory University. His areas of research are the history of the American South and the American Civil War, and he is the author and editor of five books, including three on Spartanburg. In 1986, he and his coauthor, Richard Harwell, received the Founder's Award from the Confederate Memorial Society of the Confederate Museum of Richmond, Va.

Tracy J. Revels is an associate professor of history at Wofford College, where she was the first female member of the department. A native of Madison, Florida, she holds a Ph.D. in history from Florida State University. She is the author of *Watery Eden: A History of Wakulla Springs* and *Grander in Her Daughters: Florida's Women During the Civil War*, for which she received the 2005 Rembert Patrick Award for the best scholarly book in Florida History. The award was presented recently by the Florida Historical Society.

Rodger E. Stroup '68 is the director of the South Carolina Department of Archives and History and is the State Historic Preservation Officer. A member of Phi Beta Kappa, he earned his B.A. degree at Wofford and M.A. and Ph.D. in history at the University of South Carolina. He is a past president of the South Carolina Historical Association and the South Carolina Federation of Museums. Currently he is serving on the executive council of the American Association for State and Local History.

Deno P. Trakas is professor of English and director of the Writing Center at Wofford College. He has published fiction and poetry in magazines such as *The Denver Quarterly* and *Oxford American*. Holocene Press published two of his chapbooks, *The Shuffle of Wings* and *human and puny*. *New Southern Harmonies*, a book of fiction by four regional writers, features three of his short stories; it was named Best Book of Short Fiction in North American 1998 by *Independent Publisher* magazine.

INDEX